Fahrenheit   Celsius

240
230   110
220
210   100
200
190   90
180   80
170
160   70
150
140   60
130
120   50
110
100   40
90
80   30
70   20
60
50   10
40
30   0
20
10   −10
0
−10   −20
−20   −30
−30
−40   −40
−50
−60   −50
−70
−80   −60

Metric to English

Approximate Conversions from Metric Measures

Symbol	When You Know	Multiply by	To Find	Symbol
Length				
mm	millimeters	0.04	inches	in
cm	centimeters	0.4	inches	in
m	meters	3.3	feet	ft
m	meters	1.1	yards	yd
km	kilometers	0.6	miles	mi
Area				
cm^2	square centimeters	0.16	square inches	in^2
m^2	square meters	1.2	square yards	yd^2
km^2	square kilometers	0.4	square miles	mi^2
ha	hectares (10,000 m^2)	2.5	acres	
Mass/Weight				
g	grams	0.035	ounces	oz
kg	kilograms	2.2	pounds	lb
t	tonnes (1000 kg)	1.1	short tons	
Volume				
ml	milliliters	0.03	fluid ounces	fl oz
l	liters	2.1	pints	pt
l	liters	1.06	quarts	qt
l	liters	0.26	gallons	gal
m^3	cubic meters	35	cubic feet	ft^3
m^3	cubic meters	1.3	cubic yards	yd^3
Temperature (Exact)				
°C	Celsius temperature	9/5 (then add 32)	Fahrenheit temperature	°F

Inches

1
2
3
4
5
6

Centimeters

1
2
3
4
5
6
7
8
9
10
11
12
13
14
15

SECOND EDITION

HOW TO TEACH ELEMENTARY SCHOOL SCIENCE

Peter C. Gega

Professor Emeritus
College of Education
San Diego State University

Macmillan Publishing Company
New York

Maxwell Macmillan Canada
Toronto

Maxwell Macmillan International
New York Oxford Singapore Sydney

Cover photos: © David Young-Wolff, PhotoEdit
Editor: Linda James Scharp
Production Editor: Jonathan Lawrence
Art Coordinator: Peter A. Robison
Photo Editor: Anne Vega
Text Designer: Jill E. Bonar
Cover Designer: Russ Maselli
Production Buyer: Patricia A. Tonneman
Illustrations: Academy ArtWorks, Inc.

This book was set in Goudy and New Baskerville by Carlisle Communications, Ltd., and was printed and bound by R.R. Donnelley & Sons Company. The cover was printed by Lehigh Press, Inc.

Macmillan Publishing Company
113 Sylvan Avenue, Englewood Cliffs, NJ 07632

Library of Congress Cataloging-in Publication Data

Gega, Peter C.
    How to teach elementary school science / Peter C. Gega.—2nd ed.
        p. cm.
    Also published as part of: Science in elementary education. 7th ed. ©1994.
    Companion volume to: Concepts and experiences in elementary school science. 2nd ed. ©1994.
    Includes bibliographical references and index.
    ISBN 0-02-341333-6
    1. Science—Study and teaching (Elementary)   I. Gega, Peter C. Science in elementary education.   II. Gega, Peter C.   Concepts and experiences in elementary school science.   III. Title.
LB1585.G39 1994
372.3'5'044—dc20   92-43309
                                               CIP

Printing: 2 3 4 5 6 7 8 9   Year: 4 5 6 7

CREDITS

Chapter 1 opener: Michael Siluk; Chapter 2 opener: Barbara Stimpert; Fig. 2-18: Education Development Center; Chapter 3 opener: Barbara Stimpert; Chapter 4 opener: Robert Finken; Chapter 5 opener: Barbara Schwartz/Macmillan; Fig. 5-1: Michael Houghton/Studiohio; Fig. 5-2: Bausch and Lomb; Fig. 5-3: Ken-A-Vision Manufacturing Co., Inc.; Chapter 6 opener: Jean-Claude Lejeune; Fig. 6-7: Barbara Schwartz/Macmillan; Fig. 6-8: Copyright Optical Data Corporation, 1987; and Chapter 7 opener: Barbara Schwartz/Macmillan.

Preface

This book shows how to teach science to children, ages 5 to 12. It begins with why science is basic to children's schooling and explains the foundations that give it form and substance. Each chapter develops a broad competency or a cluster of related teaching skills through step-by-step descriptions and use of many real-life examples. (Incidentally, all the examples reflect my personal teaching experiences or firsthand observations with elementary schoolchildren.) The chapters and several exercises that are included should enable you to

- Decide what science is basic, useful, and learnable for children.
- Recognize and assess differences in children's thinking.
- Use closed-ended and open-ended teaching activities.
- Improve children's thinking in several ways.
- Locate and use a variety of resources to teach science.
- Arrange and manage learning centers, microcomputer centers, and projects.
- Organize and assess science teaching.

The first of five appendices presents a sampler of science activities and some open-ended investigations to show the kinds of concrete experiences children need to learn science. The other appendices include information about useful publications, science supply sources, and a summary of children's thinking in several stages of their development.

A companion book, *Concepts and Experiences in Elementary School Science,* second edition (New York: Macmillan, 1994), features a large inventory of concrete activities and investigations. The contents of both books can be found in one comprehensive volume, *Science in Elementary Education,* seventh edition (New York: Macmillan, 1994).

I greatly appreciate the help given to me in preparing these materials by Christine Ebert, University of South Carolina; John P. Huntsberger, University of Texas—Austin; Linda Cronin Jones, University of Florida; Ernest W. Lee, University of North Carolina—Greensboro; and Nedra C. Sears, East Central University.

Peter C. Gega

Contents

7 How to Organize and Assess Science Teaching 160

A Sample Investigations and Activities 191

B Professional Bibliography 228

C Some Major Project-Developed Programs 231

D Commercial Suppliers of Science Materials and Equipment 236

E Summary of Children's Thinking in Three Piagetian Stages 238

Index 240

HOW TO TEACH ELEMENTARY SCHOOL SCIENCE

Science in Elementary Education

When you were a child, you and all the other girls and boys wanted to know a great deal about the world around you. Children still do. Sooner or later, they will ask questions like

Why doesn't a spider get stuck in its web?

How does a bird get in the egg?

How can you tell the difference between a boy tree and a girl tree?

and

Where does the dark come from?

What makes the wind blow?

Where do the people on TV go when you turn it off?

If you had asked these questions as a child, how thoughtfully would your teachers have handled them? Would you have been able to explore some of your own interests? Or was learning more restricted? Were you guided to think through some problems for yourself? Or were answers always given?

How your teachers worked with children reflected their notions about science teaching and how they thought it could benefit their pupils. The same applies today with you. Your school or district office can give you some instructional materials. But your concepts and values about science teaching will strongly affect what children actually learn in your classroom.

Notice the contrasting approaches taken by several teachers—one pair each at the primary-, middle-, and upper-grade levels—as they prepare to introduce a hands-on activity.

In two separate primary-level classrooms, the children are supposed to experience the same listening activity. They have brought in empty shoe boxes and numerous small objects: marbles, jacks, crayons, paper clips, pencils, and the like.

Teacher 1 explains what to do. Each child will work with a partner. One child will secretly place an object in the box and replace the lid. The partner will try to identify the object by tilting the box back and forth, listening with an ear held close to the box. The teacher then says, "Will you be able to guess what your partner put into the box? After you do, take turns."

Teacher 2 has asked her class to bring, besides shoe boxes, *matching pairs* of small objects. Each child will also work with a partner. Each child is to display six different objects in a row before her or his partner, then secretly select from the matching objects one that matches a displayed object. This is to be put into the box and lid replaced. The teacher says, "See if you can figure out which one of the six objects in front of you matches the object secretly placed in your box. Listen to the noises the object inside makes as you tilt it back and forth. Also look carefully at the objects in front of you. Which one is most likely to make the sounds you hear?"

Here we have two very different notions of what the lesson is about. The first teacher sees the activity as a fun way to engage the children in a listening experience that is little more than a guessing game. The second teacher sees the activity as an interesting chance for children to make observations that require them to use their minds. Visibly displaying concrete objects enables the children to connect the *appearance* of objects with their probable *sounds*. This teacher also realizes that she has to limit the number of objects displayed to avoid confusing her young pupils. If six objects prove to be too many for some to consider, she is ready to reduce this number at any time. Among other things, this teacher shows knowledge of how children learn science and a sensitivity to what's possible at their developmental level.

In two separate middle-level classrooms, pupils are going to make magnets out of common iron nails. Each teacher has some nails, paper clips, and several magnets for the activity. Both intend to use the same activity described in the textbook:

Can you make a magnet out of a nail?

Materials: magnet, iron nail, paper clips

1. Place one end (pole) of the magnet on the nail near its head.

2. Rub the whole nail's length with the magnet in one direction. Then lift the magnet off the nail.

3. Do steps 1 and 2 again. Rub the nail 10 times, always in one direction.

4. Touch the nail to some paper clips. What happens?

Teacher 1 directs the children to do the activity as written. The children find that the nails attract from two to four paper clips. A monitor quickly retrieves the materials and the class begins a related reading assignment in the science textbook. After the reading, pupils write answers to questions posed in the book.

Teacher 2 also conducts the activity as written, then says, "Wait a minute. How do we really know that rubbing the nail with a magnet made it a magnet? Maybe it was a magnet *before* you rubbed it." Protests and a lively discussion follow until it dawns on the children that they are operating solely on faith. They decide it makes sense to first check any nails for magnetism before rubbing them with a magnet. Maybe nails have a "little bit" of magnetism to start with, some say. Now that things are loosened up, further questions are raised by pupils and teacher: Why did some nails pick up more clips than others? What would happen if you rub the nail more, or fewer, times? In *both* directions? How long will a nail hold its magnetism? Can you make a nail lose its magnetism? My nail lost most of its magnetism—what's wrong? What would happen if you cut the nail in half? Would it be only half as strong? And so on. The teacher invites pupils with questions to write them on the chalkboard. Most can be answered by experimenting with the materials on hand. A few questions may call for locating and carefully reading reference materials, or conferring with people who are most likely to have valid knowledge about magnetism.

The first teacher in this example is willing to provide a concrete experience for pupils, but subordinates it to getting general information about magnetism through routine and unfocused reading. What's missing is an understanding of the nature of science, and how to get children thinking in purposeful, scientific ways.

Teacher 2 takes an otherwise humdrum activity and uses it to provoke curiosity, generate real experiments, critically examine procedures and assumptions, and think carefully about exactly what to read or whom to confer with for further information students need to answer *their own questions*. The children's minds are opened to further possibilities for investigation in ways that resemble how intelligent and educated persons, including working scientists, operate.

In two separate upper-level classrooms, two teachers are scheduled to teach the same three lessons. Here's how each begins each lesson:

Teacher 1: Does cold air hold less moisture than warm air?
Teacher 2: Why do our lips and skin seem so dry today?

Teacher 1: Does air have weight? What is air pressure?
Teacher 2: When you drink pop through a straw, what makes the liquid go up the straw?

Teacher 1: Can sunlight cause a chemical change in things?
Teacher 2: How many of you have seen colored clothing that has faded?

Maybe you're aware that the first teacher in each case has simply stated the science principle that will be taught in the form of a question. So in the first lesson, for example, the children will learn that *cold air holds less moisture than warm air.*

Teacher 2, in contrast, begins with an *application* of the principle. She tries to begin (and end) most lessons by referring to children's everyday experiences. To her, the most significant, understandable, and unforgettable science is what students can apply in their lives. Science principles, or *generalizations* as we'll refer to them in this book, typically have many real-life applications. When we begin and end lessons with applications, it enables children to reflect on their experiences.

It's easy to see that the second way of teaching in each example is likely to be more interesting and productive than the first way. This kind of teaching is exhilarating. You feel a growing sense of excitement, competence, and fulfillment as your pupils respond enthusiastically and grow. Yet if you're like most persons who select elementary teaching as a profession, science is not likely to be your strongest subject. So it's only natural to wonder if you are up to the job.

Perhaps you'll be surprised to learn that my university colleagues and I have observed many student teachers, as well as experienced teachers, using methods like those in the better examples you have just read. Generally, these persons have taken only the few science courses required for graduation, plus a course on the teaching of elementary school science. What they *do* have, in abundance, is good judgment. An internal set of guidelines enables them to judge between what science is basic and what is trivial, what is useful and what is ornamental, what is learnable and what is obscure.

An effective way to develop sound judgment in any subject is to study its *imperatives*—the powerful, essential ideas and processes that give the subject its value. When we heed and work in tune with clear imperatives, good results are likely to come our way. When we ignore them, the opposite result is likely no matter how hard we try.

There are three sources of imperatives in science education: those that come from science as a discipline, those that reflect society's needs, and those that reveal how children develop and learn. Your keen study of these imperatives can enable you to judge what is basic in science, what science is useful to nonscientists in our society, and what sci-

ence children can learn. This can also help you to put into perspective the specific teaching methods of following chapters and gain confidence from seeing the big picture.

SCIENCE IMPERATIVES

The imperatives from science as a discipline are found in *how* scientists go about finding out—*process;* and *what* scientists have found out—*knowledge.* Although the two in practice are inseparable, it will be convenient now to look at each separately. Let's consider knowledge first.

Knowledge

You and I try to explain, predict, and control our experiences by generalizing about the patterns or regularities we observe:

> *Muscles get sore when overworked.*
> *Quality and price go together.*
> *Actions speak louder than words.*

Knowing the generalization about sore muscles may cause you to say, "I overworked yesterday, that's why I'm sore!" (explain) or, "I'm probably going to be sore tomorrow" (predict) or, "I'm not going to overwork today" (control). Can you see how you might also use the other two generalizations for these three purposes?

Scientists, too, observe patterns and generalize about them. But they usually do so with far more precision and reliability. This is a big reason nonscientists can profit from the study of science and its methods.

Scientists use an ingenious array of tools and organized ways to search for patterns in objects and events. The generalizations they invent to explain what they observe may look like these:

> *Plants have adaptations that enable them to survive changing conditions.*

Fossil remains show that some life forms have become extinct.

Eclipses happen when the earth, sun, and moon are aligned.

However, few scientists pretend to fully "explain" or understand natural events. What they do is to *describe* natural events and, when they can, to predict or control them. What they may call "explanations" (concepts, generalizations, principles, laws, theories) are really descriptions—often brilliantly conceived and useful, but descriptions after all. How well a description enables them to "explain," predict, or control events becomes the chief measure of its worth.

Consider the concept of mammal, for example. Like other concepts, this one stands for a class of things with similar properties. Suppose a small whale gets tangled in a fishnet below the ocean's surface. Can you predict what will soon happen to the whale? You might think: "Whale—that's a mammal. Mammals are lung breathers. It will probably drown." Notice how the concept of whale as mammal brings up a property (lung breathing) associated with all mammals. This enables you to make a reasonably certain prediction. Or if a friend asks, "A whale *drown?* How?" you can explain by using the same property. Your understanding of the concept might also prompt you to influence or control the event, by swiftly cutting the net, for instance.

The generalizations of science help us in a similar way. The statement "Most matter expands when heated and contracts when cooled" interrelates several concepts. This generalization enables us to relate and explain a number of apparently different events: a sidewalk that cracks and buckles in hot weather; telephone wires that sag in summer but do not in winter; why we can loosen a tightly screwed jar lid by running hot water over it; the reason rocks rimming a campfire break apart when we douse the fire (and rocks) with water; and so on.

The learning of key concepts and generalizations invented by scientists is imperative in science education because it dramatically increases brainpower. Notice that in Figure 1-1 a large variety of animals could be classified as mammals. But only a comparative handful need be studied to get a handle on the concept.

Once we understand the physical properties of mammals, it's easy to classify even unfamiliar animals found in zoos, stories, or on television. Despite not knowing their names, we already know a great deal about them.

A similar transfer of learning happens with properly learned generalizations. Although few events may be studied to learn the generalization (Figure 1-2), many more may be applied. This explains why persons who organize their thinking into concepts, generalizations, sequences, and other patterns broaden and deepen their understanding throughout their lives. In contrast, persons who study unrelated facts quickly forget what they have been taught.[1] Learning the patterns of nature allows us to continually apply, or transfer, these learnings to new objects and events. The new facts collect and stick to well-learned patterns almost like iron filings to a magnet. This is not to say that teaching for transfer is easy. Pupils must often see applications made within a variety of contexts and at increasingly complex levels. Still, everyone reaps benefits from the cumulative work of scientists of today and years past, for only the relatively short time it takes to learn about that work.

---

[1]Robert F. Biehler and Jack Snowman. *Psychology Applied to Teaching.* 5th ed. (Boston: Houghton Mifflin, 1986), pp. 427–28.

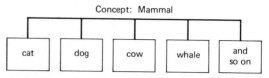

FIGURE 1-1

Concepts stand for a class of things with similar properties.

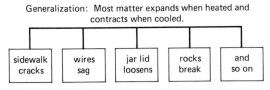

FIGURE 1-2
Generalizations enable us to relate and explain apparently different events.

Incidentally, have you already inferred how you might test to see if concepts and generalizations can be applied by pupils? You'll want to ask questions that contain examples of objects or events that have *not* been studied. If the child can link *unstudied* examples of a studied concept or generalization, chances are that transferable learning has occurred.

Scientists search for patterns, but they also look for inconsistencies in the patterns. Under certain conditions, for example, plants may *not* adapt and survive. The occasional deviation from the usual allows scientists to sharpen their generalizations and theories. In the same vein, we may find when shopping that quality does not always accompany higher prices. Figuring out under what conditions this happens improves our previous notion and makes us cagier shoppers.

Children, too, can learn to refine their generalizations. A second-grade class placed various small objects in water-filled pans to see which would sink or float. Some children summed up what they had learned by saying, "Light things float and heavy things sink." On hearing this, the teacher had them compare on a balance the weights of some things that had floated and sunk. A few objects that floated were heavier than some that had sunk. This made everyone look at the objects more carefully. Still, no one seemed to know what to say. When the teacher drew attention to the objects' sizes, the children soon concluded, "Things that are light for their size float. They sink when they are heavy for their size." Not bad, considering that the children had to think about two variables together, size and weight. (More on this mental operation in Chapter 2.)

It is hard when dealing with natural events to foresee all the conditions that might cause them to change. This is why scientists see their generalizations and theories as *tentative*—always subject to change with new data. It also explains why generalizations may be stated in *probabilities,* a frequent practice when dealing with living things: "Persons who eat fatty foods run a greater risk of heart attacks than those who do not."

Parsimony.   Scientists may offer competing explanations or theories to account for a natural phenomenon. This is likely when the phenomenon can only be observed indirectly (the makeup of the earth's core, for instance), or has happened in the distant past (extinction of the dinosaurs, for example), and so cannot be fully tested. When competing theories account for the data equally well, scientists prefer on principle the simplest one. This principle of *parsimony*—literally, the word means the quality of being stingy or miserly—helps to keep the scientific enterprise more manageable and economical than it would be without it.

In an upper-grade class I visited recently, the teacher was well acquainted with the principle of parsimony. Several children were reporting their explanations of hidden electric circuits they had tested. They had connected a battery-operated circuit tester in various ways to wires hidden in a cardboard folder and inferred the locations of the wires. While terminal connectors for the wires were visible, the actual wires were not.

One child explained how three hidden wires connected in a certain pattern would account for the times the circuit-tester bulb had lit up. Another pupil showed how only two hidden wires could give the same results. Although both explanations were "correct," the class quickly saw the wisdom of preferring the simpler one when the teacher brought up the point. Later, the teacher told me that the pupils themselves had cited the principle of parsimony within several further discussions during their instructional unit on electric circuits.

Spiral Approach. If you switch to a higher grade after several years of teaching, don't be surprised if a previously taught generalization shows up again in your curriculum guide. Because a science generalization consists of several concepts and accounts for many facts, it usually takes more than one exposure for pupils to learn it well. So curriculum developers may plan for children to study the generalization several times, at increasing levels of complexity and abstraction, and in different contexts, during grade levels K–6 or K–8.

Consider, "Heat is a form of energy that is transferred in several ways." It may be studied in one of the primary grades as simple heat conduction from the source through solid materials, such as metal, plastic, wood, and cloth. The question, Why do people use cloth pot holders? and other matters dealing with safety around hot objects may be emphasized. (Children are especially vulnerable during the primary years.) In one or two of the intermediate grades, radiation and convection might be introduced, besides a more refined treatment of conduction. Upper-grade pupils, in turn, may tackle heat as molecular energy. Each of the experiences and smaller ideas contribute to the overall generalization about heat transfer.

Figure 1-3 shows how this generalization may be scheduled in a science curriculum that spans grades K–8. Notice how the generalization "spirals" up through nine grade levels but is substantially taught only three times. In curriculum development, this is known as an *interrupted spiral approach* to teaching concepts and generalizations. The approach embodies the need to restudy ideas at higher levels of complexity while it avoids needless repetition.

Not every curriculum treats these ideas in this way. Some may address a major idea at almost every level. Others may be more sparing. But at least two general practices seem clear: Most curricula are organized around

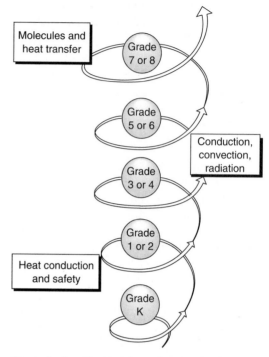

Generalization: Heat is a form of energy that is transferred in several ways.

FIGURE 1-3
An interrupted spiral approach to teaching concepts and generalizations.

the major concepts and generalizations of science, and study of these ideas is developmental. That is, children will study the broad ideas more than once, and with increasing complexity, during the several elementary grades. You can see how important it is for teachers from all school levels—elementary, junior high, and senior high—to plan together in selecting or constructing a curriculum.

Following are main points from the preceding pages on science as knowledge:

■ It is natural for people, scientists and nonscientists alike, to generalize about the regularities they observe.

■ Science is an organized search for regularities or patterns and inconsistencies that may occur in them.

- Scientists invent concepts and generalizations to explain the patterns they observe and, when possible, to predict and control objects or events that fit the patterns.

- Learning science concepts and generalizations increases intellectual power because we can apply this knowledge well beyond the facts studied to learn them.

- Varying conditions may produce inconsistencies in the patterns scientists observe; so the generalizations they invent may be stated as probabilities and change with new data.

- When competing generalizations or theories explain an event equally well, scientists use the principle of parsimony to select the simplest one.

- The learning of concepts and generalizations is ongoing and integrative; so science curricula present them at least several times, with increasing refinement and complexity, within the elementary grades.

One purpose in Appendix A of this book is to identify and develop in teachable ways some of the key concepts and generalizations used by scientists. You'll also find most of these ideas within the elementary science curriculum you teach. The knowledge that comes from science as a discipline is a powerful force in shaping the modern curriculum.

Process

Although the basic concepts and generalizations of science are always subject to change with new data, their high quality generally makes them last a long time. The quality is no accident. The processes and attitudes scientists use in seeking regularities have been screened over many years to get the best results. Scientists realize the futility of trying to construct immutable laws or truths. But they also understand that the quality of their knowledge is linked to the quality of the processes used to produce it. So scientists continually try to sharpen their observations and how they think about them.

Such an approach breeds deeply a continuing curiosity, the willingness to listen to others' ideas, the caution to suspend judgment until enough facts are known, the readiness to try innovations, and many other qualities we collectively label "scientific attitude." This attitude does not come from some special quality of nobility or goodness in scientists, of course, but from their constant awareness that their thinking can probably be improved. The next several pages present principles that guide their thinking and attitudes. As you'll see, these can also benefit nonscientists, both children and adults.

If the scientist's question "*What* do I know?" is linked to *knowledge*, "*How* do I know it?" reflects the habits of mind and attitude called *process*. At the heart of process is the nature of acceptable *evidence*. Science itself is often defined as a search for *observable* and *reproducible* evidence.

Observable Evidence.   In guiding children, help them to understand that only data that can be detected by the senses is "observable evidence." Sometimes the senses must be extended by instruments. The microscope allows us to see organisms too small for the unaided eye. A radio permits us to detect silent radiations from a broadcasting tower. But however aided, the senses must confirm that something tangible exists.

Reproducible Evidence.   Scientists assume that, under the same conditions, natural events are "reproducible." That is, they will recur either naturally or, if conditions are the same, in the laboratory. Any qualified scientist should be able to observe or produce the event if the necessary conditions are made public. In the same vein, your pupils should be able to reproduce each other's findings when questions arise about data. You can see how this and the preceding test make it harder for thoughtful children to be misled by questionable data or, later in life, to accept the abracadabra of self-appointed spiritualists and psychics.

Interacting Objects. For a further test for evidence, envision a room where you live. Is the air temperature near the ceiling warmer or cooler than that near the floor? You probably will say warmer. Why? A common explanation we hear is that "warm air rises." Think about it. Does it go up all by itself? Is it immune to gravity? A more acceptable answer is that something is pushing it up. Cooler, heavier air displaces warmer, lighter air. In a confined space such as a room, the warm air is pushed up because there is nowhere else for it to go. Children can learn that this is the reason we may leave a window partly open at both top and bottom to have fresh air. Fresh, colder air enters at the bottom and pushes warmer air out the top. (Outdoors, colder air displacing warmer air is the primary cause of winds.)

What we have is a cause-and-effect relationship between two interacting objects: cold air and warm air. (In science, any material substance—solid, liquid, or gas—may be considered an "object.") Children can find evidence of the interaction by first measuring air temperatures near the floor and ceiling. Then they can close and open the window, each time holding strips of tissue paper at the top and bottom of the window, to observe directions of air flow.

To establish a cause-and-effect relationship, then, acceptable evidence must describe interacting objects. What most people call science "explanations" are typically descriptions of interacting objects. In science, the most powerful tool to discover cause-and-effect relationships is the experiment.

Correlation and Causation. Does breaking a mirror bring bad luck? Most schoolchildren have had experiences with common superstitions, claims of magic, astrology, and the like. These practices offer many chances to teach the difference between a genuine cause-and-effect connection and mere *correlation without causation*. For example, because two events—

breaking a mirror and then badly stubbing a toe—happen closely together, there is no logical reason to assume that one event caused the other.

One reason people outside the scientific community adopt seemingly plausible but untrue ideas comes from their concept of authority. To the nonscientist, an "authority" may simply be someone who by personality, position, or unsubstantiated eloquence attracts much attention. But in science, what counts is tested evidence. Any ballyhoo of untested ideas gets a fishy eye whether it comes from a distinguished veteran or a novice.

Nature of "Proof". Is it better to "test" hypotheses or to "prove" them? In elementary science, it's wise to avoid the term *prove*. Seldom can we experimentally prove anything in an elementary classroom. More important, the idea itself is antiquated. The modern view is that well-designed experiments and observations yield powerful data that lend power to the ideas behind them. Poorly designed experiments and slipshod observations yield less-powerful data and theories. Since all forms of evidence may be improvable, how can any corresponding hypothesis or theory be finally "proved"?

It is also wise to avoid saying to children that they are right or wrong when they give ideas and explanations. This behavior sets us up as an arbitrary authority who accepts or rejects proposals. Instead, we can simply ask, What is your evidence? This invites everyone to examine the data. Which of these two ways do you prefer?

"Failure" as Evidence. The perseverance of scientists is well known. Many grind on fruitlessly for years to find evidence that will support a hypothesis or solve a problem. Where is the reward? Their tenacity almost seems contrary to human nature. The makeup of science as an organized discipline helps us to see why this happens.

For the most part, science is a cooperative enterprise whose practitioners are expected to share their findings with others through publications and meetings. Persons who spread the results of careful work save time, money, and energy for everyone else with a common interest even when they announce no breakthroughs. This narrows the search and so benefits all. Also, careful work—the pursuit of plausible hypotheses with acceptable procedures—continually impels researchers forward because of its potential. As a scientist friend of mine says, "If you keep making a decent effort, sooner or later something good might happen." Besides this, recognition, promotion, and grant money often flow to researchers who share careful work. Although success is preferred, intelligent "failure"—which is the far more frequent outcome of investigation—is rewarded, too.

In your science teaching, you'll often find it useful to organize pupils into small groups that work independently to test a hypothesis or solve a problem. At times, some groups may report that they have failed to find supporting evidence for their ideas. Here, you might do what many effective teachers do: recognize their shared efforts as positive contributions, as well as the work of more successful groups. Commend them when possible on the intelligence of the methods they used, and discuss how to improve those processes. This raises morale and shows everyone a core value in science. It also resembles in a way what happens when scientists report research at their conventions.

Science Processes and Objectivity. The quality of the evidence we collect usually depends on the quality of the thinking processes we use and how objectively they are applied. The processes used by scientists (detailed in Chapter 4) as they seek and work with data include the following:

■ Observing

■ Classifying

■ Communicating

■ Measuring

■ Inferring and predicting

■ Experimenting

"Objective" persons use such processes in an impersonal manner—without bias, without allowing their desires and expectations to influence the process or outcome. Probably the chief way that scientists promote objectivity is to require that all reported findings be achievable by others under the same conditions. Procedures within each process can help make such replication possible.

For example, consider a "double blind" medical experiment in which a drug is being tested. The experimenters set up the test so that neither they nor the patient groups sampled know who is receiving the drug or who is being given the placebo. (An independent third party keeps track.)

Of course, objectivity is much harder to get with children than with highly educated adults. One common tendency you may have already observed, especially with primary-level pupils, is the subjective way they may view nonhuman objects. The child's environment often promotes fantasy over reality. Children commonly read stories or see TV cartoons in which animals talk, the sun smiles, and steam locomotives suffer pitiably as they huff and puff up a steep mountainside. Giving human characteristics to nonhuman objects is called *anthropomorphism*. Children usually have no trouble deciding whether such events are true or fictional. But sometimes they make anthropomorphic inferences without realizing it. These can take several forms.

Children may be quick to imbue some animals with human personality traits. But is a lion truly "braver" than a mouse? A fox "sly"? A wolf "nastier" than a dog? This is *personification*. No doubt some movies children see contribute to this form of anthropomorphism.

Sometimes children ascribe a conscious purpose to nonhuman things. Do plant roots really "seek" water? Do female birds find food for their young because "they don't want them to die"? This is *teleology*.

A third form of anthropomorphism, especially common in young children, is to endow almost any object with life and human feelings. I've had several primary-level pupils tell me it rains because "the clouds get sad and cry." Others, responding to the question, "Where is the sun at night?" have said, "It's tired and goes to sleep." This is *animism.*

Science educators today view anthropomorphic statements in the context of children's early attempts to explain their world. As children grow, these statements decrease and also become more easily correctable. Anthropomorphism in all its forms can be overcome by pupils when they learn how to make proper inferences from their observations. How to teach all the science processes and apply them objectively are described in detail in Chapter 4. The processes are also used in every investigation in Appendix A. Marginal notes show where each is used, so you can observe in context how they are applied.

The Importance of Processing Data.

Much factual material may be learned by children from books and other ways of being told about it. But to learn the science processes, they *must work with data.* For instance, pupils may be told how the period of a pendulum (to-and-fro motion) is determined, and some may understand and remember this. But pupils who are given a few materials and guided to figure this out for themselves will soon be counting the number of swings per minute (measuring), trying various possibilities to change the swing rate (experimenting), taking notes of what they did (communicating), making graphs (more communicating), and drawing conclusions from their findings (inferring). They are also more likely to remember and apply the principle of pendulums throughout their lives (clocks, playground swings, metronomes, oscillating water sprinklers, and so on).

Perhaps what makes processing data so effective in improving children's thinking is that they can actually observe the consequences of good and bad thinking. The objects they work with will usually "tell" them if

they are on the right track: snails will eat only what they are adapted to eat, toy boats will sink like real boats when they are not buoyant, green plants will die when deprived of light, and so on. Science is a good subject in which to demonstrate observable consequences because it presents so many opportunities to test ideas with concrete materials.

Interactive Nature of Process and Knowledge.

Process thinking is typically neglected in science education. One reason is that many teachers are unsure about how to teach it. In reaction, some curriculum writers press process teaching so hard they neglect subject-matter content. This approach runs against the inseparable nature of process and knowledge.

The science processes are not like computational skills in arithmetic. Nor are they like decoding skills in reading, which, once learned, may be applied in any subject-matter context. Cognitive psychologists say that the quality of the science processes we use is "domain specific." That is, *our ability to apply a process in a situation is strongly linked to our understanding of the organized field of subject matter that pertains to the situation.*[2] A physician's observations of subtle weather signs are likely to be no more useful than a meteorologist's observations of subtle disease symptoms, if each tries to do the other's work. Their subject-matter background of concepts and generalizations is what gives purpose, meaning, and significance to what they observe in their chosen fields. Background knowledge is inseparably mixed with the process of observation. The same can be said of the other processes they use in their work.

This means that a curriculum must give children continual opportunities to learn thinking processes within a wide variety of subject-matter areas and conditions if the processes are to be generally useful. So the

---

[2]Ellen D. Gagné. *The Cognitive Psychology of School Learning* (Boston: Little, Brown, 1985), pp. 145–150; and Barry K. Beyer. *Practical Strategies for the Teaching of Thinking* (Boston: Allyn and Bacon, 1987), p. 164.

trend today is to guide children to apply thinking processes in all the school subjects. Because process and subject-matter concepts are open-ended, pupils can get better at processing data and learning concepts throughout their lives. An effective science curriculum gives chances to teach process thinking within all topics at all grade levels. How you can identify and maximize these opportunities is an important objective of this book.

Following are the main points of the preceding pages on science as process:

- Science is a search for publicly observable and verifiable evidence.

- Evidence must describe interacting objects to establish cause-and-effect relations.

- Correlation is not the same as evidence of causation.

- Acceptable evidence is always subject to change with new data; so nothing is finally "proved."

- "Failure" gives evidence that narrows the search for further evidence.

- The search for evidence requires the objective use of science processes.

- Knowledge and the science processes are interactive; so effective curricula present opportunities to teach the processes within all topics and grade levels.

You can see that the imperatives of science as an organized discipline can set the foundation and tone for a quality science program. But there is much to choose from, and very few of our pupils will become scientists. What's likely to be useful for most people within our society?

SOCIETAL IMPERATIVES

As you saw on page 4, you are likely to teach better and stimulate more interest and appreciation in lessons when you apply science learning to everyday life. It's fun for pupils to learn how eyeglasses work when they study light energy and the eye. And it's interesting when studying electrical energy for them to make their own flashlights from simple materials. A well-planned curriculum usually contains many of these everyday applications.

At the same time, there are many broad concerns, problems, and changes that continually crop up in our society. Coping with them raises the need to educate people and change attitudes. It's only natural to look to the schools for help. Is it important for future adults to learn that the survival of many plant and animal species is threatened by humans? That our supply of safe, drinkable water continually decreases? That science-related careers are possible for women and men of all races, ethnic groups, and national origins?

The growing awareness of how *science, technology, and society* (STS) interrelate has generated an STS movement in science education. This causes numerous science programs to embody an "applications first" policy—to keep foremost how science impacts our lives. Science education today typically reflects many of society's concerns, including cultural literacy, energy and environmental problems, the ever-growing importance of technology, and career awareness for students at all levels.

Science and Cultural Literacy

Every society wants its contributing members to be culturally literate, that is, to have enough background knowledge and ability to communicate, produce, and improve the general welfare. When the culture of a society is primitive, knowledge is limited and fixed. People are self-sufficient. They can continue for many years doing the same things in the same self-sufficient ways.

In advanced societies such as ours, knowledge must multiply quickly. Interdependence increases as people develop narrow specialties to earn their way. Under such conditions, people need a common core of knowledge. How else can they efficiently communicate with one another, and address matters of public policy? The challenge compounds because of our country's large population and the cultural differences of persons who have settled here from many lands.

The need for cultural literacy arises at every hand. Turn on a TV and find references to toxic waste dumps, test-tube babies, AIDS, nuclear power, and artificial hearts. Pick up a newspaper and read stories about vaccines, fossil fuels, sonic booms, ozone depletion, radiation, and gene splicing. Shop for a new automobile and consider horsepower, fuel injection, disk brakes, and quadriphonic radio systems. Employers expect even more background knowledge. You can see that our functioning in this society, and even our well-being, are linked with cultural literacy.

Science literacy is the part of cultural literacy that enables us to live intelligently in a society that leans heavily on science and technology. It is not gained overnight. The student who is achieving science literacy is gradually

1. Developing positive attitudes about science and taking an active interest in natural phenomena and technological achievements.

2. Learning fundamental concepts of science and how the applications of these concepts affect our daily lives.

3. Learning techniques that compose the scientific methods to validate knowledge and to develop thinking skills for lifelong learning.

4. Using attitudes and knowledge about science to live as an informed citizen in a technologically advanced nation.[3]

All children need a rich array of firsthand experiences to grow toward a full measure of science literacy. It's especially important for disadvantaged children to have such experiences at school. They are less likely than advantaged children to have other opportunities for such growth. Quality science programs can expand their horizons and benefit other children as well. Possibilities increase for advanced study later that can lead to many occupational choices and benefits to society.

Energy and Environmental Education

Most thinking persons now realize that we must continue to move from a position of exploiting the environment to conserving or using it wisely. Not only are resources of the planet limited, but almost every year we see a greater demand on these resources from other nations. The immensity of the changes needed in the United States as we shift to environmental awareness is revealed in our yearly consumption of energy. With five percent of the world's population, the United States recently used *twenty-five percent* of the world's energy.

The history of material progress everywhere closely parallels a rise in energy use. More and more demand has been made on the earth's dwindling energy *stocks;* in modern times, these have been mainly the fossil fuels. As such fuels disappear, more attention will be turned to tapping into the relatively inexhaustible energy *flows:* solar, wind, and tidal energy, and the heat energy trapped beneath the earth's surface (geothermal energy). Material progress and swelling populations have also brought air, water, and land pollution and growing problems with managing solid wastes.

Education in environmental awareness is critical for massive changes to happen, especially in a democracy. Uninformed people are not ready to support essential research and development, to use less, to recycle materials, or to alter long habits that harm the environment. What is needed now as never before are people who understand that the earth is a closed system with natural self-renewing cycles. These cannot be overloaded without harm to the earth's inhabitants.

Working harmoniously with nature does not mean that the quality of life *must* go

---

[3] *Science Model Curriculum Guide, K–8* (Sacramento: California State Department of Education, 1987), p. 1.

down. Creative, imaginative people should continue to solve (or resolve) energy and environmental problems. But cooperation and common objectives among many persons are needed to apply solutions.

Nobody properly expects children to take on and solve such worldwide problems. However, the kinds of habits and understandings to effect major changes are best begun early and then reinforced over a number of years.

Many useful activities and information on energy and environmental education may be found in practically all modern elementary school science programs. This should continue indefinitely.

Technology and Career Awareness

Solutions to energy and environmental problems will flow in good part from applied science or *technology*. So will advances in health care, business, communications, agriculture, and many other areas.

As you saw earlier, scientists invent ideas to explain, predict, and *control* phenomena. Technology is the branch of science that is mainly concerned with controlling, or managing, objects and events in improved ways.

Where will the people come from to fill the many technical jobs that will be available? Only a tiny percentage of people can become research scientists. But many thousands can become professional engineers or skilled technicians with satisfying careers and substantial pay. The need for engineers' useful inventions and creative solutions to technical problems should continue indefinitely. So should a strong demand for technicians to conduct laboratory tests, treat waste water and solid wastes, service and program computers, repair electronic devices, operate medical equipment, and the like. Far more technical workers will be needed in the future.

Traditionally, women have avoided many jobs in technology. Sex-role stereotyping is still deeply etched into our culture. But attitudes are changing. Elementary school science programs can contribute to this change.

Science textbooks and other teaching materials now show women and men in a variety of science-related jobs and describe what they do. Becoming aware of a variety of occupations and having realistic role models open up a broader range of choices for pupils when the time comes to make career decisions.

Technology and the Curriculum

Some old notions about teaching science die hard. Don't be surprised to hear remarks like these in the school lounge:

"Even a new science textbook is dated by the time it's distributed."

"No science curriculum should be adopted for more than four years."

"I can't teach science. Who has time to keep up with it?"

People who talk like this have the wrong idea about teaching *elementary school* science. Contrary to their view, the basic ideas and processes we need to teach usually last a long time. As you know, scientific thinking may change with new information. But many ideas we use today—gravity, motion, adaptation, interdependence, rules of evidence, and the like—can last for generations in unchanged or only slightly altered forms.

Where, then, are fast changes likely to happen? In *technology* (from copper telephone wires to fiber optics); in specific *facts* (from 186,198 miles per second for the speed of light to 186,282 miles per second); and in the thinking of scientists engaged in *frontier research* (from few subatomic particles to many).

Basic concepts and generalizations in effective science programs are often linked to technological applications: aeronautics, rocketry, telecommunications, electric circuitry, soil conservation, food processing, and the like.

Learning about these applications helps to keep study alive and interesting. It can also change the ways children view many of the useful gadgets around us. Children who see some everyday devices as understandable and interesting develop different self-concepts than those who see them as mysterious and bewildering.

Yet a worthwhile *elementary* curriculum will probably always be rooted in the basic ideas and processes of science because it yields a bigger payoff: pupils understand more basic science and so more applications, including technology.

If you are concerned about teaching technology, please remember that its complex forms are typically reserved for junior high school and beyond, where teachers are subject specialists. Let the textbook or curriculum be your guide. Most authors are sensitive to what young children can understand. And the simple applications they present are likely to be both interesting and well grounded in basic science.

CHILDHOOD IMPERATIVES

Science as a discipline and as applied to society's concerns comprises the bulk of what makes science education valuable to most persons. But we are dealing with the very young. How do we match what there is to be learned with what children actually need and can do?

Perhaps you have heard the expression, "To a child who's discovered the hammer, all the world is a nail." It captures nicely the broad curiosity and inner need of children to try things out for themselves whenever they are free to do so. Science education is of great value to children because it richly enhances these and other attributes that loom so large in their development. But the nature

of childhood also makes us recognize several other realities.

For example, because broad generalizations and skills are so useful in science study, it is tempting to increase their scope so they apply to more and more phenomena. When we deal with children, though, there is always the question of when to stop. Explanations become continually more abstract and remote from common experience as their "mileage" increases. As a generalization or process approaches the most advanced scientific model, it is less likely that children can learn it or will even want to. To persist is simply to have them bite off more than they can chew. So teaching generalizations about molecules in the primary years, for example, or insisting that *all* variables be controlled in upper-grade experiments is likely to be self-defeating.

It is important for children to understand and see the purpose of what they are doing. Also, they need to reach short-range goals as they head toward those farther away. To do otherwise cuts down pupil interest and personal significance in what is taught. Because children are relatively inexperienced and intellectually as well as physically immature, they usually learn best when working with concrete and semiconcrete materials, limited generalizations, and the here and now. This is most obvious and necessary with younger pupils, as primary teachers are quick to tell us.

So science and applied science as practiced by adults usually must be modified to fit what we know about children's capacities. Ideas and processes need to be simplified, known interests and needs of children considered, and their physical coordination and dexterity weighed. What they can apply now must be assessed, as well as complementary learnings from the other goals of early general education.

It is unlikely that any publisher or curriculum office can develop a program in advance that suits every child or class. To bring a suitable match between pupils and curriculum requires our intelligent intervention.

This, in turn, requires us to understand in some detail the imperatives of childhood, particularly how children learn science. The whole second chapter is given to that important objective.

HOW SCIENCE CONTRIBUTES TO WHOLE LEARNING

So far you've examined some imperatives to help you judge the good and bad in science teaching. But your work as an elementary-school teacher goes far beyond the teaching of science. No subject in the curriculum stands alone. After all, we want to provide a basic *general* education in the elementary school. What can science give to meeting objectives in other subjects? How is this done? Now is a good time to put science, with its exciting potential for enriching your overall teaching, into perspective.

It is only common sense to realize that learning in science often calls for skills from other parts of the curriculum to be applied. When pupils look up information about caves in an encyclopedia, they are reading. When they measure and graph changes in a growing plant, they use mathematics. They use language skills to organize and report their findings in experiments and observations. When children plan and draw a large panel picture to illustrate conservation practices, this is art. Such integration of subjects is both desirable and usually necessary if you want to promote useful, whole learning.

There are also times when several content subjects or parts of subjects are integrated with science. Energy and environmental education, and topics in social studies, health, and safety are the most likely areas of the curriculum to be treated in this fashion. Drawing on content from several subjects makes it easier for cohesive, whole understandings to form in pupils' minds when they study such questions as Where do we get our water? What can people do to conserve energy? Why did they build Megalopolis City in that location?

A main responsibility of the elementary school has been and is to teach pupils skills in reading, language, and mathematics. From time to time over the years, some of the public and even some educators have taken a narrow view of how to do this. In many schools, pupils are being saturated and bored by an isolated approach to these skill subjects.

There *is* probably some need to study each subject separately and sequentially, particularly in the early stages. But this approach by itself does the job only partway. It ignores how the skills are applied and learned in the world outside the classroom. There, the three Rs are used far more flexibly and broadly. They are needed in varied ways and in many different subject-matter situations. A curriculum that allows children to apply these skills in several areas reflects that fact.

There are several reasons some people cling to a narrow view of the three Rs. Consider reading instruction, long regarded as the most important of the elementary school subjects. When pupils' reading scores on tests decline or do not advance at an acceptable rate, a commonsense remedy is to give more time to the subject. This often comes at the expense of science and social studies. But the remedy prescribed can speed *decline* in reading scores after the primary grades rather than advance them.

Why? Reading consists of decoding (phonics, structural analysis, and so on) and comprehension. Decoding instruction is distinct, linear, progressive, and above all, limited. The skills can be mastered by most primary pupils so that further instruction, once the elements are learned, is unlikely to do any good. Comprehension, though, is unlimited or open-ended. No one can "master" it because it largely depends on the quality and extent of one's world knowledge.[4] Most of the general reading material in the world reflects concepts from science, social studies, and literature. So an important way to improve reading comprehension is to increase the time and quality of instruction in these content areas rather than in reading alone. Still, good results do not come right away.

The teaching of decoding during the primary grades usually raises pupils' reading test scores immediately when decoding is sampled because there is a high correlation between what is taught and what is measured. But gains in reading *comprehension* test scores from increased content teaching are likely to appear slowly, be cumulative, and show occasional inconsistencies at different grade levels. Why? Test items must be drawn from a far larger pool of possibilities. In time, though, the probability of significant gains in reading comprehension is high.

Increasingly, top organizations in education are throwing their weight behind subject-matter content as a way to boost performance in the three Rs, and to push up overall literacy. The California State Department of Education explains its view in this way:

> The shift of emphasis from mastering basic skills to understanding thoroughly the content of the curriculum is intentional. Research indicates that children will learn more—and more effectively—if teachers focus lessons on content and the connections among subject areas. Students learn to apply skills by reading, writing, and discussing curriculum content. The essential learnings emphasize central concepts, patterns, and relationships among subject areas and reinforce inquiry and creative thinking.[5]

Science and other content areas give more than just chances to apply the three-R skills. Subject-matter content also supplies situations from which appealing, natural *purposes* for the three Rs arise. The skills by themselves lack these situations. So purpose has to be artificially supplied from the outside by the teacher ("For practice today, do all the division problems on page 151 of our math book."). Or, purpose is contrived within the textbook. Consider some word problems you have seen in mathematics textbooks ("Terry wants to find out how much more the larger wagon costs") and tired examples in language textbooks ("Pretend a friend is in the hospital and you want to write a letter").

Some of the foregoing is fine, but you can see that a steady diet of this alone soon pales. That's why an elaborate system of extrinsic rewards—gold stars, Happy Face stickers, and other reinforcers—often must spice up a strongly-focused three-R curriculum.

The need to apply three-R skills arises more naturally within a science program. Sometimes this happens incidentally ("You can find some answers to your questions about satellites in this book" and "You might write Dr. Thompson to see what she thinks"). Or, it is usually easy to slant science activities toward the skills you want reinforced—experience charts for beginning readers, metric measurements and calculations for math concepts, and so on.

The research[6] on science as a vehicle for helping children learn the basic skill subjects is massive and convincing. Science programs based on manipulative materials are espe-

[4]Jeanne S. Chall, *Stages of Reading Development* (New York: McGraw-Hill, 1983), p. 8; and *What Works—Research About Teaching and Learning* (Washington, D.C.: U.S. Department of Education, 1986), p. 53.

[5]*Science Model Curriculum Guide, K–8* (Sacramento: California State Department of Education, 1987), p. vii.

[6]See, for example, Ruth T. Wellman, "Science: A Basic for Language Development," in *What Research Says to the Science Teacher,* Mary Budd Rowe, ed., vol. 1 (Washington, D.C.: National Science Teachers Association, 1978), pp. 1–12; and Sandra R. Kren, "Science and Mathematics: Interactions at the Elementary Level," in *What Research Says to the Science Teacher,* vol. 2, Mary Budd Rowe, ed. (Washington, D.C.: National Science Teachers Association, 1979), pp. 32–49.

cially helpful in building reading and language readiness levels in primary pupils. Firsthand experiences in science expand pupils' vocabularies and reading comprehension at all levels. Similar growth is found in mathematics as children work with various geometric forms and measure real objects and events.

Good science teaching develops in children the kinds of attitudes, ways of thinking, and a solid knowledge base that promote success in the real world. Devoting too much time to the three Rs traps children into a narrow and superficial outlook that reduces their capacity to learn further and solve real problems. Fortunately, increasing numbers of educators and parents see the consequences. That's why in recent years there has been a steady growth of more balanced and integrated approaches across the curriculum, including various forms of "whole-language" teaching, that evoke personal meaning in what is learned and an I-can-think-when-I-try feeling in learners.

How to integrate science and other subjects, with emphasis on the three Rs, is detailed in Chapters 4, 5, and 6. Units of instruction, described in Chapter 7, offer an ideal and systematic way to integrate into science as many experiences in the three Rs or other subjects as you judge best.

SUMMARY

Your view of science teaching makes a big difference in what pupils actually experience, even when you and fellow teachers supposedly teach the same curriculum. Three compelling influences can improve your teaching as you learn more about them: science as a discipline, society's needs, and the characteristics of children. Understanding these imperatives enables you to judge what is basic, useful, and learnable.

Science is an organized search for patterns or regularities. Scientists construct concepts and generalizations to explain the patterns they observe and, when possible, to predict and control objects and events within the patterns. Nonscientists also do this, but usually with far less precision and reliability. Evidence in science is acceptable only when it is collected and processed under objective rules generally agreed to by the scientific community. To conduct scientific investigations requires an integrated knowledge of process and content in the topic of study.

When problems and changes emerge in a society, coping with them raises the need to educate people and change attitudes. Some recent matters that affect science education are society's increased concern for science literacy, energy and environmental education, and technology and career awareness.

Science as a discipline, and the science that adults find useful in our society, must be modified to suit children before we can expect them to learn it. Ideas and processes need to be simplified, known interests and needs of children considered, and their physical coordination and dexterity weighed. What they can apply now must be assessed, as well as complementary learnings from the other goals of early general education, if the science curriculum is to be appropriate for children.

Effective teaching often combines science study with opportunities to integrate and apply the other school subjects. It fosters whole learning in children—the attitudes, ways of thinking, and integrated knowledge base that transfer successfully into the larger world.

SUGGESTED READINGS

American Association for the Advancement of Science. *Science for All Americans, Project 2061.* Washington, D.C.: AAAS, 1989. (One of the most authoritative descriptions of science literacy.)

Cole, K. C., "The Essence of Understanding." *Discover* 5 (4):57–62 (April 1984). (What does it mean to "understand" something from a scientific point of view? A thoughtful and interesting essay.)

Kronholm, Martha, and John Ramsey. "Issues and Analysis." *Science and Children* 29 (2):20–23 (October 1991). (An example of how to approach science-related social issues.)

Penick, John E., ed. *Focus on Excellence: Elementary Science Revisited.* Washington, D.C.: National Science Teachers Association, 1988. (Thirteen of the best school science programs in the country and how they developed.)

Waks, Leonard J. "The Responsibility Spiral: A Curriculum Framework for STS Education." *Theory Into Practice* 31(1):12–18 (Winter, 1992). (How educators can identify, select, organize, and sequence learning activities to promote effective science/technology/society education.)

Yager, Robert E. "A New Focus for School Science: S/T/S." *School Science and Mathematics* 88 (3):181–90 (March 1988). (Describes the interrelations of science, technology, and society for school programs as conceived by leading science educators.)

2

How Children Learn Science

Let's look again at two of the children's questions with which we began the first chapter:

Why doesn't a spider get stuck in its web?

and

Where do the people on TV go when you turn it off?

Compare the levels of sophistication behind these questions. The child who asked about the spider, for example, is mulling over an interesting discrepancy. If a fly gets stuck on a sticky web, then why not the spider itself? This is high-level thinking. But what of the question about television? Do some children of school age—remember, they may have more than a thousand hours of viewing experience—really believe there are tiny people inside a television set? Surprisingly, some do, in a hazy half-conscious way. At the primary level, it's not rare at all.

There is a wide range of thinking ability among elementary school children. You'll find large differences even within a single class of children of the same age. The ability to assess and understand children's thinking can help you to teach anything, but especially science and mathematics.

CONTRIBUTIONS OF PIAGET

What can children learn in science? And how does their ability to reason grow? Jean Piaget, the world-famous Swiss developmental psychologist, is the researcher who has given most for our understanding of children's thinking. His books[1] and research suggest

---

[1] Among others, *The Language and Thought of the Child* (New York: Harcourt, 1926); *The Psychology of Intelligence* (London: Routledge and Kegan Paul, 1950), *The Construction of Reality in the Child* (New York: Basic Books, 1954). Also, Barbel Inhelder, *The Child's Conception of Space* (London: Routledge and Kegan Paul, 1956), and *The Early Growth of Logic in the Child* (London: Routledge and Kegan Paul, 1964).

that the ability to think develops in several noticeable "stages." Please understand that the idea of *stages* is solely a convenient theoretical construct. Improvement in thinking tends to be gradual and incremental, rather than abrupt and massive, as children move from one stage to the next. All children normally go through the earlier stages in the same fixed order. But not everyone moves from one stage to the next at the same time or achieves all stages in every field of study. A child may think in one stage for some things and a different stage for others. This is why it's preferable to label a specific sample of an individual child's *thinking* as being representative of a stage, rather than the child. However, when describing the typical behaviors of a large group of children within the usual age range of a given stage, it's customary and convenient to label the children as belonging to a certain stage.

As teachers, our concern is with children at the *preoperational stage,* from about 2 to 7 years old; *concrete operational stage,* from about 7 to 12 years old; and *formal operational stage,* from about 12 on.

Preoperational means that children in this stage are not yet able to do certain kinds of thinking Piaget calls *operations.* (Details shortly.) The latter part of the stage, which lasts from about four to seven years, is known as the *intuitive thought substage.* Since this is the time when most children begin school, we'll start our study of children's thinking at the intuitive period of their mental development.

"Intuitive thought" captures well how four- to seven-year-olds think. They typically use their sense impressions or intuition rather than logic in forming judgments. They also find it hard to remember more than one thing at a time.

Concrete operational children, on the other hand, can do much logical thinking. Their handicap is that the ideas they consider must be tied to concrete materials they can manipulate. Or, at least, they must have had some firsthand experience with the materials to think about them.

In the stage of formal operations, children are able to think much more abstractly; there is far less need to refer to concrete objects. With experience similar to adults', they can handle formal logic, that is, use the same mental operations as many adults.

As an elementary school teacher, your work is mainly with children who are in the intuitive and concrete operational stages of mental growth. It will be worthwhile for you to study in some detail how they grow from intuitive thought, to concrete thought, and to the beginnings of formal logical thought. Learning how children think can give you some fascinating chances to reflect on what they do or say. It can make you more sensitive to individual differences. Best of all, it can help you to guide each child in learning science. The next section will describe, in order, typical behaviors of intuitive thinkers, concrete thinkers, and formal thinkers.

Intuitive Period Behaviors

What can you expect of many children ages four to seven? We'll consider their thinking in four related areas. (The same four areas will also be examined later in describing the concrete thinker and formal thinker.) We begin with intuitive children's notions about causes of events.

Cause-and-Effect Thinking. The logic of intuitive children as to causes can be unpredictable. They may think nothing of contradicting themselves to "explain" some event. If you ask them why an object sinks in water, they may say it is "too small" to float. Another time, it is "too large." If you point out this inconsistency, the typical child may shrug and say, "Well, it is."

Four- to seven-year-olds often give magical explanations for events: "The sky is held up by angels." Or they may suppose that lifeless objects have conscious awareness and other

human qualities. Clouds move because they "want to." There is thunder because "the sky is angry." Natural events may happen to serve a human need or purpose: "It rained because the farmers needed it."

Relative Thinking. Of special interest is the self-centered view of intuitive children. This affects how they relate to other people. Ask them to point to your *right* arm when they are face-to-face with you and they point to your *left* arm. They find it hard to put themselves in another's position. The same problem with orientation may come up when they put on clothing. Left arms are often thrust into the right sleeves of coats and jackets.

This egocentric quality also surfaces in their language. They take for granted that everyone understands (and is interested in) what they are saying. They assume that words mean the same to others as they do to them. If the listener gets confused, intuitive children may simply repeat the original message more loudly. The idea has not yet developed that we need to say things in certain ways to communicate clearly.

Their egocentrism may also affect their perception of objects. So the moon and sun follow *them* as they walk. It doesn't occur to them that others also see the same apparent motion.

Four- to seven-year-olds find it hard to interrelate several ideas at one time. Take time, distance, and speed. If two model windup cars start together on a path, you know the faster will travel farther in the same time. But intuitive children cannot properly interrelate the time/speed/distance variables. Unless they have seen one car overtake and pass the other, they focus on the stopping points. When asked to explain the different end points, they typically say that one car must have traveled longer than the other. The other possibility seldom occurs to them.

The relative nature of other physical properties also dawns slowly in this stage. Some objects are always "heavy," others are always "light." Some are always "large," others are always "small." Little by little, properties of objects such as size, texture, hardness, volume, thickness, and the like are viewed in relative terms: "Peggy's tall, but short next to her Mom."

Classifying and Ordering. The abilities to classify and arrange objects or ideas in some logical order are basic to thinking in both science and mathematics. By analyzing likenesses and differences, we can make more sense out of our environment.

Intuitive thinkers usually learn to sort objects well. But they are limited to considering only one property at a time. They can put all the objects of one color in a pile and those of another color in a second pile. They can also go on to subdivide these objects by using another descriptive property.

In Figure 2-1, for example, the objects shown have two different colors and two different shapes. An intuitive child has sorted the objects by color, blues and nonblues (reds). The child can also go on to subdivide the blues by shape. This means he or she might sort out the blue circles from the larger group of blue circles and blue triangles. You will find such skill is fairly common even at the lower primary level.

Is this true classification? Piaget would not think so because the intuitive child cannot keep the part-whole relationship in mind. Let me explain further. If you ask, "Are all the blue objects triangles?" the child will say, "No." This, of course, is true. There are blue circles as well as blue triangles. But if you ask, "Are all the triangles blue?" the intuitive child is likely to say "No" again, which is wrong. The notion of class inclusion is too abstract to grasp at this stage.

Intuitive children don't see that the blue triangles are included as a part of a larger class of blue objects. How can all of a smaller group be at the same time only a part of a larger group? This is too abstract to grasp. Similarly, it's hard for them to realize that they can live at the same time on a street *and* in a town *and* in a county *and* in a state *and* in a country.

The ability to order or arrange objects in a series—small to large, thick to thin, and so on—grows fast during the intuitive stage.

Let's consider how these children might seriate different-sized sticks from smallest to largest. Four- or five-year olds may only be able to order at random a few sticks in some consistent sequence. Six-year-olds usually do better, but they rely on trial and error. They will continually size up each stick with the next, then replace each as seems needed, perhaps several times. Only during the last part of the intuitive stage, around age seven for many children, is trial and error replaced by a more systematic attack. These children may look first for the largest and smallest pieces, then arrange the others with the end objects always in mind. Again, the key to success is the ability to hold two or more things in mind at the same time.

Conservative Thinking. Perhaps the most widely known findings of Piaget are the intuitive child's notions of *conservation*. By "conserve" Piaget means the ability to realize that certain properties of an object remain unchanged or can be restored even though the object's appearance is changed. Take a paper bag, for instance. Even if you crush it, you realize that it still weighs the same and can be opened again to its original capacity. The informed adult, of course, has little trouble with most conservation concepts. But the reasoning of intuitive children can be surprisingly different. Examine next the ways in

FIGURE 2-1
An intuitive child can sort objects by color (blues and reds).

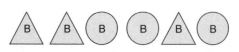

which they may fail to conserve number, length, amount, area, weight, and volume—each important for science and mathematics understandings.

The conservation of *number* is easily tested. If you put a dozen checkers in two matched rows, these children are quite sure each row contains the same number of checkers. That is because they see a one-to-one correspondence between the checkers. But spread out one row or bunch it together and the children become confused. Now it will seem that there are comparatively more (spread-out row) or fewer (bunched row) checkers in the altered group.

The ability to conserve *length* is necessary before you can ask children to measure meaningfully. Intuitive thinkers will agree that two identical strings are the same length when laid out together. But move one ahead of the other, and they may now say it is longer. This is not simply a misunderstanding of the term "longer." It literally seems longer to them.

Their thinking shows the same limits when they are tested for the conservation of *liquid substance*. If you show intuitive children two identical glasses filled with water, they will probably say each contains the same volume of water. But suppose you pour the contents of one glass into a taller, narrower glass. They are likely to say now that the taller glass contains more water than the remaining filled glass.

These pupils also show the same perception with conservation of *solid substance*. Suppose you show them two identical balls of clay. They will agree each is made up of the same amount of clay. Now flatten out one into a large disk, and they probably will say the disk has more clay than the clay ball. It seems larger to them.

Appearance again fools intuitive children when they are asked to conserve *area*. Two toy buildings side by side on a paper lot seem to take up less space than when the buildings are placed far apart.

Similarly, they cannot conserve *weight*. They believe a solid object weighs more after it is cut up in the form of several smaller pieces. Or, if a soft plastic ball is compressed into a smaller ball, they feel that it now weighs less.

Intuitive children also believe that changing an object's form affects its overall size or *volume*. A clay object submerged in a half glass of water causes the water to rise to a level that equals the volume of the clay object. They do not realize that no matter how the object is reshaped in solid form, it will displace the same volume of water.

Do you see the common thread in these ways to check on the child's conservation of number, length, substance, area, weight, and volume? All give the learner a choice between a perceptual impression and logic. Intuitive children usually choose their perception.

They fail to conserve because of two reasons. When an object's appearance is changed in several dimensions, they center on one and ignore the other. It is too hard to consider more than one thing at the same time. They cannot compensate for the changed dimension. The taller glass of water means to them that there is more water. But you and I see that the taller glass is also narrower. We can compensate for one dimension by thinking of the other at the same time.

The second reason some children fail to conserve these key concepts is that they cannot reverse their thinking. You and I know that what is done can be undone, at least mentally. We can easily change directions in our thinking and imagine a reversed or restored condition. But intuitive children lack this flexibility as they focus on the object's present appearance. In short, they are tied to their perception.

The inability of preoperational children to compensate when an object's appearance changes and to reverse their thinking are the chief reasons they cannot perform "operations" in the Piagetian sense. Let's see next some mental operations that are possible in the *next* stage of development.

Concrete Operational Behaviors

What thinking can you expect of many children ages 7 to 12? A comparison of the child in the stage of concrete operations with the intuitive thinker reveals many differences. Consider again the four areas mentioned before: cause-and-effect thinking, relative thinking, classifying and ordering, and conservative thinking.

Cause-and-Effect Thinking. Unlike intuitive children, concrete operational pupils usually avoid contradictory explanations for events. If a contradiction is pointed out to them, they try to straighten it out. They don't ignore it or otherwise show unconcern as younger children may.

Natural events are no longer seen to happen through magic or to fit some human convenience or purpose. The concrete thinker sees the need to make a physical connection between an effect and its cause. So natural objects or events are influenced by other natural objects or events.

The improvement in thinking is only slight at first. For example, they may now say "the wind comes from the sky" rather than "the wind comes to keep us cool." And a bicycle goes "because the pedals go around" rather than "because a bicycle can go." But notice the linking of physical objects in the first of each of these paired statements. This is a key difference in logical growth that first appears at the early part of the concrete stage.

In the last part of the concrete stage, the child uses explanations that reflect what you and I call "good common sense." They may not always agree with scientific evidence, but they do make sense. The explanations are logical and show judgment. For example, a 10-year-old may say to you, "It's colder in winter because the earth is farther away from the sun." This is entirely logical even though it is wrong. (The earth-sun distance is actually less when the United States has winter. The earth's tilted axis is basically responsible for seasons.)

Relative Thinking. The egocentric quality found in intuitive pupils changes significantly in the concrete stage. Now children are much more aware of viewpoints that differ from their own. And they are more concerned with what others think. So they try to get evidence to support their ideas and spend time attempting to convince their peers.

Concrete thinkers can mentally put themselves in another's place. They realize that someone opposite to them will see direction in an opposite way. Also, the relationship between time and distance as a ratio that determines speed begins to form at this stage.

They can do experiments, but they are usually aware of only a few of the changeable conditions (variables) that might affect the results. The relationships they consider still must be linked to concrete or pictorial objects before they can deal effectively with them. Take this problem, for example:

Bill is shorter than Jane.

Bill is taller than Mary.

Who is the tallest of all?

The concrete operational thinker typically must draw stick figures to get the answer.

Classifying and Ordering. The first true classification appears in the concrete stage. These children recognize the class-inclusion principle. They understand that if all *robins* disappear, there still would be other *birds* left. But if all *birds* disappear, there would be no *robins* left.

However, classifications that require increasingly abstract organizations are beyond them. Suppose you show them some objects that have several properties and ask them to classify them. They may easily organize them into four groups according to four different properties. But if you ask them to classify the four groups into three groups and logically justify the new groupings, this is harder. Forming the three groups into two groups is still harder. This ability usually appears only by age 15 or so, in the formal operations stage.

The concrete child's ability to order (seriate) objects is fairly systematic now, but continues to grow and is by no means complete. It takes until about age nine or later before one can consistently place in series objects of different weights. And the ability to seriate objects by the volume of water each displaces, or to seriate by viewing solid objects, is not consistent until the formal operations stage.

The concrete thinker's improved ability to seriate objects means he or she can better follow a succession of steps or changes in some process. The intuitive child tends to see each step as a separate entity, but the concrete thinker is aware of and understands the connection between the steps. So the steps in making ice cream, or developing a photo, for instance, are much more meaningful to the concrete thinker.

Conservative Thinking.   Perhaps the most obvious and dramatic difference that appears in concrete thinkers is their ability to conserve number, length, and so on. This is because, unlike intuitive children, they can consider more than one thing at a time. They can reverse their thinking and hold in mind a sequence of changes. But the ability to conserve develops gradually.

Table 2-1 shows the usual sequence of children's concept development. However, the ages shown may vary somewhat when the same children are tested by different testers, since test procedures, children's responses,

TABLE 2-1
Usual sequence of concept development.

Conservation Concept	Age of Conserver (Years)
Number	6–7
Length	7–8
Substance (solid and liquid)	7–8
Area	8–10
Weight	9½–10½
Displaced volume	12–15

and interpretations of responses may not be wholly uniform. Notice that the displaced volume concept is not conserved until the stage of formal operations. This is probably because, of the concepts shown, it is the most abstract. It incorporates something from most of the others.

Formal Operations Behaviors

Some children begin to show evidence of formal operations at about age 12 or even earlier. But they are not likely to be classifiable as formal operational until they are 15 or 16. Even then, few students can operate consistently at the formal level, particularly when the material to be learned is new to them. This is also true of adults. *Probably most adults and adolescents think at the concrete operational level most of the time.* What the schools can do about this is a matter for much research.

The chief difference between the concrete operational child and the formal operational child is the latter's superior ability to deal with abstractions. Like a skillful checkers player, the formal thinker can think through several moves ahead without touching a checker. A concrete thinker, on the other hand, is limited to considering one move at a time. Even then, this child may need to physically move about the checkers into one tentative position or another before deciding what to do.

Cause-and-Effect Thinking.   The beginning formal thinker thoroughly enjoys developing theories or hypotheses to explain almost any event. At the same time, the child is developing the skill to separate the logic of a statement from its content. Consider, for example:

The moon is made of green cheese.

Green cheese is good to eat.

Therefore, the moon is good to eat.

The logic of this proposition is sound. However, we cannot say the same for its factual assumption! The concrete thinker would reject this proposition outright because of its content. ("That's silly!")

Another critical difference between the concrete and the formal thinker is the way each considers the various conditions (variables) that may affect an experiment. Suppose a child is presented with five jars, the liquid contents of which may be mixed in any combination.[2] Only one combination of three jars produces the desired yellow color. The concrete thinker tends to combine two liquids at a time. But then the child may stop or just dump together at random three or more liquids. The formal thinker, however, typically thinks through all the combinations in a systematic way before starting. First come the pairs, then the triple combinations, $1 + 2 + 3$, $1 + 2 + 4$, $1 + 2 + 5$, and so on.

It is during the formal operations stage that children can control variables by holding them constant in mind. This enables them to do quick "thought" experiments. "If all things are equal except . . . , then . . . " becomes a convenient way to appraise hypotheses. This is not typical of concrete thinkers.

Relative Thinking. Children in the formal operational stage become able to understand relative position and motion to the point where predictions become possible. So, for example, a study of the interactions of various bodies in the solar system is meaningful. These boys and girls also understand higher-order abstractions—they can define concepts with other abstract concepts. ("Light energy is the visible part of the electromagnetic spectrum.") They can also explain concepts with analogies and similies. ("An orbiting satellite is like a ball on a string that you whirl around your head.")

Interestingly, the beginning formal thinkers' vigorous habit of using logic to organize and explain everything in the physical world

brings out again an egocentric quality in their relations to others. They cannot understand at first why everyone is not as logical as they. "If pollution is ruining the cities, then why isn't the gasoline engine outlawed now? The government is *crazy* if they let this go on!" They are still years away from the adult's perception of reality found in the French proverb, "To understand all is to forgive all." Later they will combine their commendable idealism with a knowledge of what is possible.

Classification and Conservation. You may recall that the formal thinkers are able to reclassify grouped objects in a way not available to concrete thinkers. That is, they can recombine groups into fewer but broader categories with more abstract labels. Also, they can classify things in a hierarchical way. In other words, they are able to form subgroups right down to the individual members and keep the interrelations in mind. This is much more difficult for concrete thinkers.

Here's an example. Suppose some formal thinkers have tested six white powders to learn more about their properties. They might arrange their data as in Figure 2-2.

Besides the ability to conserve the displacement of volume mentioned before, formal thinkers can also conserve solid volume. They realize that a building twice as high as another needs only half the base to equal the overall size of the other building.

Notice that this concept is like the conservation of solid substance concept usually achieved at age seven or eight. Yet the conservation of volume comes unexpectedly late. This shows the value of finding out what is really going on rather than simply following what others assume.

For a summary of children's thinking within the Piagetian stages, please see Appendix E.

Next is the first of several activities within this and the following chapters. They are intended to help you gain further useful knowledge, sharpen skills, and apply key principles. The length of the first exercise—it is by far the longest in the book—reflects its importance.

---

[2]The prototype of this experiment is described in Jean Piaget's and Barbel Inhelder's *The Psychology of the Child* (New York: Basic Books, 1969), p. 134.

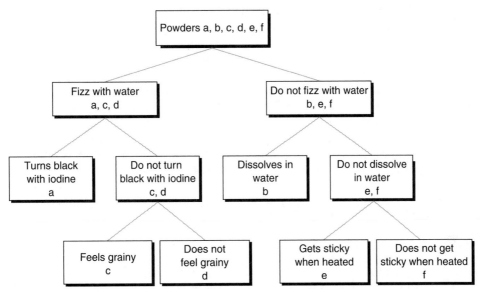

FIGURE 2-2
Formal thinkers are able to classify things into subgroups and keep the interrelations in mind.

EXERCISE
2-1

Assessing Thinking Through Piagetian Tasks

Your understanding of children's thinking can be greatly improved if you try your hand at assessing some of their ideas. You can start by discovering where they are in forming the important concepts of number, length, solid and liquid substance, area, perimeter-area relationship, weight, and volume. Your growing skill in interpreting how children think about specific concepts will be far more useful than merely labeling their general stages of mental growth.

The methods suggested here will be like those developed by Piaget and associates. The tasks described take too long to use with more than a few children. However, the experience you will get in administering these tasks will help you later on to use more informal everyday techniques as you work with pupils.

If your time with and access to children are limited, and you are interested in primary-level teaching, try at least two younger children of different ages (five and eight, for example) with any three of the following tests: conservation of number, length, solid substance, liquid substance, and area.

For minimal upper-level testing, try two older children of different ages (9 and 12, for example) and any three of these tests: conservation of perimeter-area relationship, weight, displaced volume A, and displaced volume B.

You will need to work with each child separately. Everything in each task should be done directly by the child or, when necessary, by you in full view of the child.

The usual sequence of development in conserving a concept is this: First, the child depends almost completely on perceptions in forming judgments. Then, there is a transition period when the child shifts uncertainly between perceptions and logic. Finally, the child is sure of his or her logic—thinking controls perceptions. With this in mind, after administering each task, decide whether the child is a nonconserver (N), in a transitional state (T), or a conserver (C) as to the concept involved. Before you begin, it will be helpful to read, "How to Evaluate Your Task Administration," found at the end of this exercise.

Conservation of Number

Materials: eight red and eight black checkers (or paper disks or buttons).
Procedure:

1. Arrange eight black checkers in a row. Leave some space between each (Figure 2-3).

FIGURE 2-3

2. Ask the child to make a row of red checkers by putting one red checker next to each black one (Figure 2-4). Ask if now there are as many red as black checkers or fewer and why the child thinks so. If the child establishes equivalence, continue. Otherwise, stop at this point.

O O O O O O O
O O O O O O O

FIGURE 2-4

3. Next, move the red checkers farther apart from each other. Ask if there are now more black or red checkers, or if there is the same number (Figure 2-5). Then, ask why the child thinks so.

O O O O O O O
OOOOOOO

FIGURE 2-5

4. Finally, bunch the red checkers close together and repeat the same questions (Figure 2-6).

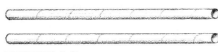

FIGURE 2-6

Note: The child who answers consistently that the number of checkers remains the same and satisfactorily tells why each time is a conserver (C) as to this concept. The child who says that the total number changes with each shift is a nonconserver (N). The child whose answers are inconsistent or who fails to give a satisfactory reason for each statement is in a transitional (T) stage. A similar appraisal can be made for each of the following tasks as well.

Conservation of Length

Materials: two identical soda straws (or strings or pipe cleaners).
Procedure:

1. Place the two straws together as in Figure 2-7. Ask the child if they are the same or different length, then why she thinks so. If the child says they are the same, continue. If not, stop the activity here.

FIGURE 2-7

2. Move one straw ahead about one-half length as in Figure 2-8. Repeat your questions.

FIGURE 2-8

3. Bend one straw into a Z shape (Figure 2-9) and repeat again the questions. To clarify, you might ask if an insect would have to crawl the same or a different distance on each straw.

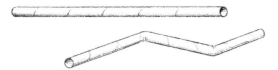

FIGURE 2-9

Conservation of Solid Substance

Materials: two ball-shaped identical pieces of clay; knife.
Procedure:

1. Ask the child if the two clay pieces have the same amount of clay (Figure 2-10). If the child thinks not, have him remove some clay from one until they do seem equivalent. If equivalence cannot be established, discontinue the activity.

FIGURE 2-10

2. Let the child flatten one ball. Ask if both clay pieces contain the same or different amounts of clay, then ask why he thinks so (Figure 2-11).

FIGURE 2-11

3. Have the child shape the flattened clay back into ball form and reestablish equivalence.
4. Tell the child to roll one clay ball into an elongated "snake" form (Figure 2-12). Ask the same questions as in step 2 above.
5. Again, have the child shape the distorted clay back into a ball shape. Reestablish equivalence.
6. Now cut in half one of the clay balls. Point to the ball, then to the two pieces. Ask if the ball is made up of more or less or the same amount of clay as the two pieces. Find out why the child thinks so.

FIGURE 2-12

7. You may want to continue cutting one clay ball into smaller and smaller pieces. Ask the same questions as in step 6, but be sure you reestablish equivalence before each cutting.

Conservation of Liquid Substance

Materials: two identical drinking glasses; also one tall narrow glass; also one glass of greater diameter than the others; pitcher of water; food coloring; medicine dropper. Procedure:

1. Put a drop of food coloring in one of the paired drinking glasses. Pour water into both glasses exactly to the same level, about three-fourths full (Figure 2-13). Ask the child if both glasses contain the same volume of water, then why she thinks so. If the child does not think they are equivalent, she may add water with the medicine dropper until satisfied. Continue only after equivalence is established.

FIGURE 2-13

2. Let the child pour the colored liquid into the tall, narrow glass. Ask if this glass contains the same or a different volume of water as the glass of clear water, then why she thinks so (Figure 2-14).

FIGURE 2-14

3. Have the child pour back the colored water into the original glass and observe the paired glasses. Reestablish that the volumes of colored water and clear water are equivalent.

4. Now let the child pour the colored water into the wide-diameter glass (Figure 2-15). Ask again the same questions posed in step 2.

FIGURE 2-15

Conservation of Area

Materials: two identical sheets of green construction paper; eight small, identical wood blocks or white paper squares.
Procedure:

1. Place the two green sheets side by side. Tell the child to pretend that these are two fields of grass on which cows feed. Ask if there are the same or different amounts of grass on the two fields for the cows to eat. Be sure the child believes the fields are equal before continuing.

2. Put a wood block or paper square on the lowest left-hand corner of each field. Explain that each block represents a farm building. Ask the same questions as in step 1. Establish equivalence again before continuing.

3. Place a second block next to the first block on one sheet, but on the other sheet place another block far from the first block (Figure 2-16). Ask the same questions as in step 1.

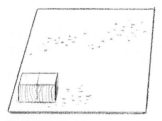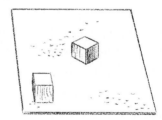

FIGURE 2-16

4. If the child establishes equivalence, add one block at a time to each green sheet. On one sheet, place each block to form a row. On the other sheet, the blocks should be scattered. Ask the same questions as in step 1. Be sure the child establishes equivalence each time before you add blocks and ask the questions.

Conservation of Perimeter-Area Relationship

Materials: two identical 12-inch strings whose ends are tied to form two separate, identical loops.
Procedure:

1. Put one loop on top of the other, so the child sees that the loops are identical.

2. Have the child arrange the loops into two identical circles, side by side. Be sure equivalence is established: Is the first circle as big around as the other? Is there just as much space inside?

3. Now pull the second loop into a narrow, oval shape. Ask: Are the two circles still as big around, or is one smaller than the other? Why do you say that? Is the space inside still the same or does one have less space? Why do you say that? (The perimeter stays the same in each case, but the area changes in the second case. The oval shape has less area inside. This can be checked by placing the loop over graph paper and roughly checking the number of blocks enclosed by the loop in both cases. Interestingly, intuitive thinkers often do better on detecting the larger area than concrete thinkers, who may allow their logic to overcome their perception.)

Conservation of Weight (Mass)

Materials: two identical balls of clay; knife; equal-arm balance.
Procedure:

1. Place the two clay balls before the child. Ask him if the balls are equal in weight. The child may use the balance as needed until agreeing that the balls weigh the same.

2. Let the child flatten one ball into a pancake shape. Ask if the weights are now the same or different, then why he thinks so. Afterward, the child may use the balance as desired to discover the equivalence. If equivalence can be established, continue.

3. Cut the pancake-shaped piece into two pieces. Ask if the weight of the two pieces together is the same or different from the weight of the unchanged clay ball. Then, ask why he thinks so. Afterward, if needed, the child may use the balance as desired to discover the equivalence. Listen for any comments as this is done.

Conservation of Displaced Volume

Note: This concept may be tested in two ways. In Example A, two clay objects of the same weight but apparently different volumes are used. In Example B, two film cans of the same volume but different weights are used.

A. Materials: small clay ball; knife; tall, narrow drinking glass half-filled with water; rubber band; spoon.

Procedure:

1. Place the glass of water before the child. Have her gently submerge the ball in the water and notice that the water level rises. The glass can be encircled with the rubber band exactly at the water line to mark the level (Figure 2-17).

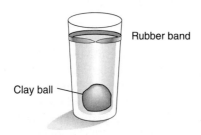

Rubber band

Clay ball

FIGURE 2-17

2. Remove the clay ball with a spoon. Hold the wet ball briefly over the glass, so if it drips, the water will go into the glass. Now let the child flatten the ball. Be sure, however, that it is still small enough to be submerged again in the water. Ask the child to what level the water will rise when the object is placed again in the water. Then, ask why she thinks so.

3. If equivalence is established, cut the flattened ball into two pieces. Ask to what level the water will rise when the two pieces are placed in the water. Then, ask why she thinks so.

B. Materials: two identical plastic film cans (fill one with pebbles, the other with pennies; both cans must be sinkable); tall, narrow drinking glass half-filled with water and encircled with a rubber band; spoon.
Procedure:

1. Have the child inspect and then heft the two film cans in his hands to note comparable sizes and weights. He should conclude that the cans are identical except for weight.

2. Let the child fully submerge the lighter can. Have him adjust the rubber band so it marks the water line. Then, remove the can with a spoon.

3. Ask him how high the water will rise compared to the rubber band if the heavier can is submerged. Ask why he thinks so.

4. Now let the child fully submerge the heavier can. How can he explain this finding? (A conserver will say that the volume or size of the can, not weight, affects the rise in water level.)

How to Evaluate Your Task Administration

It's very possible for two persons to get widely different results when administering the tasks to the same child. Please keep in mind that the tasks are not like a standardized test. They are best suited to a clinical interview setting. Here, the interviewer may use similar questions with different children to begin a task. But follow-up questions must be varied to best get at what each child seems to be thinking at any time. So exactly what questions to ask after you begin is a matter of intelligently following the child's lead.

The language used in an interview must be meaningful to the child if you want worthwhile results. It helps to keep all directions and words as simple and short as possible. If you are not sure the child will understand some terms or directions, try to clarify these before you begin. Some persons continually elaborate on words or procedures during the task. This extra talk often adds to the child's confusion and makes it harder to respond naturally.

In most of the conservation tasks two sets of materials are compared, both before and after a change is made to one set. It's necessary that the children you test believe by themselves that the paired sets are equivalent before a change is made. Otherwise, the whole point to the change is destroyed. So you'll want to avoid leading the children into making this judgment. It's all right to help children tell you what is on their minds, but they must decide for themselves if equivalency exists. For the same reason, it's important for the children to manipulate the materials whenever possible.

The tasks are best done in a relaxed, gamelike setting conducted by someone with an accepting, uncritical, but neutral manner. Avoid saying "Good," or "That's right." To acknowledge an answer, just repeat it or say, "Thank you." Children are also quick to pick up subtle cues about how to act given off by grown-ups. A frown, sigh, change of pace, or voice inflection may cause the child to react to you and not the materials. There is no one correct answer in these tasks. The purpose is to find out where the children are—what is on their minds. Their natural unguided responses are the best clues to their understanding. (Incidentally, you may find that all these points are helpful to keep in mind *whenever* you want to discover what children are thinking.)

A good way to evaluate your task administration is to make a videotape or audiotape of your performance. The following questions can help you to analyze what happened. They are based on the preceding paragraphs.

1. What in the interview shows that your words and directions were clear and brief?

2. What shows that the child established that the paired materials were equivalent before the change was made?

3. What shows that you tailored your follow-up questions to the pupil's responses?

4. What shows that you reacted to pupil responses in an accepting and nonevaluative (avoiding praise or criticism) way?

APPLYING PIAGET'S THEORY TO CLASSROOM SCIENCE

Piaget and colleagues have dealt chiefly with tracing the course of mental development. They have not tried to find how best to teach school subjects to children, but the ideas shaped from their research have strongly affected modern science programs. Three of their most persuasive ideas follow. More and more educators agree that they are essential for helping the child grow in scientific thinking.

1. Schoolchildren in all stages need to share their experiences with others, consider other viewpoints, and evaluate these social interactions thoughtfully.

2. Children need to explore the physical properties of a wide variety of objects. Not to do so in the early years of schooling is wasteful and crippling in later stages of mental operations. *Some effects are likely to be permanent,* because further chances for such explorations may not appear or may be avoided later in life.

3. Besides handling objects and exploring their properties, children must perform mental operations with them. That is, they need to change objects or events for some purpose, organize the results, and think about these operations as much as their development allows.

The Benefits of Sharing Experiences

Children who are exposed to various viewpoints will evaluate their own more realistically. Of course, this is not as likely with the typical five-year-old as with an older child. Yet one's egocentricity takes a beating from others at any age if it is clung to unreasonably. Children who work in groups containing boys and girls of different abilities learn much from each other. The intuitive thinker sees the concrete thinker as an influential model. And children who sometimes demonstrate formal thinking stretch the minds of the concrete thinkers.

How do the more advanced pupils benefit from these interactions? Explaining one's ideas in clear, understandable language is an excellent way to improve thinking. It forces analysis and organization, and exposes what one needs to work on.

Pupils sometimes do a better job of explaining things than teachers. A pupil who has just caught on to some process may remember the reasons for an earlier state of confusion. This may make the child more able than the teacher to communicate to another child who is confused.

So let children work together often when you teach science—in pairs, small groups, and occasionally as a whole class. And don't hesitate to have children of different ability levels work together. We'll take up in some detail how to do this in following chapters.

The Need for Many Concrete Materials

Words—spoken or written—are helpful to most children only to the extent that they are based on concrete materials. Children who are allowed to "think with their hands" are doing what comes naturally. The intuitive and concrete thinkers *must* work with real materials before they can grasp abstractions. It is the only basis from which they can think, if the findings of Piaget and others mean anything.

One of your most important jobs is to arrange for a wide variety of materials children can manipulate. "That's easy to say, but hard to do," is the reaction I get from some people after making this point. Part of the problem is a misunderstanding of what is needed to teach elementary science successfully. Test tubes, expensive microscopes, Bunsen burners, and the like have little or no place in the activities suggested by most science educators today. Instead, we use materi-

TABLE 2-2
Readily available concrete materials.

Disposable pie pans	Wire clothes hangers
Flashlight batteries and bulbs	Mirrors
Buttons and beads	Marbles
Paper clips	Empty cereal boxes
String	Bottle caps
Paper cups	Plastic bags
Milk cartons	Clothespins
Popsicle sticks	Drinking straws

als such as those listed in Table 2-2. Every one of these materials, and much more, are available from around the home and school, and usually just for the asking.

Another part of the job is organization. How can your class help gather the materials? How can they be stored so they are neat, yet easily checked in and out? And what about inventory and replacement? We will take up details of these and other important points in Chapter 5.

Perhaps the really troublesome part of the materials problem is not knowing how to get the most out of the materials you have. Children in some classes go through materials so fast that their teachers are run ragged trying to keep up. The next chapter will help you to avoid this common problem.

The Need to Think While Doing

Everyone knows that children "learn by doing." But Piaget would put it somewhat differently: They learn by *thinking* about what they are doing. Because intuitive, concrete, and formal thinkers differ in how they operate mentally, we must arrange experiences that fit what they can do.

In general, this means that primary-level children learn best when their science activities stress perception. Intuitive thinkers can use all their senses to help them describe and organize in simple ways the properties and interactions of living and nonliving things. Children in the middle grades (ages eight and nine) usually work well with problems and ideas that refer them to concrete materi-

als. Upper-grade children (ages 10 on) still need a concrete base to work from, but are often able to develop some abstract ideas (transfer of energy, interdependence, water cycle, and so on) from their experiences.

How necessary is it for us to stick to these guidelines? Can the several stages of mental growth be accelerated? These questions occur to many teachers, but the answers are unclear. Piaget says that we should link the learning environment to the child's present stage. This gives the child a firm footing for each succeeding stage. The child should then slip back less often and should operate more successfully than peers who have had a less complete background in each preparatory stage.

Some American psychologists are more optimistic about acceleration than Piaget. Jerome Bruner thinks it is possible through good teaching to "tempt" children into the next stage.[3] Robert Gagné would move children along more quickly by analyzing and breaking down each desired behavior into smaller, more easily learned subbehaviors.[4] In a well-designed study, Richard Anderson found that an above-average group of first graders performed some mental operations usually associated by Piaget with the formal operations stage.[5]

---

[3]Jerome S. Bruner. *The Process of Education* (Cambridge: Harvard University Press, 1960).
[4]Robert M. Gagné. *The Conditions of Learning* (New York: Holt, Rinehart and Winston, 1977).
[5]Richard C. Anderson. "Can First-Graders Learn an Advanced Problem Solving Skill?" *Journal of Educational Psychology* 56 (1965): 283–94.

Despite some favorable results shown by these researchers and others, no one knows how broadly learning transfers to new situations when children's thinking appears to be accelerated.

Since children learn best by working with concrete materials, thinking about what they do, and sharing these experiences, the teacher's role needs to be compatible. This means we need to do less telling and more listening, for example. A classroom geared to "hands-on" learning activities offers a variety of chances to find out what children are really thinking. It also gives us many chances to guide children in helpful and understandable ways. It is during these times that Piagetian theory is valuable in interpreting what is going on. Read this description of a class of seven-year-olds written by an insightful observer:

FIGURE 2-18
Discovering how to measure capacity.

As part of a unit about sand, second graders were asked to put an assortment of empty containers in order from largest to smallest. The containers varied in size and were of regular and irregular shapes. After much argument as to which container was bigger, most agreed that height (tallness) could be used to establish an order.

They then were asked whether or not there was a good way to order them when the containers were turned on their sides. The children thought that now they would have to change the order.

Then the class looked for ways to make an order for biggest that would work standing up or lying down. A few thought the biggest container would hold the most sand. How to find out which this was and which was next biggest and so on was a problem. [See Figure 2-18.]

Each youngster's approach was quite individual. One child started filling containers and overturning the contents on trays to compare the size of the piles. Another youngster measured how many handsful of sand were in a container. Another took a tiny cap and found out how many capsful it took to fill a small cup.

Then a girl thought of pouring the sand from one container to another. Her enthusiasm was contagious, but most of the others could not follow her idea because it was so

different from their own thinking. A few children did follow her example. They would pour the sand confidently from one container to another, but with no regard for the overflow of sand. When asked which of two containers held more sand, sometimes one was singled out, sometimes another.

From an adult's standpoint it would seem that pouring sand from one container to another would be the easiest way to compare volumes. However, it appeared that unless children have had a great deal of experience—through water play, balancing volumes of materials, or other activities—this is an unknown strategy to them.

It took the children a long time to sort out what mattered, and in what way it mattered. In trying to solve the problem children said things like:

"I poured sand into the jar from the full vase and it didn't come up to the top. Does that mean the vase is bigger because it was full? Or, is the jar bigger, because I could put more sand in it?"

"If the sand flows over that means there is lots of sand, so maybe the container is the big one. If the sand doesn't fill the jar, the amount of sand looks smaller, so maybe that jar is smaller."

"If I pour sand from one container to another and some sand spills, I don't know whether or not I did it right or whether the spilled sand means these are different-sized containers."

"I poured all the sand from this tall one into the pail and didn't even cover the bottom."

When pouring from container to container it appeared to the children that the volume of sand changed as well as the size of the container. They observed the sand and the container as a single thing; when the sand looked too small, that meant the container was too small; when there was a lot of sand, that implied that the container was big. The notion of *too much* was not available to them because everything was changing.

It took a great deal of practice, talking, and thinking before the children realized that in each case of pouring, the amount of sand remained the same. What looked like less sand meant really that there was more container space.[6]

Although the foregoing describes a class at work, you can see that the teacher was actually observing and working with *individuals*. Reaching each child is another important application of Piaget's theory. But you cannot sit down with every child and administer a battery of tasks to find out what each is thinking. So you need to rely on activities that allow you to circulate around the room, first observing, then guiding, individuals at work. It also means that the children themselves should have some freedom to pick and plan activities.

CHILDREN'S CONCEPTS AND MISCONCEPTIONS, AND CONSTRUCTIVIST THEORY

Piaget's theory continues to be a powerful tool in understanding how children's thinking changes over time. In recent years, cognitive psychologists and science educators have added much to Piaget's work. The new contributions show more specifically how learners process subject-matter information and how teachers can tune into the process. What follows is a blending of ideas from Piaget and more recent findings.

Underlying both bodies of research is the notion that all people normally try to make sense of their world. While most of us operate with far less precision than scientists, we still seek to explain, predict, and control our experiences.

In this view, children do not simply receive or absorb incoming information as presented by the teacher or textbook. Nor do they "discover" concepts just by manipulating hands-on materials. Instead, when children are challenged by something they want to learn, they try (with varying degrees of success) to consider any incoming data in the light of whatever related information is already stored in their long-range memories from previous experiences. In other words, they *construct* new knowledge and derive meanings by combining incoming information with what they already know. This view of learning, called *constructivism*, explains why two pupils may get different meanings from the same written paragraph or even the same concrete activity.

Each child may be using a slightly different mental schema, a theoretical concept developed by cognitive psychologists. A *schema* is a remembered network of related information organized around a familiar topic, event, or procedure. When we observe a situation that is even slightly familiar, we draw upon the schema to help us interpret the situation. To link this definition to a word, think of *context*. A schema is what we know, or can apply, in a given context.

Suppose you read, "He rose trembling before the commencement audience, stumbled to the microphone on rubbery legs, then awkwardly tucked his instrument under his chin." No one has to tell you directly about stage fright here or that graduation

[6]*ESS Newsletter,* March 14, 1968, Elementary Science Study, Education Development Center, Inc., 55 Chapel Street, Newton, Mass. 02160. By permission.

ceremonies often feature solo performers. And you are unlikely to perceive this person as a polished professional or mistake his instrument for a piano. Will he overcome his fear and do well, or will his performance be a disaster? What will happen to his self-confidence in either case? Will the effects be temporary or permanent? How will his family react? You could go on and on. Drawing on your contextual knowledge about such an occasion allows you to glean a lot from only a little given information.

If you were able to infer much about the case of the hapless musician, chances are you used more than one schema. A schema may be linked to others and form a larger network of related knowledge to draw on. A well-organized memory may have thousands of *schemata* (plural form) combinable in more thousands of ways. This enables us to interpret and act on a huge assortment of experiences.

When confronted with something new, we try to make sense of it by seeing how well it fits into an existing, relevant schema. In other words, we try to use what we already know. This is *assimilation*. If the new experience will not fit a present schema, we must modify the schema or develop a new one. This is called *accommodation*.

Here's a familiar example. Suppose you want to examine a new book in some bookstore. A book-related schema stored in your memory causes you to expect to read each page from left to right and the book itself from front to back. This happens as expected and so you assimilate the experience.

But let's say you observe someone nearby examining another book. She apparently is reading pages from *right to left,* and the book from *back to front!* You cannot assimilate this into your present book-related schema unless it provides for the several foreign languages that are written in that way. Instead, you may fruitlessly search your memory structure for other schemata that will explain what is happening, and seek confirming behavior:

Maybe she is joking. But why doesn't she smile? Maybe she's browsing. But she looks *like she's reading.*

And so on. Suppose the woman, seeing your puzzlement, explains her behavior. This causes you to modify or accommodate your previous book-related schema. The next time you see a similar event, you'll easily assimilate it.

Assimilation and accommodation work together in learning. We adapt our behavior from new information that jibes with our present schemata and that which causes us to revise our thinking.

No child begins school with a blank mind. Schoolchildren have been busily constructing concepts and related schemata since infancy. Some of what they pick up comes from formal schoolwork, of course, but their schemata are chiefly based on their everyday experiences and common sense. The result is a mixed bag of valid and invalid understandings. Several things about this state of affairs are especially important to understand.

One or several concepts usually make up the core of a schema. If a child's concept is wrong, the associated information that collects around the concept is also likely to be wrong or wrongly applied. What's more, children may hold hard to their concept.

During 10 years of writing elementary school textbooks, I received many letters from children. Here's one from a sixth grader, exactly as written:

Dear Mr. Peter C. Gega,

  I am a student at Junction Aveneu School and I would like to tell you something on page 72 in the first paragraph in Exploring Science Red Book. It says that a bee is an animal, but it isn't, it is an insect. I would like you to correct this page with the proper word.

  Sincerely, Mike H.

Another pupil in Mike's class wrote: "I have read that a bee is an insect but *not* an animal."

Sixth-grade children are usually well able to understand that a small group of objects can belong, at the same time, to other larger groups. So, unlike intuitive-level pupils, they are not baffled by the class inclusion concept. What's going on here is different.

It's more likely that our two letter-writers have picked up from early, everyday experiences an incomplete concept of animal and have long acted accordingly despite school instruction. They are not alone. Children commonly expect an animal to have four legs, be larger than insects, live on land, have fur, and be able to make noise.[7] All in all, do you suppose the second writer actually read that "a bee is an insect but *not* an animal"?

Pupils are especially likely to cling to their commonsense schemata when there is no way to directly observe what is being taught. This often happens when we try to teach abstract concepts— ideas pupils cannot verify for themselves by using their senses—such as potential energy, light waves, molecule, atom, and photosynthesis.

Consider photosynthesis. Children learn early that living things need food to live. They often care for pets and may tend houseplants. They may even hear adults casually remark, "Let's feed this plant some fertilizer."

It's easy for children to infer that green plants *get* their food from water, soil, and fertilizer. This notion can prevent them from understanding that plants *make* their own food, using water, carbon dioxide, and sunlight in the chemical process of photosynthesis.[8] Even after pupils have engaged in hands-on activities—covering leaves with black paper to block sunlight, for example—the old notion may persist. There is no direct way for them

to observe photosynthesis. Unless the teacher is aware of their misconception and is skillful, the children may simply assimilate what they experience into their present commonsense schemata and draw the wrong conclusion.

When we help pupils to form a new schema (accommodate), it may have no effect on another, apparently related schema. This is frequent at the primary level.

Young children typically perceive the earth as generally flat, and gravity as vertically down. They know well that, when something falls, it goes down to the ground and stays there. With careful instruction about the shape of the earth using globes, photographs taken from satellites, and so on, you can help many pupils achieve a more realistic concept of the earth's shape. However, if you ask them where people live on the earth (globe), don't be surprised if many say, "On top." Why not also on the sides and bottom? "Because they would fall off."[9]

Children's schemata are usually consistent with their Piagetian level of cognitive development. When they are asked to explain something that is beyond their level, they can only respond with ideas that make sense to them now.

I was once working with a fifth-grade class when the question came up, How does a ship captain know when the ship crosses the equator? (Receiving timed radio signals from three space satellites or measuring relative positions of three stars are two methods. Understanding either, except in the haziest way, requires some formal operational thinking and technical knowledge.) Some of their explanations are shown in Figure 2-19.

One child thought that maybe there was a long rope tied to floats strung across the ocean. (Did the child use his "swimming pool" schema here?) Of course, there would have to be openings to let the ships through.

[7]Roger Osborne and Peter Freyberg. *Learning in Science* (Auckland, N.Z.: Heinemann, 1985), p. 30.

[8]Edward L. Smith and Charles Anderson. "Plants as Producers: A Case Study of Elementary Science Teaching," Research Series No. 127, Michigan State University, Institute for Research in Teaching, East Lansing, Mich., 1983.

[9]Joseph Nussbaum and Niva Sharoni-Dagan. "Changes in Second Grade Children's Preconceptions About the Earth." *Science Education* 67: 99–114 (1983).

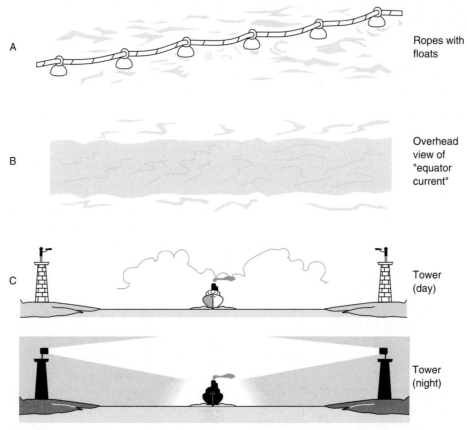

A — Ropes with floats

B — Overhead view of "equator current"

C — Tower (day)

Tower (night)

FIGURE 2-19
How does a ship's captain know when the ship crosses the equator? Fifth graders may offer different explanations, depending on their personal schemata.

Another pupil thought she had read that there was a narrow ocean current at the equator. Perhaps the "equator current" would be a visibly darker green band of water in a lighter-green ocean.

Some children felt it would be possible to have two very tall towers on opposing points of land. Lookouts with telescopes could spot when ships crossed the "line." Then they could radio the ship's captain to announce the event.

How about at night? Well, if the ship's lights were on, the tower lookouts could still see the ship. Or a big searchlight mounted on each tower could be switched on. That way, the ship's officers themselves could tell when they crossed the line.

And if the weather was bad? Hm-m-m. Then they couldn't tell at all.

Notice the thoughtful intelligence behind the children's hypotheses. Although all are operating at a concrete level, they are using their limited schemata for all they are worth.

Would "proper" instruction at this time help? Not much. Interestingly, one boy's father worked on a tuna clipper, which had a radio/satellite navigation device. The child had observed it in action several times, with explanations from his parent. The boy was able to describe the device's appearance, its purpose, and even a bit about how it was operated. But he couldn't satisfactorily tell how it worked. He got confused and soon gave up.

As teachers, what are we to make of these and other examples of children's thinking? How can we apply the powerful ideas of schema theory with Piagetian theory to sharpen our teaching and benefit our pupils?

1. Remember that most pupils are likely to have formed some ideas about objects and events before you teach them. This may influence what they learn for better or worse. So it is good practice to probe their ideas before you teach *and* when they form conclusions about what they have learned. At both times, children need to do most of the talking if you want to find out what they have assimilated or accommodated.

2. If you want your teaching to stick, instruct in ways that help pupils to *construct* schemata and enrich or reshape their present schemata.[10] Teaching that guides pupils to build organized structures of knowledge— concepts, generalizations, patterns, sequences, classification systems, and the like—does this. Well-organized schemata allow more usable information to be stored in memory, then efficiently retrieved and applied as needed.

3. The quality of pupils' thinking—including problem solving—is strongly related to the subject-matter information they can apply to a situation.[11] Children can only intelligently work with objects or events that they can relate to their schemata. They do well when challenged with problems at their cognitive level. And they work well when their lessons begin and end with references to their world of experiences and interests.

Let me add a note to paragraph three for you to consider. Almost any top-notch teacher will tell you that children *love* to use their minds when they are often successful. It makes them feel competent, confident, "grown up." They *love* to be around a teacher who arranges experiences that foster such feelings. And there's more. They have much incentive to *cooperate* when given these experiences. A curriculum that pupils see as worthwhile is likely to be the best discipline system you'll ever have and promote worthy self-images as well. Praise, reward, recognition, and most of the other positive behavior management techniques we learn as teachers are needed and have much merit when properly used. But nothing comes even close to the internal satisfaction, real competence, lifelong motivation for learning, and self-discipline that come from frequent success at using one's own mind.

ASSESSING CHILDREN'S KNOWLEDGE OF CONCEPTS AND CAUSES OF EVENTS

How can you find out about pupils' common-sense concepts and schemata? One good way is to informally ask them about familiar objects and events: animals, plants, air, clouds, rain, thunder, and so on. If the children have misconceptions, you can be reasonably sure that these do not result simply from lack of first-hand experiences.

To assess for concepts of an object, it's often effective to ask for a definition, then examples, and then nonexamples. Here is an interview I did with a six-year-old:

Q: What do you look for to tell if something is a *plant?*
A: Well, it's green and stuck in the ground. It can be stuck in a pot, too. A plant has leaves. And it grows bigger if you water it.
Q: What are some examples of plants you have seen?
A: Plants in my house and bushes and flowers in my Mom's garden.

[10]J. D. Bransford. *Human Cognition: Learning, Understanding, and Remembering* (Belmont, Calif: Wadsworth, 1979).
[11]Lauren B. Resnick. "Mathematics and Science Learning: A New Conception," *Science* 220 (April 29, 1983): 477–78.

Q: Anything else?

A: No.

Q: Is there anything that grows in the ground that is *not* a plant?

A: Yes.

Q: What grows in the ground and is *not* a plant?

A: Grass.

Q: Why isn't grass a plant?

A: It doesn't look like a plant. Grass is grass.

Q: Anything else that grows in the ground that is *not* a plant?

A: I don't know.

Analysis: If this child is consistent (intuitive children often are not), a plant will need to be green, have leaves, be stuck in the ground or a pot, and grow to be classified as a plant. His concept is incomplete, rather than wrong. Especially revealing is his answer that grass is not a plant because "It doesn't look like a plant." His list of plant attributes is composed of objects that look reasonably alike. General appearance is very important to intuitive thinkers in organizing objects. (Note: For the same reason, it's hard for young children to perceive a porpoise as a mammal when it "looks like a fish.")

Considering this child's limited and perception-bound attributes for a plant, we may be able to make some predictions. What do you think this child would say if you presented him with pictures of an untrimmed carrot, a cabbage, and a seed?

Beverly F. Bell, a researcher in New Zealand, discovered that almost one-half of 29 children, at the relatively advanced ages of 10 to 15, thought that a carrot and a cabbage were vegetables but not plants. More than one-half said that seeds were not plant material.[12]

Children's explanations about *causes* of objects and events are particularly interesting. An early book by Piaget offers fascinating

views of what many children believed a half century ago about the causes of rain, lightning, and so on.[13] Much of what children today believe is surprisingly similar.

To assess for children's understandings of cause-and-effect relations, it is again helpful to ask for a definition of the object or event. This can clarify what the child is thinking about. Next, you can ask about the cause. If the child immediately launches a causal explanation, though, a definition may not be needed. Here is an interview with a bright eight-year-old girl:[14]

Q: What do you think *thunder* is?

A: It's a big loud boom in the sky.

Q: What do you think makes thunder happen?

A: Well, in space there might be friction between two meteorites.

Q: What is friction?

A: When two things rub together real fast. The meteorites make sparks from the friction.

Q: Is that what thunder is?

A: No! That's the lightning! Sometimes when it rains we have lightning and thunder.

Q: Well, what makes the thunder?

A: You have a big boom when the two meteorites smash together.

Q: Must it rain to have thunder and lightning?

A: No, it only has to be cloudy.

Q: Are there meteorites in the clouds?

A: No, they're in space.

Q: But you have to have clouds for thunder and lightning?

A: Yes.

Analysis: Unlike younger or less able pupils who might see thunder as suiting some human purpose or happening through magic,

---

[12]Roger Osborne and Peter Freyberg. *Learning in Science* (Aukland, N.Z.: Heinemann, 1985), p. 7.

[13]Jean Piaget. *The Child's Conception of Physical Causality* (New York: Harcourt Brace Jovanovich, 1930). For a more recent printing and a companion volume, see *The Child's Conception of Physical Causality* (Totowa, N.J.: Littlefield, Adams, 1972) and *The Child's Conception of the World* (Totowa, N.J.: Littlefield, Adams, 1975).

[14]Based on an interview by Terry Williams.

this girl aptly describes two interacting objects. Even though she is wrong about the causes of thunder and lightning, she is using a previously stored schema and some logic to build what she thinks is a plausible explanation. Also, notice her apparent confusion between correlation and causation at the end of the interview. She believes that clouds must be present for thunder, even though she says that thunder is caused when meteorites collide in space.

EXERCISE 2-2

Interviewing Children for Concepts and Causes of Events

Following is a list of some natural objects and events about which elementary-age pupils have probably formed some notions. To learn more about children's thinking, you might interview two or more who are several years apart in age. As you listen to what they say, compare their conceptual understanding to what educated adults believe. State each suggested question below in language that makes sense to the child, if it does not now. Also, let the child's responses influence your follow-up questions. To avoid guiding responses, be noncommittal and accepting, not directive or reinforcing.

Concepts About Natural Objects and Events

The questions below have children define concepts and give examples. There are four concepts. To avoid confusion, select and work with only one concept, or one concept at a time if you do more. Note each child's responses. Clarify your thinking by writing a short analysis, like that on page 46, for each child you interview.

animal
plant

1. What does the word *animal* (plant) mean to you? What do you look for to tell if something is an *animal* (a plant)?

2. What are some examples of *animals* (plants)?
[At this point it is often revealing to also ask specific questions, such as Is a snail (earthworm, spider, bird, goldfish, butterfly) an animal? Why or why not?
Is grass (a tree, a bush, a carrot, a potato, a bean seed) a plant? Why or why not?]

3. What are some living things that are not *animals* (plants)?
[If you have asked specific questions after 2, it may be more appropriate to begin 3 with, What are some *other* living things that are not . . .?]

air
energy

1. What does the word *air* (energy) mean to you?

2. How can you tell if there is such a thing as *air* (energy)? What do you look for?

Cause-and-Effect Relations

The questions below have children begin by first defining a concept, and then thinking about cause-and-effect relations. To avoid confusion, select and work with only one concept, or one at a time if you do more. Clarify your thinking by writing a short analysis like the one on page 46 for each child you interview.

cloud

mountain

1. What do you think a *cloud* (mountain) is? What do you look for to tell if something is a *cloud* (mountain)?

2. How does a *cloud* (mountain) get to be a *cloud* (mountain)?

3. What makes *a cloud move in the sky?*

thunder

rain

1. What do you think *thunder* (rain) is?

2. What do you think makes *thunder* (rain) happen?

Although we must carefully heed the work of researchers, a little theory—good theory, that is—goes a long way. It's time for specific methods. What *activities* can we use to boost children's learning, now that we have some key principles in mind? The next chapter tackles that question.

SUMMARY

How effectively we teach science to children is linked to our understanding of children's characteristics, including how they learn. Jean Piaget's theory proposes that elementary schoolchildren go through three intellectual stages as they grow: intuitive, in which children are ruled by their perceptions; concrete operational, in which their thinking is tied to concrete experiences; and formal operational, in which abstract thinking becomes a practical possibility. (A larger summary of Piaget's theory can be found in Appendix E.)

Research in human learning continues to verify and augment Piaget's research. According to constructivist theory, based on this combined research, people continually develop personal explanations to make sense of their experiences by reflecting and constructing on what they already know. Children as well as adults appear to derive meaning from an experience by referring to a schema—a body of related information stored in the long-range memory from previous experiences. Learning proceeds by fitting new information into a schema (assimilation), and modifying or forming a new schema (accommodation). Existing schemata may help or hinder new learning; so teachers should be aware of such knowledge to plan suitable lessons. Teaching that helps children to build organized structures of related information in their memories improves their ability to retrieve and apply the knowledge.

SUGGESTED READINGS

Chaille, Christine, and Lory Britain. *The Young Child as Scientist: A Constructivist Approach to Early Childhood Education.* New York: Harper Collins, 1991. (How younger children construct knowledge.)

Eggen, Paul D., and Donald P. Kauchak. *Strategies for Teachers.* 2d ed. Englewood Cliffs, N.J.: Prentice-Hall, 1988. (Gives a detailed information-processing approach to teaching content and thinking skills across the curriculum.)

Hyde, Arthur A., and Marilyn Bizar. *Thinking in Context.* White Plains, N.Y.: Longman, 1989.

(Shows the inseparable connection between content knowledge and thinking skills in reading, mathematics, science, and social studies.)

Neale, Daniel C., et al. "Implementing Conceptual Change Teaching in Primary Science." *Elementary School Journal* 91(2): 109–131 (1990). (How eight primary teachers changed pupil misconceptions to valid understandings.)

Roth, Kathleen J. "Science Education: It's Not Enough To 'Do' or 'Relate.'" *American Educator* 17 (22): 46–48 (Winter 1989). (A thoughtful essay on three approaches to teaching conceptual understanding.)

Saunders, Walter L. "The Constructionist Perspective: Implications and Teaching Strategies for Science." *School Science and Mathematics* 92(3): 136–44 (March 1992). (A detailed analysis of constructivism in science teaching.)

3

How to Use Closed-Ended and Open-Ended Activities

Children can learn science in several ways. But generally the most effective way is through hands-on activities, on which we'll concentrate in this chapter.

There are two basic kinds of activities you can use to meet the wide variety of individual differences and objectives faced in classrooms today—*closed-ended* and *open-ended* activities. For a quick view of what each is like, see these two problems:

$$3 + 3 = ?$$
$$? + ? = 6$$

Notice that the first problem has only one correct answer. The second has many answers. Closed-ended problems and activities lead to a single, or narrow, response. They foster *convergent* thinking. Open-ended activities and problems lead to a wide variety of responses. They produce *divergent* thinking. Both types of activities and thinking are needed in learning and solving problems.

In Appendix A of this book and elsewhere in science programs, you'll find that closed-ended activities tend to be short and tightly focused. Open-ended activities are usually longer, and branch out to many related questions besides the beginning problem focus. To make it easy for you to identify each kind of experience in Appendix A, I've labelled the closed-ended type *activities* and the open-ended type *investigations*.

Closed- and open-ended activities also differ in other ways. To see how, let's consider each kind in turn. We begin with some common closed-ended examples involving children 5 to 12 years old. In each case the children are active—they do things.

CLOSED-ENDED ACTIVITIES

In a primary class children are learning that vibrations are needed to make sounds. It is obvious that a guitar string moves to and fro when plucked. But what vibrates when a drum is struck? A child is directed by the teacher to sprinkle some sand lightly on the drumhead of a toy drum. The child next strikes the drumhead with a stick. The sand is seen to bounce up and down briefly as the drumhead vibrates. The harder the drumhead is struck, the louder the sound. This also makes the sand bounce higher.

In a middle-level class some children are learning that limestone is a common rock that can be detected by putting acid on it. The acid bubbles when it contacts the rock. A few pieces of limestone have been borrowed from the school district's materials center. Several children put these rocks into small cups of vinegar, which is a weak acid. Nothing happens at first. Moments later they see streams of tiny bubbles rising from the submerged rocks.

In an upper-level class some children are learning about air pressure. One child reads how to use unequal air pressure to crush a metal container. To demonstrate this, the teacher heats a clean, uncapped metal can (such as that used to hold fluid for duplicating machines) for a few minutes on a hot plate. The air inside warms and expands. Some of this heated air escapes through the uncapped opening. The can is then removed from the hot plate, the cap quickly screwed on, and the can allowed to cool. As the air inside the can cools, it requires less space than before because some air has escaped; so it exerts less pressure inside. The children delightedly watch the can slowly cave in as the stronger outside air pressure exerts its force.

Notice that each of these closed-ended activities illustrates some idea or procedure with concrete materials. Everyone can participate if there are enough materials or if pupils take turns. Working with concrete materials helps the children to form realistic concepts or learn useful techniques. Therefore, these activities are often found in science textbooks and the curriculum. Sometimes they are presented as teacher or pupil demonstrations. Here are more concrete but closed-ended examples you will run into from time to time.

Primary Level. Children learn that their bodies give off heat. They are told to feel the heat radiating from their faces by holding the palms of their hands close to each cheek.

Middle Level. Children read that the echo-chamber effect of sounds in an empty house disappears when soft drapes are added. They experience a similar effect when they speak into a solid metal wastebasket before and after lining it with a soft cloth.

Upper Level. Children learn how to tell directions by using the sun, a pencil, and a wristwatch. The pencil is pushed into the ground upright. The wristwatch is placed so that the pencil's shadow covers the hour hand. The hour hand is pointed away from the sun. The pupils are told that north is exactly halfway between the hour hand and the numeral 12.

For further examples of closed-ended activities, turn to Appendix A, "Sample Investigations and Activities," at the back of this book. Inspect some of interest to you to get a sense of how they are organized and what they can do.

Once a closed-ended activity has made its point, there is little need for one to go on with it, at least in its beginning form. So the activity comes to a close, and the child goes on to something else.

Closed-ended activities, when taught well, help children to construct a solid subject-matter background that is rooted in experience. But these activities are not enough for the whole job. As you have seen, the scope in each activity tends to be limited. Outcomes are predictable and specific. Children follow someone else's ideas or procedures—those of the teacher, book, film, or other authority source. To boost children's thinking pro-

cesses, independence, and creativity, you need to offer open-ended experiences.

OPEN-ENDED ACTIVITIES

Most good teachers encourage children to try their own ideas about how to investigate and organize objects or events. This allows children to discover or find out things for themselves and opens up the scope of study. It broadens study because children usually come up with their own suggestions. Some suggestions lead to others, so there is almost no end to what may be investigated or organized.

Objects and events in science are described and compared by their observable properties—weight, shape, hardness, resistance to rust, location, speed, order of appearance, and so on. Open-ended activities allow pupils to study objects and events in two very useful ways. Pupils can (1) observe similarities and differences in the *properties* of things, and (2) discover *conditions* that can produce or change properties.

Note the contrast in each pair of these questions you might ask your pupils:

1. What materials will rust? (Observing a property.)
2. In what ways can you get some objects to rust? (Discovering conditions.)

1. How fast does water go up the stems of different flowers?
2. How can you speed up (or slow down or prevent) water rising in flower stems?

1. What things does a nail magnet pull (attract)?
2. How can you make your nail magnet stronger (or weaker)?

1. On what things do molds grow?

2. What conditions must be present for molds to grow?

1. Which objects can be charged with static electricity?

2. What's the longest time you can keep an object charged with static electricity?

1. How long do different cut flowers stay fresh if you keep them in water?

2. How can you lengthen the time a cut flower will stay fresh?

1. What foods attract ants?

2. In what ways can you attract the most ants?

1. In what places can we find sow bugs?

2. In what conditions do sow bugs best live?

1. How many single pulleys can you find around the school?

2. How can you rearrange single pulleys to make work easier?

1. Which juices contain vitamin C?

2. How might a juice lose its vitamin C?

Now that you have compared both kinds of questions, here are a few details to better understand their uses. When children examine the present properties of comparable things, they learn that properties usually exist in varying degrees: some magnets are more powerful, water rises faster in some plant stems, some juices have more vitamin C, molds grow more easily on some materials, and not all places where sow bugs are found are exactly alike.

As pupils inspect these variable examples of things, they may observe, describe, contrast, measure, and classify them according to specific properties. They may also use a procedure and tool—slitting open a plant stem with a pin to see what is inside, for instance—along the way. Even so, they just want to find out what the existing properties are like. *This feature makes open-ended investigations of things with comparable properties very suitable for intuitive-level pupils, and others who lack experience with the materials being examined.*

But when pupils investigate the *conditions* that might produce or change a property of an object or event, their intent is different. Now they seek cause-and-effect connections. *This feature makes investigations of conditions that may produce or change properties more suitable for pupils at or beyond the concrete operational level.* As you saw in Chapter 2, younger children have trouble with cause-and-effect relations.

Naturally, even older elementary school-children cannot seek causes in the strict ways of scientists. Adult researchers must isolate critical variables to invent, test, and modify scientific theories. Instead, children simply try to find out what changes result when they perform one-at-a-time operations on objects. Both younger and older children do this. However, the operations younger pupils perform to cause change are often just hit-or-miss. Older pupils are more apt to use a concept or schema to guide their operations.

We can teach pupils to state such operations as narrow questions. For instance, if you ask, "What can you do to make a nail magnet weaker?" it's natural for children to say things such as

> *Drop it on the sidewalk.*
>
> *Heat it.*
>
> *Leave it alone for a while.*

With a little coaching from you, pupils can change these statements into narrow operational questions:

> *Will dropping a nail magnet on a sidewalk make it weaker?*
>
> *Will heating a nail magnet make it weaker?*
>
> *Will a nail magnet get weaker if you just leave it alone?*

This does three things for children: they do the thinking, the purpose of the upcoming activity is clear to them, and so is the general procedure. If a few more details are needed in the procedure—who gets and does what, for example—these can now be easily added.

This method does something for you, too. It puts in your corner the greatest science authority in the universe. The only one, in fact, that never makes a mistake. It's a pleasure to teach in ways in which *nature* supplies the answers to children's questions.

To nail down the difference between questions that guide pupils to observe the variable *properties* of comparable things and questions that guide them to discover *conditions* that may produce or change a property, try Exercise 3-1. Find answers at the end in a section entitled "Comments."

EXERCISE 3-1

Which Open-Ended Questions Are for Observing Property Variables? Discovering Condition Variables?

1. What flat materials will magnetism pass through if you put them one at a time between a magnet and a paper clip?
2. How can you make your string telephone work better?
3. What can you do to get a liter of liquid as warm as possible with 30 minutes of sunshine?
4. What foods does a land snail eat?
5. What is the longest time you can keep brine shrimp alive?
6. How much liquid do different kinds of apples contain?
7. In what ways can soil be prevented from eroding?
8. What materials conduct electricity?
9. What do you think will make plants grow faster?
10. Which objects can you identify just by touch?

Comments

Questions 1, 4, 6, 8, and 10 now invite children to inspect comparable examples of objects for variable properties. Here's how they might look if rewritten for pupils to discover variable conditions that might produce or change properties:

1. How can you prevent magnetism from going through objects?
4. How can you get a snail to eat food it usually won't eat?
6. Under what conditions might apples have less liquid than usual?
8. In what ways can you make conductors of electricity nonconductors?
10. In what other ways besides touch can you identify these objects?

Questions 2, 3, 5, 7, and 9 now invite children to find conditions that might produce or change properties of objects. Here's how they could be rewritten to have pupils simply study examples of objects with comparable properties:

2. What different examples of string telephones can we find?

3. How warm will different objects, including liquids, get if we put them in the sun?

5. How long will brine shrimp from different places live?

7. In what places is the soil eroding?

9. How fast do different plants grow?

How to Develop Open-Ended Investigations with Questions

If you want children to come up with their own ideas, ask *broad* questions that will cause them to state what specific points they want to tackle. Broad questions are designed to put as much responsibility for thinking as possible on the pupil—where it belongs. At the same time, we can never be sure of what a pupil's responses will be. This unpredictable, divergent quality in the responses to broad questions is what makes them so interesting.

What happens when youngsters cannot come up with their own ideas? Then we need to help them by asking *narrow* questions— those that zero in on only one example or condition.

The key to knowing how to ask broad and narrow questions in an activity is to identify *which* examples of objects or *which* conditions pupils might vary. To illustrate, let's begin with a typical primary-level, closed-ended activity found in science textbooks:

Find out about rusting. Get an iron nail. Wrap it in damp newspaper. Wait one or two days. What happens to the nail?

This activity shows simply and concretely what rust is. But it is too restrictive in its present form for either good concept building or to sharpen pupils' thinking skills.

The property of rusting is centered here on only one example, a nail. What are some *other examples* of objects young children might want to try, using the same damp newspaper test? Consider some everyday items—safety pins, comb, spoon, penny, and so on—made of aluminum, plastic, steel, copper, rubber, and so on. Let the class gather them.

If the class has done the closed-ended activity, to open it just ask:

What other things do you think will rust if wrapped in damp newspaper?

If no one responds, direct one or two narrow questions to some objects brought to class that might be tested:

Will these aluminum (or plastic, or steel, etc.) objects rust in damp newspaper?

Or you might specifically name some objects:

Will these safety pins (or pennies, or hair curlers, etc.) rust in damp newspaper?

After pupils gain more experience, repeat the broad question:

What other things do you think will rust if wrapped in damp newspaper?

Now, more responses are likely. If not, simply shift down again to one or two narrow questions that focus on further specific objects. As your pupils build a broader concept of the properties of "rustable" objects with more experience, they will be able to make more of their own suggestions.

Another way to open up the activity is to consider some *other conditions* that might produce rust besides wrapping the objects in damp newspaper. (Remember, though, that exploring causative conditions may be hard for younger pupils. So stay sensitive to what they can handle.) Pupils could try to produce rust or to speed up rusting by putting objects in hot or cold tap water, salt water or other liquids, or in damp soil or sand. To prevent rusting, pupils could try covering objects with oil, grease, Vaseline, or different paints or leaving them in different locations. To get pupils to propose operations like these, you could ask any of these broad questions:

> *How else can you get things to rust besides wrapping them in a damp newspaper?*

or

> *How could you make objects rust faster?*

or

> *How could you keep objects from rusting?*

When pupils cannot respond because of limited experience, just shift down to one or two narrow questions that reflect the specific operations you have thought of:

> *Will a nail rust if it is under water?*

or

> *Can salt water make an object rust faster?*

or

> *Do things rust if they are painted?*

Your modeling of these narrow operational questions, and a little coaching, should help pupils state their own. After pupils gain some experience, you can again try opening up the activity with one of the broad questions posed before:

> *How else can you get things to rust . . . ?*

After you have posed many broad questions to stimulate children to test conditions,

you may notice patterns in the ways the questions begin. Here are some beginning phrases that teachers are likely to use when they challenge children to test the conditions of change:

> *How can you . . .*
>
> *How else can you . . .*
>
> *What will happen if . . .*
>
> *What conditions are best for . . .*
>
> *What could you do to . . .*
>
> *What else could be done to . . .*
>
> *What ways could be used to . . .*
>
> *In what ways could . . .*
>
> *In what other ways could . . .*

Helping children to work with property and condition variables is like riding a bicycle with changeable gears in hilly terrain. When the going gets tough, you need to gear down (ask narrow questions on single variables). When the going gets easier, you can gear up (ask broad questions that embrace multiple variables).

Realize that when asking questions you take cues from pupil responses. So the process is interactive and responses are somewhat unpredictable. That is why it's hard for authors of a text or curriculum to provide in advance exactly what to do or say in an open-ended activity. They are generally tied to a narrower, sequential approach that presumes certain pupil responses to closed-ended activities. This is no fault of the authors; it just goes with the medium.

"But what if I can only think of one or two variables?" teachers ask me sometimes, "Can I still open up activities?" Usually, yes. Most children can generate other variables *they* want to explore after being helped with just one or two narrow questions. Or if they already have some background, you can often fruitfully *begin* with a broad question.

Please understand that pupil suggestions for variables to test need not be "correct." We want to find out what they are now thinking and improve it if needed. Children who believe that certain objects will rust and who discover they will not, or who unsuccessfully try other ways to cause rust, are learning to sharpen their future ideas and actions. To use Piaget's term, they are learning to "accommodate."

Broad, open-ended questions typically require much thinking, and it's essential that children have enough time to do so. Mary Budd Rowe has found that many teachers ask questions and react so quickly to silence that pupils are unable to thoughtfully respond.[1] But teachers who ask a question and wait about five seconds for a response (Wait Time I), and wait again about five seconds after the first response before reacting to it (Wait Time II), get improved results. The quality and length of pupil responses increases, and they listen and react more to each other's statements rather than only to the teacher's comments.

To get similar results in your classroom, use wait time and make remarks like these before you ask thought-provoking questions:

I'm going to give you time to think before calling on anyone.

Before you raise your hand, think carefully for a while about what you might say.

Now for some practice in asking broad and narrow questions. Exercise 3-2 on sprouting bean seeds is almost identical to the previous rusting activity. If you have trouble forming your own questions, just reread the rust-activity section on pages 55–56.

---

[1]Mary Budd Rowe, *Teaching Science as Continuous Inquiry.* 2d ed. (New York: McGraw-Hill, 1978), pp. 273–83.

EXERCISE 3-2

Forming Broad and Narrow Questions

Here's another typical closed-ended activity found in children's textbooks:
Find out about sprouting seeds. Soak a bean seed overnight in water. Plant it in soil. Keep the soil damp. Wait five or six days. What happens to the seed?

1. What broad question can you ask to open up this activity so pupils can explore further examples of objects with comparable properties? (Hint—"What other . . .")

2. Despite your broad question, your pupils cannot think of more objects to try. What narrow questions can you ask that focus on single objects to try? (Hint—First think of further examples of objects like the one tried in the beginning activity.)

3. You now want pupils to explore several conditions that might produce or change the property (sprouting) studied in this activity. What broad question can you ask to do this? (Hints—"How else can you . . . ," "In what other ways can you . . .")

4. You find that your pupils still lack enough background to ask operational questions about conditions. What narrow questions can you model that will include operations they might try? (Hint—First think of some single-condition variables.)

Comments

1. Some broad questions to explore further examples:

   What other seeds will sprout in this way?

   What, besides a bean seed, do you think will sprout like this?

2. Some narrow questions to focus on further examples to try:

   Will *sunflower* seeds sprout in this way?

   Will *radish* seeds sprout in this way? And so on.

3. Some broad questions to explore various conditions:

   How else can you get seeds to sprout besides planting them in damp soil?

   How can you speed up (slow down) the sprouting of seeds?

   How can you prevent seeds from sprouting?

4. Some narrow questions to test single-condition variables:

   Will bean seeds sprout under water?

   Will an *unsoaked* bean planted in damp soil take longer to sprout?

   Will half of a bean seed sprout in damp soil?

Learning about the variable properties of many different objects helps pupils to build a conceptual background and organized data base. That is, it helps them to *construct* schemata. Trying to discover the conditions of change requires pupils to *use* their schemata to solve problems. In doing so, they often find that they also need to pick up more data. The new data are then assimilated or accommodated, depending on what they presently know. The result is improved and additional schemata, which allow your pupils to become even better problem solvers.

Combining Knowledge of Properties with How to Produce or Change Them

When children lack background, finding out about the conditions of change is difficult. After all, they must learn what properties of objects exist before they can discover how they or nature may produce or change the properties. It's a good idea to have children study properties first and then explore whatever conditions of change they can handle. Often, study of one aspect naturally leads to the other.

For example, after two of your pupils demonstrate a tin-can string telephone, you might say to the class, "How many different kinds of string telephones can we make? Don't worry now about how well they are going to work." This will prompt them to use a variety of substitute materials. As children try out each other's phones, some will obviously be more effective than others. Now you can ask, "How can you make your string telephone work better?" and have some assurance that the class has enough background for intelligent problem solving. Pupils could instead build background through reading or consulting some other source of information. But they are likely to find answers rather than raw data they can process for themselves. Which way seems better to strengthen their ability and confidence in problem solving?

When pupils do have background, you may be able to launch an immediate investigation into conditions that produce variation or change. Suppose your class reads the following activity in a textbook:

> Find out how much dust falls on your desk top through the day and week. Tape a piece of sticky tape upside down on a small white card. Place it on a corner of your desk. Observe just before you go home each day how much dust sticks to the tape. A magnifier will help you see.

Chances are concrete operational pupils will already know enough about dust to respond intelligently (but not necessarily correctly) to open-ended questions such as

> Where do you think you might collect the most dust in this classroom? The least dust? Where in the school? Where on the school grounds? When do you think there would be the most dust? The least dust?

Forming specific operational questions (Will more dust collect by a closed or open window? Will more dust collect on the floor or on top of the tall cabinet? Will more dust collect by the air vent or away from it? etc.), keeping careful records of locations and times tested, and carefully comparing sticky strips would give pupils enough data to answer all these open-ended questions and more.

Experimental and Nonexperimental Activities

You can see that varying a condition to produce or change a property in an object or event tends to be experimental, whereas examining existing properties tends to be nonexperimental or observational. However, children may do more than simply "observe" existing properties. As pointed out earlier in this chapter, they may also group, order, describe, measure, and compare the properties, for example. This can be just as interesting and challenging to pupils as experimenting to discover the conditions of

change. Note the following nonexperimental situations.

In a primary-level classroom three different kinds of open-ended activities in science are going on. In one corner some pupils are sorting leaves by their properties—size, shape, veins, edges, and so on. The teacher then invites them to play a game:

> Sort your leaves into two groups according to some property. Will your partner be able to tell which property you used? Take turns. Try a different property each time.

In another part of the classroom other primary pupils are exploring the property of shape with a "feely box." This is a medium-sized cardboard box that has a hole cut in each side for a child's hands. Matched pairs of small objects (for example, blocks, jacks, different-sized Cuisenaire rods, toy soldiers) have been brought in by pupils and supplied for the activity. One of each pair is displayed outside the feely box. The rest are inside the box. A child reaches into the box and tries to find, solely by touch, the mate of an object that a partner points to. When found, it is removed and compared to the outside object. Occasionally the "used-up" objects are replaced by other paired objects to provide a continued challenge.

Still other primary children are working with small milk cartons, containing varying amounts of sand, to explore the property of weight. The cartons are in sets of three; each set is painted in a different color. The children are trying to put in order, from lightest to heaviest, three cartons of each set. They check their work with a simple balance. After stopping by and observing for a while, the teacher says:

> How can you pour some sand out of each carton and still keep the same order? How can you check your work?

In the middle-level class some pupils are classifying rocks according to the property of hardness. They are using the scale listed in Table 3-1. The teacher says:

TABLE 3-1
Scale of hardness.

Hardness	Test
Very soft	Can be scratched with your fingernail.
Soft	A new penny will scratch it. Your fingernail will not.
Medium	A large iron nail will scratch it. A penny will not.
Hard	It will scratch glass. A nail will not scratch it.

TABLE 3-2
Users of fossil fuels.

Buildings	Machines
Schools	Trains
Movie theaters	Airplanes
Government offices	Ships
Factories	Private autos
Hospitals	Trucks
Churches	Taxicabs
Houses	Buses
Apartments	Motorcycles

How much will someone else agree with the way you grouped your rocks? How could you check?

A discussion follows on possible procedures. Pupils exchange rocks with partners but do not reveal their test results until the partners themselves have tested the same rocks. Then, both sets of findings are compared. Partners try to iron out differences by retesting, arguing, and describing more carefully what they mean. Some children even try to refine the scale. More rocks are introduced as needed to broaden experiences still further.

In an upper-level class pupils learn that our country must depend on a dwindling supply of fossil fuels for some time before other forms of energy become fully available. But what happens if we begin to run out of fossil fuels sooner than expected? Or, what if pollution in some places gets too bad to continue using such fuels at the present pace? If fossil fuels must be cut back, where should the cuts be greatest? (This highlights the *value* given to the properties of some objects—automobiles, trains, and so on.)

With the help of the children, the teacher makes a list of some buildings and machines that use fossil fuels (Table 3-2). The teacher says:

Let's each arrange these in order from the ones you would cut least to those you would cut most. Also be ready to say why you ordered each in this way. Then, let's discuss our choices and see how they compare.

Themes and the Scientific Search for Patterns

It is easy to feel snowed under by a world stuffed with variable properties and conditions of change everywhere you look. How do you make sense of it all? Or, as one teacher said, "How do you find your way without being an Einstein?" People who feel this way are not likely to seek open-ended science experiences. What's needed is a way to help them see a "forest" every here and there, rather than only trees, trees, trees. Here is where *themes* can be useful.

Themes are large, overarching ideas designed by science educators to cut across content subjects, and so unify what may appear at first to be unrelated facts. They can make understandable and economical what otherwise is confusing and overwhelming. For some examples of themes, please see Table 3-3.

Thematic teaching has become both popular and varied in recent years. For clarity, we need to distinguish the science themes of Table 3-3. which are conceptual, from the *topical* themes that some teachers use to apply and integrate several subjects across the curriculum. "Whales," for example, is a

TABLE 3-3
Some widely used conceptual themes in science.

properties	matter	systems and interactions
change	diversity	patterns of change
order	interactions	material objects
cycles	systems	energy transfer
ecosystems	energy	stability
energy sources	balance	evolution

theme that some teachers use to integrate a high-interest science topic with elements of reading, language, mathematics, art, and music. "Indians of the Southwest" is an even broader topical theme. It allows teachers to select and integrate parts of the entire curriculum so pupils can gain a broad understanding of several Native-American cultures.

Don't expect children to quickly grasp all conceptual themes in science, especially younger pupils. They may need some time and instruction to make broad connections. But most teachers, with just a little experience, can readily use themes to help students see the big picture. You'll find about six in most programs. They also make it easier to locate many possibilities for open-ended explorations across the science curriculum.

Although themes in science programs are devices to guide teachers and students, scientists also invent them to guide their thinking. Three of many themes that scientists and educators alike work with—properties, interactions, and energy—can show you the right direction. Authors of textbooks and curriculum guides also steer by these themes. So knowing them can also better your understanding of how these teaching aids are organized. We've already touched on several of these ideas in earlier chapters. What's needed now is to see how they work together.

Let's begin with what you may be most familiar with—*properties*. Scientists realize that, although individual objects and events vary greatly, many have much in common when viewed collectively. So scientists continually search for *patterns* among the properties of objects and events. This makes it far easier

to keep track of single things. For example, individual rocks vary greatly, but most rocks can be classified as sedimentary, igneous, or metamorphic from common properties in each group. (Because classification is so useful it is often a central objective when scientists observe properties.)

You know, too, that properties of objects change. Yet, as you saw in an earlier example with warm air "rising" (page 10), nothing can change by itself. Scientists realize that any change in an object is evidence that one or more other objects have *interacted* with it. A rounded rock found in a stream bed shows signs that it was tumbled by the stream and rubbed against its bed. To be confident that this happens generally, scientists search for a *pattern of interactions* in similar situations. Or, if needed, they experiment when possible to change other rocks of that type in the same way they think it happens naturally. The experiments are repeated by others to check for the same pattern of results.

Finally, scientists realize that *energy* is needed to change or preserve an active balance in living and nonliving things. Gravity is the force that moves the stream that tumbles the rock. Tracing how energy drives interactions allows scientists to better describe the conditions for change.

In science education, as in science, the variable properties, interactions, and energy sources of objects are carefully observed and changed (when possible) to find out about them. Pupils' knowledge of these three kinds of variables usually improves with additional examples to observe. Their ability to change the variables depends on their learning the conditions of change.

Patterns in properties, interactions, and energy—or similar themes—thread through modern elementary science programs, even when they are not clearly identified. The usual sequence is to begin with properties of objects and events, then move to interactions that change or produce properties, then trace energy sources behind the interactions. (To remember the sequence is as easy as P–I–E.)

The sequence may appear at any grade level. But it is not always complete, nor is each pattern equally treated. Properties are stressed at the primary level. Study of interactions happens more often after the primary grades because it's harder for younger pupils to make cause-and-effect connections. Energy in interactions, being abstract, is studied most intensely in the upper grades.

See next how the three themes cut across the entire curriculum of life, earth/space, and physical sciences. Patterns of properties, interactions, and energy crop up repeatedly as you look for them. These patterns represent much of what the subject matter of elementary science is all about. So getting a feeling for them can truly help you to "find your way."

P–I–E Themes and Some Common Patterns of Variables

In the *life sciences,* children observe the variable properties of living things with all their senses but find that each sense detects only some properties. Touch is useful to detect an object's texture, for example, but not its color. They learn how to group similar body parts, foods, plants, and animals. They see that plants have many uses, that animals develop in several ways. Living things interact with their environment as they respond to light, touch, heat, or cold. Certain needs must be met to stay alive, such as proper temperature, clean air and water, light, food (animals), soil materials (plants), and adequate space. Living things interact with each other in predator–prey and food web connec-

tions, in communities and ecosystems. Energy from the sun makes all of this possible.

In the *earth/space sciences,* children discover the variable properties of earth materials—soil, rocks, air, and water. The earth has a certain size and shape; it rotates and revolves and is part of a solar system whose members share only some properties. Earth materials interact, as when moving air and water erode rocks and soil. Other regular interactions occur at a distance among objects in space and cause predictable eclipses, moon phases, and tides. Gravity and sunshine are seen as the main energy sources behind the interactions.

In the *physical sciences,* children explore energy more directly. They find it has several accessible forms—light, heat, sound, magnetism, and electricity. Each form has some unique and some common properties. Each may be converted through an interaction into another form, as when sunlight strikes a table top and warms it. Energy can trigger physical and chemical changes in matter, as when ice cream melts and wood burns. Children also learn how to send a flow of energy from one object to another, and how to vary or even prevent the energy flow, as they work with batteries and bulbs, everyday sound and heat insulators, mirrors, and string telephones.

Broad questions based on the foregoing variables can generate hundreds of open-ended experiences for children, as you will find sampled in Appendix A of this text.

Open-Ended Activities and Piaget

In Chapter 2, you saw three important ways in which teachers are trying to apply Piaget's research. According to Piaget each way is essential for helping the child grow in scientific thinking. Look again at these points and consider some added comments:

1. *Children need to explore the physical properties of a wide variety of objects.* It's possible for this to happen with both open- and closed-ended activities, but with which is it likelier to happen?

2. *Children need to perform mental operations as they work with science materials.* That is, they need to change objects or events for some purpose, organize the results, and think about these operations as much as their development allows. Isn't it plain that open-ended activities are well suited to these functions?

3. *Schoolchildren in all stages need to share their experiences with others, consider other viewpoints, and evaluate these social interactions thoughtfully.* From what you have seen so far, which are more likely to do this, open- or closed-ended activities?

The benefits work for both you and your pupils. Multiple approaches to problems allow you to cope more easily with individual differences. A single activity can serve children at several ability levels because they view it in different ways. Children's attention is held longer because the more they dig, the more they find. Fewer activities overall are needed because pupils get more from each experience, and the scramble for materials is reduced.

Even when many materials are called for, getting them is less of a problem. Probably the child's improved motivation is responsible. In following authority, most people feel it is up to the authority figure to get what is needed to put across what they are supposed to learn. But it is different when people go after their own purposes. Children *want* to search for materials that will test their position or their ideas. How far interested girls and boys will go in their searches can be very impressive.

EXERCISES
3-3 to 3-6

How Well Can You Identify and Develop Open-Ended and Closed-Ended Activities?

Most science programs offer a mixture of closed-ended and open-ended activities. However, the number of closed-ended activities far outweighs the other kind. This does not mean that closed-ended activities are bad. As you have seen, they can be valuable in constructing concepts and learning procedures. But used alone, they are very limited in improving children's thinking and ability to function independently. So it will be to your advantage, and the children's, to correct the imbalance. One way to do this is to know where to find open-ended activities. We will discuss this shortly. Another way is to be able to spot the limited activities that have the potential to be expanded.

Almost any activity can be made into an open-ended investigation. However, we are dealing with children. Some activities are easier to work with, have more appeal, and offer more possibilities to improve thinking than others.

Try the following exercises, which include descriptions of six useful but closed-ended activities. Only three have broad open-ended *potential*. The exercises are designed to help you spot and then develop these three activities by practicing what you may have learned so far in this chapter. You will need paper and a pencil. Compare your ideas with the comments that appear after each part of the exercise.

3-3 Which one in each of the three following pairs of closed-ended activities is more likely to be made into an open-ended investigation? (Remember that an open-ended investigation offers many variables to consider, either in the form of observing existing properties or changing them.)

Primary Level

1. Children place an object in water to see whether it will sink or float, to learn something about buoyancy.
2. Children make an outline of their bodies and draw where they think some main bones are, to start learning the bones' locations.

Intermediate Level

3. Children make artificial rocks with plaster of paris and portland cement, to learn more about how some rocks are formed.
4. Children observe how long it takes for an ice cube to melt, to learn more about how heat energy is transferred.

Upper Level

5. Children touch the pulse point on their wrists and count the number of pulses for one minute, to learn how fast hearts beat.
6. Children examine and manipulate a working model of the human heart, loaned by the school's instructional materials center, to learn how the heart works.

Comments

For the primary level, (1) has many more possibilities than (2), which is very limited. There is only one correct answer for where bones are located in the normal body.

For the intermediate level, the better choice is (4). Making rocks with plaster or cement (3) involves following a recipe provided by an authority. There is not much children can vary without fouling up the procedure. If things do go wrong, children can only guess as to why, and this may have no relation to how real rocks are formed.

For the upper level the better choice is (5). Learning how the human heart works (6) is valuable, but it does not generate variables children can manipulate. Other kinds of hearts could be examined—sheep and cow hearts, for example. However, dissection and comparative anatomy are better reserved for later study in properly equipped laboratories with skilled biology teachers.

3-4 Consider now the three *potential* open-ended investigations just identified. What variables for each can you think of that can be tested by children at their level? Hints are given to help you begin.

Primary Level

Children place an object in water to learn whether it will sink or float. (You want to vary the objects and water.)

Intermediate Level

Children observe how long it takes for an ice cube to melt. (You want to change the melting time of ice. What can you vary to do this?)

Upper Level

Children touch the pulse points on their wrists and count the number of pulses for one minute. (You want pupils to observe and produce variations in pulse rates.)

Comments

Primary Level

Some sink and float variables: sizes of objects; kinds of materials objects are made of (plastic, wood, metal, rubber, glass); how pliable the objects are for small hands to shape or change; depth and kind of water (fresh, salty, muddy).

Intermediate Level

Some variables that might change the melting times of ice: still air versus wind; immersion in different liquids and volumes of liquids (fresh, salt, muddy water; alcohol, etc.); air temperature; wrapping the ice in foil or other materials; crushing the ice; changing the shape of the ice (by freezing water in various molds made from kitchen foil).

Upper Level

Some variables to learn how fast hearts beat: children or adults of the same and different age, weight, height; sitting versus standing position; before and after eating or exercise; different times of day; adults before and after smoking.

3-5   It's good to remember variables such as the foregoing while you work with children. If they need help, you have some ideas to supply. These are often best given as narrow operational questions.

Are you able to state a narrow question for each variable children might try? Use the foregoing "Comments" variables in Exercise 3-4 for your narrow questions. Some examples follow to help you start:

Variable: Size of objects. Narrow question: Will the big or small object float, or will both float?

Variable: Medium that ice melts in: air, water, etc. Narrow question: Will an ice cube melt faster in air or water?

Variable: People's height. Narrow question: Do people of the same height have the same pulse rate?

Comments

As you look over the following narrow questions and compare them to yours, please also refer back to the "Comments" variables in Exercise 3-4 that were used to form the questions. There's no need for you to pose exactly the same questions as mine. What we're after is the basic method.

Primary Level

Will more of these plastic or wood (metal, rubber, glass) objects float? Will squashing the foil into a small ball (or other manipulation) make it sink? Will making the water deeper make some things float that sank before? Will more things float in fresh or salt water?

Intermediate Level

Will a fan blowing on an ice cube change its melting time? Will putting a cube in salt water make it melt slower (faster) than it would in fresh water (muddy water, alcohol, etc.)? Will a cube melt faster in warm or cold water (in sun or shade)? How much longer will a cube last if you wrap it in foil (wax paper, newspaper, etc.)? Will a crushed cube melt faster than a regular ice cube? If you refreeze the water from a melted ice cube into a thin pancake shape, will it melt faster than a regular ice cube?

Upper Level

Do people of the same age (weight) have the same pulse rate? Does sitting give a different pulse rate than standing? Is your pulse rate the same before and after eating (exercise)? Is your pulse rate different at different times of the day? Is an adult's pulse rate the same before and after smoking?

3-6 Besides narrow questions, it's useful to ask broad questions. A broad question, you'll recall, is often easy to ask after pupils have explored a narrow question:

> Will magnetism go through paper? (Narrow.) What else besides paper will magnetism go through? (Broad.)

This sequence may be worthwhile when children are very young or inexperienced with the materials they will use. When they are on more familiar ground, you may find it better to open up a lesson right away with broad questions.

Consider again the three potential open-ended experiences we began with:

Primary Level

Children place an object in water to see whether it will sink or float.

Intermediate Level

Children observe how long it takes for an ice cube to melt.

Upper Level

Children touch the pulse points on their wrists and count the number of beats for one minute.

What broad questions can you pose that might make these activities open-ended investigations from the beginning? Please state one or two for each activity now.

Comments

As you compare your broad questions with mine, think of the responses children might make to the questions. Are they likely to come up with some of the same kinds of variables and narrow questions you have seen in Exercises 3-4 and 3-5? This is a better test of the quality of your questions than simply how well they match mine.

Primary Level

Which objects do you think will float? How can you sink the things that floated? How can you make float the things that sank?

Intermediate Level

What could you do to make ice melt faster? In what ways can you slow down the melting of ice?

Upper Level

How might the pulse rates of different people compare? What is there about people, or what they do, that might affect their pulse rate? What are some things that might affect a person's pulse rate?

Did you find it easier to identify the potential open-ended activities than to develop them? That's to be expected now, so don't be discouraged. The ability to develop these activities thoroughly takes some firsthand experience with the materials involved and some understanding of the subject matter. We will take up how to get this background shortly.

The Relativity of "Openness"

Many activities found today in science books and curricula cannot be properly categorized on an either/or basis; that is, they are neither totally closed- nor open-ended. Many authors realize the need for children to extend or apply what is learned, and they know how to ask broad (open-ended) and narrow (closed-ended) questions. Does this mean the two categories are useless? Far from it. However, it does mean that many activities are likely to be closed or open only in a relative sense.

As you saw in Exercises 3-3 to 3-6, some activities can generate a wide variety of variables, and some can generate far fewer. Even with relatively closed-ended activities, it is often possible and desirable to ask broad as well as narrow questions. One type sets up the other. Your ability to do this can boost children's learning, regardless of what kind of hands-on experience you offer.

HOW TO PRACTICE

To improve your ability to develop questions and hands-on learning experiences, examine the investigations and activities in Appendix A of this book. The investigations typically have a broader scope than the activities and are more open-ended. Check how broad questions are often used to open up the discovery part of each investigation. Notice how narrow questions are used to zero in on single variables as needed. Study, too, how the child is guided to explore materials or a procedure *before* the broad and narrow discovery questions are posed. This experience is usually required before children (and many adults) can see possible chances to observe or manipulate variables. You will find it worthwhile to go through the investigations yourself if you lack background in either the materials or content.

Examine and try the activities, also. They often include broad as well as narrow questions. Some of the activities are relatively open-ended. They could easily become full investigations depending on pupil responses.

Finally, try some investigations and activities with children. Note how they respond to the questions. You may want to amend some or come up with many of your own questions as you interact with pupils. This might bring the best results.

SUMMARY

Science is a purposeful search for patterns among objects and events in the physical world. In searching for patterns, scientists uncover numerous facts, many of which at first seem unrelated. To help organize facts, especially from several different science areas, scientists and educators invent conceptual *themes*. Three such themes are *properties, interactions,* and *energy.* The use of themes also enables teachers to see many chances for open-ended investigations. To find patterns among the variable properties, interactions, and energy sources of material objects, scientists thoughtfully observe and experiment with (when possible) the variables. They develop theories to support their findings and guide further searches. Their purpose is to explain, predict, and control phenomena.

Our purpose is to teach the patterns that scientists discover, and their ways of thinking, that children are most likely to understand and use in our society. To do so, we set up closed-ended and open-ended learning activities. Closed-ended activities are appropriate to directly teach specific subject-matter ideas and procedures through demonstration and illustration. Their scope is limited, and exact outcomes and pupil responses are often predictable. Open-ended activities are best used to discover, through investigative and indirect teaching methods, a broader scope of variables. Children are much more likely here to learn scientific ways of thinking as well as subject matter, but their responses and exact outcomes of lessons are less predictable.

In science education, as in science, the variable properties, interactions, and energy sources of objects are carefully observed and changed (when possible) to find out more about them. Pupils' knowledge of property variables usually improves as we give them additional *examples* to observe. Their ability to change the variables depends on their learning the *conditions* of change.

Varying a condition to change or produce a property in an object or event is usually experimental. Experiments require a higher level of operational thinking than intuitive-level and early concrete-operational children can independently demonstrate. So seeking causes of changes in properties through experiments is done more often beyond the primary grades. Examining existing properties is nonexperimental or observational. Activities in which pupils observe and compare properties are ideal for younger children, and others who may lack experience with the properties of the objects and events being studied.

To guide children's learning, we ask narrow and broad questions. Narrow questions focus their thinking on single variables and will dominate in closed-ended activities. Broad questions open their thinking to multiple variables and will dominate in open-ended activities. A combination of both kinds of questions ordinarily works best in learning activities, whether closed- or open-ended.

SUGGESTED READINGS

Birnie, Howard H., and Alan Ryan. "Inquiry/ Discovery Revisited." *Science and Children,* April 1984, 31–33. (How to vary the open-endedness of inquiry activities.)

Blosser, Patricia E. *How to Ask the Right Questions.* Washington, D.C.: National Science Teachers Association, 1991. (Many helpful ideas in this monograph, including closed and open questioning techniques.)

Hawkins, David. "Messing About in Science." *Science and Children* 2 (February 1965): 5–9. (One of the developers of a national curriculum project describes an open-ended approach to learning science. A classic.)

McCormack, Alan J. *Inventor's Workshop.* Belmont, CA: David S. Lake, 1981. (Clear examples of using variables to "open-end" activities.)

Shaw, Jean M. "A Model for Training Teachers to Encourage Divergent Thinking in Young Children." *Journal of Creative Behavior* 20 (2): 81–88 (1986). (Ways to use questions that promote divergent thinking in primary-level children.)

Wasserman, Selma. "Teaching Strategies: The Art of the Question." *Childhood Education* 67(4): 257–59 (Summer 1991). (Four guidelines for using questions to improve class discussions.)

How to Improve Children's Thinking

The last chapter sets the stage for this one. You've just seen how to help children observe or change objects and events by asking broad (open) and narrow (closed) questions. Such questions can stimulate children to think—to process data. But to use questions well you need more details. There are several kinds of processes used in science. You can learn how to ask broad and narrow questions that are right for each kind. This chapter presents the processes and the kinds of questions and experiences that spark children's thinking.

Recall that for children to grow in their thinking, they need to explore many objects and events and share their experiences. Most important, they need to perform *mental operations* as they do these things. Everyone is for improving children's "mental operations," just as everyone is for health, happiness, and Friday afternoons. But this can mean anything unless we pin it down. Just what is it that we do to help pupils think within different activities? Must we learn entirely new ways of thinking to help children?

No educated person begins teaching with a blank mind. Over the years you've probably picked up more good thinking habits than you're aware of. You now use many of the thinking processes children need help with, just as you now practice most of the three-R skills they need. This chapter can help you to build on what you do already and apply it to teaching.

The science processes we'll take up are observing, classifying, measuring, communicating, inferring and predicting, and experimenting. Before we examine the processes in detail, it's important for your understanding to put them into perspective. Here are some relevant points from previous chapters:

1. Remember that the basic mission of scientists is to construct *knowledge* about how the world works, so they can explain, predict, and control phenomena. Science processes are the means by which scientists seek data and construct knowledge. A similar outlook works well in science teaching. Regard the processes as tools that enable children to gather and reason about data to make better sense of their world. Little is gained overall unless children's use of processes also results in improved conceptual knowledge.

2. The processes are most productive when guided by a valid conceptual framework. In other words, quality process thinking and accurate knowledge of subject matter are interactive—one helps, and also depends on, the other.

3. The ability to use science processes tends to be "domain specific" when applied to real world problems. Being a good problem solver in one field doesn't guarantee that you will be so in another. So process thinking needs to be groomed across the science curriculum and in all the academic subjects.

4. To learn process thinking requires pupils to work with raw (unprocessed) data. Probably the best learning experience to promote such thinking in children is the hands-on, open-ended investigation, as guided by a knowledgeable teacher.

Open-ended investigations usually give the chance to teach a variety of science processes. But in some investigations, one process will dominate. Following each introduction to a process are several titles of investigations from Appendix A of this book in which you can see the process applied. To quickly find where a process is used, just look at the marginal notes on the pages indicated.

Now let's consider the processes, one by one.

OBSERVING

The process of observing is the taking in of sense perceptions. It is the most basic and broadest of the processes. In a way, all the others simply refine it. Our job is to help children to

- Use all of their senses when they observe objects or events.
- Notice how things may be alike or different.
- Become aware of changes.

Pupils can learn that each of the senses is a gateway to observing different properties of objects. *Seeing* allows them to notice properties such as sizes, shapes, and colors of objects and how the objects may interact. *Hearing* makes knowable properties of sounds such as loudness, pitch, and rhythm. *Touching* teaches the meaning of texture, and is another way to discover sizes and shapes of objects. *Tasting* shows how properties such as bitter, salty, sour, and sweet can be used to describe foods. (At the same time, pupils can learn not to taste an unknown substance, since it could be harmful.) *Smelling* calls for associating objects with odors because odors are otherwise hard to describe. So something smells "like perfume," "like a lemon," "like cigar smoke," and so forth.

Properties, children find, enable them to compare and describe likenesses and differences among objects. This leads to explorations that require several of the other processes, such as classifying and communicating, which we will examine in other sections.

You can ask broad and narrow questions to guide learning in observing or any of the other science processes.

In a primary-level class children are examining bean seeds that have been soaked to make them easy to open. The teacher gets everyone to observe by saying:

What do you notice about your seed?

Later, some narrower questions are posed:

How many parts did you find?
How does the seed feel to you without its cover?
What does it smell like?

In a middle-level class pupils are raising tadpoles in a large jar. On Monday morning,

they rush to the jar as soon as the classroom opens and see a small sign that reads:

What changes do you observe since Friday?

During sharing time everyone learns what the pupils have noticed. Then, the teacher asks a narrow question to zero in on an interesting change that has been missed:

How has the water level changed since Friday?

In an upper-level class children are comparing plastic but real-looking cat bones and rabbit bones from a kit. The teacher says:

In what ways are the two sets of bones alike? Different?

The need for a few narrower questions comes up later during a discussion:

How do their back leg bones compare?
How do their skulls compare?

For some examples of *observing* applied in investigations, see:

The Makeup of Colored Liquids (p. 192)
A String Telephone (p. 194)
A Bottle Xylophone (p. 196)
Mealworms and What They Do (p. 212)

CLASSIFYING

We have already seen in Chapter 2 how children at different developmental stages handle the process of classifying and its variation—arranging objects or events in order according to some property. (It will help to review pages 24, 26, and 28.) Our concern now is to see what happens in classrooms.

Most intuitive thinkers can select and group together real objects by some common property, such as color, shape, and size. They can use a different property each time they make a new group.

In a primary-level class some children remove from bags small objects they have brought from home. The teacher says:

Think of one property, such as a certain shape. Sort all the objects that have that property into one pile. Leave what's left in another pile.

Later, to open up the activity, the teacher says:

What other properties can you use to sort your objects?

Other children in the primary classroom are grouping pictures according to whether they show living or nonliving things. Later, they will be asked to take the pictures of living things and group them into animal and plant categories.

Many middle-level children can classify an object into more than one category at the same time and hold this in mind.

In a middle-level class some children have classified animal pictures into three groups with two subgroups each: mammals, birds, and fishes have each been divided into meat eaters and plant eaters. They have done this in response to their teacher's question:

How can you group these animals by kind and by what they eat?

Some upper-level students can do the foregoing and can also reclassify according to other properties that fit their purposes.

In an upper-level class several pupils have a large collection of animal pictures. They start off by dividing them into groups such as mammals, birds, fishes, and so on, but then decide that this will not further their purpose. They want to alert people to animals of different locations that are threatened with extinction. How to do this?

After talking with the teacher, they decide to classify their pictures according to the animals' natural homes or habitats: woodlands, grasslands, marshlands, and so on. These pictures are then subgrouped into endangered and nonendangered animal cat-egories. Later, they subdivide further for in-state and out-of-state animals. Only classmates with similar advanced classifying skills and knowledge will fully understand their request for more pictures:

Can you bring in ones that show animals that are dying out in different environments in our state or other states? We're really short on grassland reptiles.

This example hits a major point about classification: It is done to fit a purpose. What works to fulfill the intent of the classifier is what counts. Objects can be classified in many different ways.

There is a second point worth remembering when we go to classify things: We can think of a property as being present or not present, but we can also think of it in a quantitative way. Consider age, for example. If we think of people as young or old, we have put everyone into two groups. But we can also arrange people in order, from young to old, according to years. It is when we think of a property in a quantitative way—that is, by the *amount* of the property present—that we can arrange objects in some order.

So, younger pupils may group magnets by shapes. They may also arrange several magnets in order by how powerful they are. Older children may group materials as to whether they conduct or do not conduct electricity. They may also test how well some materials conduct electricity by checking the varying brightness of a flashlight bulb used in the test. The materials then may be ranked in order from the worst to the best conductor.

For some examples of *classifying* applied in investigations, see:

A Bottle Xylophone (p. 196)
The Properties of Leaves (p. 210)

The first example shows serial ordering. In the second, classifying sets up everything.

MEASURING

Thinking about properties in a quantitative way naturally leads to measuring them. To measure is to compare things. At first, at the primary level, children may be unable to compare an object with a standard measuring tool, such as a meter stick or yardstick. Instead, they find out who is taller by standing back to back. They find out which of two objects is heavier by holding each object in their hands. They measure how far a soap bubble traveled by stretching a string between the bubble blower and the wet spot and marking the string.

There is good reason to start off measuring in this way. Remember that intuitive thinkers *do not conserve* several concepts that deal with quantity. Changing the appearance of an object still fools them. Children who think that merely spreading out some material gives them more, for example, have to be treated differently from children who conserve quantity. (Now is a good time to review pages 24 and 25.) This means that most young children cannot work meaningfully with standard units of measurement such as centimeters, inches, and so on until about age seven.

Intuitive thinkers can build readiness for working with standard units by using parts of their bodies or familiar objects as arbitrary units to measure things. A primary child may say that "The classroom is 28 of *my* feet wide." Or, "The classroom is 10 of *my* giant strides long." The child also may say, "The mealworm is one paper clip long." Or, "It moved as far as three spelling books during science time."

Pupils' Natural Interest

Children's observations in almost any science area can be sharpened by measuring things. But experienced teachers will tell you that children are not interested in measuring for its own sake any more than they are interested in the other science processes as such. Pupils are more interested—*much* more interested—in the physical activity and its outcome than in the processes they use.

Children get bored when a process is emphasized for its own sake. The teacher who announces, "Today we are going to improve our ability to measure weights," is seldom greeted with foot-stamping enthusiasm and shouts of joy. Things go better if the children hear, "We're running out of hamster food. How much do we need to buy for a month's supply?" *So deal with measurement and the other processes as natural ways to answer questions that come up in investigations.*

Concrete Referents

One way to improve the ability of children to measure and estimate accurately is to have in your classroom many concrete objects they can refer to when needed. Meter sticks, yardsticks, and trundle wheels are useful for thinking about length. Containers marked with metric and English units are good for thinking about liquid volumes.

Similar things to refer to are needed for other concepts involving quantity. A kilometer may be a round trip from the school to the police station; a mile, from the school to the post office. Meanings associated with time can be developed by many references to water or sand clocks (containers with holes punched in the bottom) and real clocks. Temperature differences become meaningful through using several kinds of thermometers.

Improvising Tools

By the time they leave elementary school, many children have had some experience with a variety of measuring instruments: ruler, meter stick, yardstick, balance, clock, thermometer, graduated (marked) containers, protractor, and wind gauge, to mention the more common ones. When possible, children themselves should choose the right measuring tool for the activity under way. Sometimes they can make their own tools when they need them. Inventing and making a measuring instrument can be as challenging and interesting as other activities.

Consider some fourth graders who are trying to figure out how to measure wind speeds during a unit on weather. They have fastened a small cardboard flap to the side of a wind vane so that the flap swings freely. When the wind blows hard, it pushes back the flap more than when there is a light breeze. But how can it be marked to show speeds?

Someone whose bicycle has a speedometer gets the idea to check the flap positions while holding the vane and riding at different speeds. Another child points out that this had better be done on a windless day. A few others say the bike can be ridden in several directions and the "middle" (average) flap positions noted. They are not sure how to figure averages, so the teacher helps them.

Some Advanced Concepts

Children can even begin to learn sophisticated concepts when these are approached in simple ways.

In a primary class several children estimate the number of objects a small jar may hold. Each child first fills the jar with beans and then with marbles. Of course, the beans are not exactly alike. Each time a child tries, it takes a slightly different number of beans to fill the jar. But when identical marbles are used, the number is always the same. The teacher helps the children understand one way that *variations in measurement* comes up by asking:

> *Why do you get a different number of beans each time? Why is the number of marbles always the same?*

In a middle-level class the idea of *sampling* comes up in a plant unit. The seed box

directions show that 90 percent of the seeds should grow under proper conditions. After making sure the children understand that not all the seeds in the box are likely to grow, the teacher says:

> *We'll be planting only some of these seeds. Some of them are bad, but you can't tell by looking at them. Maybe most of the bad seeds are in one part of the box. How might we avoid picking too many bad seeds?*

Sometimes there is a need for *scaling* in elementary science activities. In an upper-level class several pupils want to make a model solar system. After they read the sizes of the planets and the distances between them, the teacher helps the children realize that only planet sizes *or* distances between—not both—can be shown in a classroom model. Because of the huge distances involved, for the model to fit within the classroom, some planets would have to be made too small for easy viewing. The pupils therefore decide that size alone will be scaled in their model. Proper planet distances, according to the scale, will be written neatly in black ink on a sign placed by the model. "That puts Pluto downtown by the bus depot!" the pupils report to their astonished classmates.

Measurement and the Mathematics Program

Measurement is often used in combination with other mathematical skills in practical situations, both in and out of school. Is there a cook or carpenter anywhere who measures and only measures?

Learning how to apply mathematical skills in science teaches a more useful understanding of science and lays the groundwork for further study in later schooling. These experiences can enhance mathematics education as well. You can use science investigations to reinforce certain mathematical skills, give practical contexts to use the skills, and motivate pupils to learn more mathematics.

Understanding the foundations of the mathematics program allows you to grasp the kinds of quantitative thinking pupils can apply in their science experiences. Most programs are developed around a half-dozen or so conceptual strands, such as the following:

- Basic operations
- Measurement
- Problem solving
- Relations and functions
- Tables and graphs
- Geometry
- Probability and statistics

Not all strands are treated equally at every grade level. The basic operations strand generally threads through all grades, while the study of probability and statistics may begin at grade five or beyond. Also, the strands overlap. Seldom can one solve problems, for example, without using skills from the other strands as well.

It is usually sounder to have children apply a skill that has already been introduced in the mathematics program than to introduce it through science activity. The mathematics program is likelier to have a carefully designed sequence of subskills that makes the skill's introduction more understandable.

Following are brief descriptions of common strands in mathematics programs that complement measurement, with some examples of how skills within the strands are applied in science situations. Many of these applications, and others, may be found in the investigations in Appendix A of this book.

Basic Operations. This is the dominant strand in elementary mathematics programs. It includes counting, tallying, and the four basic processes—addition, subtraction, multiplication, and division. Examples include

- Comparing the power of several magnets by counting the number of paper clips attracted.

- Finding the average air temperature over three days.
- Counting pulse beats for 15 seconds, then estimating beats for 1 minute, hour, day, week, and year.
- Calculating one's weight on various planets by multiplying that weight by ratios supplied in a reference book.

Problem Solving. Problems may range from a simple situation that requires a single calculation to open-ended situations that call for observing, gathering data, making inferences and testing them. Skills from any or all the strands may be needed. Examples include

- Will an adult blue whale fit into our classroom. How can we find out?
- What balanced meals can you plan of no more than 1000 calories?
- How much weight will it take to balance a 40-kilogram person if the fulcrum is 2 meters from the end of a 6-meter board?
- How can you make a string pendulum swing 60 times per minute?

Relations and Functions. Here, the apparent association of one variable with another is revealed. Examples include

- Observing that lowering the water temperature reduces the breathing rate (gill movements) of a goldfish, while raising it increases the rate.
- Finding that the number of times a bike pedal revolves compared with the rear wheel changes with the sizes of gears one uses.
- Learning that the power of an electromagnet varies with the number of turns of wire around its core.
- Observing that changing the slope of an inclined plane varies the force needed to pull up an object.

Tables and Graphs. The ways data are displayed in tables and graphs make them useful for several purposes. They help pupils to make sense of numerical data and clearly communicate the data to others, to make predictions, to see relationships between variables, to hypothesize about changes in data, and to draw conclusions. You'll see several examples of how to use tables and graphs in parts of following sections on communicating, inferring, and experimenting. Some further examples are

- Making a table and graph of air temperatures over several days.
- Making a table and graph of the effect of practice on writing backward (mirror writing), as measured by the number of times the writing goes outside a narrow border, timed over five trials.
- Graphing the heights reached by several bounced balls and predicting further heights of bounced balls from the data.
- Graphing the loss of vitamin C in orange juice over time as measured by the number of drops of juice required for a blue fluid indicator to lose its color.

Geometry. Early experiences in applying geometry can build a number of skills, including pupils' spatial and aesthetic judgment, the ability to better describe objects, and the skill to make more technical measurements. Examples include

- Locating everyday objects that demonstrate geometric forms—litter can (cylinder), ice cream cone (cone), hopscotch area (squares), boat sail (triangle), shoe box (rectangular prism), ball (sphere), dice (cube), wheels (circle), church steeples (pyramid), and so on.
- Reading directions in degrees on a magnetic compass to find an object.
- Measuring angles to make a sundial.
- Using coordinates and scale to draw maps and give directions.

Probability and Statistics. This is a minor strand at the elementary level and is seldom introduced before grade five. The approach is to seek a practical awareness of probability in pupils rather than basic proficiency, which requires a formal operational level of thinking. Examples include

- Recording frequencies of seeds that sprout under varied conditions.
- Tossing a coin to simulate chances for inheriting a trait, as presented in a unit on heredity.
- Learning that a 70 percent chance of rain means a comparison of present conditions to past conditions that produced rain.
- Learning not to generalize about a whole population from measuring a sample unless the sample is representative of the whole.

Measurement and the Metric System

Gradually, the United States is joining the other countries of the world that have replaced the English measurement system with the metric system. School districts now teach both systems. Scientists everywhere have long used the metric system because it is simpler and faster; all of its units are defined in multiples of 10, as in our money system.

The three basic units most commonly used in the metric system are the *meter, liter,* and *gram.* A meter is a little longer than a yard (about 1.1 yd) and is used to measure length. The liter is a little larger than a quart (about 1.06 qt) and is used to measure liquid volume. The gram is used to measure weight or mass and weighs about the same as a paper clip.

Strictly speaking, the terms *mass* and *weight* mean different things in science. Mass is the amount of material or matter that makes up an object. Weight is the gravitational force that pulls the mass. On the moon, for example, an astronaut's weight is only about one-sixth of what it is on earth. But the astronaut's mass stays unchanged.

Prefixes are used in the metric system to show larger or smaller quantities. The three most common prefixes and their meanings are

- *milli*   one-thousandth (0.001)
- *centi*   one-hundredth (0.01)
- *kilo*   one-thousand (1,000)

Let's see how the prefixes are used in combination with the basic units.

Length   1 meter (m) = 1,000 millimeters (mm) or 100 centimeters (cm). 1 kilometer (km) = 1,000 meters (m). A millimeter is about the diameter of paper-clip wire. A centimeter is slightly larger than the width of a formed paper clip. A kilometer is about nine football fields long, or about six-tenths of a mile.

Volume   1 liter (1) = 1,000 milliliters (ml) or 100 centiliters (cl)[1]. 1 kiloliter (kl)[1] = 1,000 liters (l). A milliliter is about one-fifth of a teaspoon; a liter is slightly over a quart.

Weight (Mass)   1 gram (g) = 1,000 milligrams (mg) or 100 centigrams (cg)[1]. 1 kilogram (kg) = 1,000 grams (g). Notice that a milligram weighs only about one-thousandth of a paper clip. A kilogram is a little more than 2 pounds (about 2.2 lb).

Temperature in the metric system is commonly measured by the Celsius (C) thermometer, named after its inventor, Anders Celsius. It has a centigrade scale—that is, one marked into one hundred evenly spaced subdivisions. Zero degrees begins at the freezing point of water, and 100 degrees marks the boiling point of water at sea level.

If you have available only a Fahrenheit (F) thermometer, you can convert it to also read in the Celsius scale. Cover one side of the present scale with masking tape. Mark on the tape the points where water freezes (32°F) and boils (212°F). Then subdivide the distance between into 100 evenly spaced parts.

Before your pupils use different metric standards, have them consider the right standard for the job. The kilometer is good for measuring long distances, as when traveling by automobile or taking a long bike ride. The meter is fine for measuring the size of the playground or classroom. A book or desk top is easily measured in centimeters, while the millimeter should be reserved for very small objects.

Children usually discover that the metric system is easier to use than the English system. Yet some adults find this statement hard to believe. Why? They are often victims of poor teaching. Generations of high school students have had to memorize details of the several metric units with little exposure to concrete materials. With only sketchy practice in using or referring to real materials, what was "learned" was soon forgotten.

Another widespread practice was to present the metric system as something that needed to be *converted* into the English system. This led to dreary and confusing lessons to learn formulas for changing one set of measurements to another.

You can profit from these past mistakes by simply doing the opposite. If your curriculum calls for work with both metric and English measures, give pupils much practice with concrete materials when working with both systems. Also, treat each system separately, instead of shifting back and forth. After much practice, children become able to *think metrically*. At that time, pupils are naturally able to compare units of both systems without confusion.

Despite the proven effectiveness of teaching both systems separately, occasionally you may wish to convert a measurement from one system to the other. For example, your pupils may want to record their body weights in kilograms. But you may have only a scale that reads in pounds. Or, if you are now unfamiliar with some metric unit, it may help briefly

---

[1] Seldom used in elementary school science.

to know the English equivalent until you have had a chance to practice some yourself. For this reason, conversion tables are provided for you on the inside front cover of this book. If you use a hand calculator, conversions are swiftly attained. After a while, once you, too, think metrically, conversions will be largely unnecessary.

For some examples of *measuring* applied in investigations, see:

Pendulums (p. 204)

Mealworms and What They Do (p. 212)

How Practice Improves Learning (p. 216)

How Water Sinks into Different Soils (p. 219)

COMMUNICATING

In elementary science, communicating means putting the data (information) obtained from our observations into some form another person can understand. Of course, we, too, should be able to understand our data when we reexamine them at a later date.

Children learn to communicate in many ways. They learn to draw accurate pictures, diagrams, and maps; make proper charts and graphs; construct accurate models and exhibits; and use clear language when describing objects or events. The last of these activities is usually stressed in elementary science.

The test of success in communicating is how closely the other person interprets what you say or do with what you have in mind. So it is important to say things or to show data in the clearest ways possible. We can help children learn these ways by giving them many chances to communicate and helping them to evaluate what they have said or done.

In a primary-level class some pupils are seated on a rug. They face a bulletin board on which many pictures of vehicles are pinned. Each picture has a number, so the pictures can be quickly located. The teacher has suggested a game: A child describes the properties of a

vehicle ("I'm thinking of a green object. It has four wheels. It is small enough to fit in my garage," etc.) and the others try to identify the object ("Is it number four?" etc.). The child who identifies the object first gets to be the new describer. The original describer is rewarded by getting the picture. Wild guessing is discouraged by reminding the children to consider the data. After each identification, the teacher asks questions such as

> What did Maria say that helped you to find the picture? What else would be helpful to say? Did anyone get mixed up? How do you think that happened, Tommy?

In a middle-level class two children are working with a simple balance that has a pegboard-type (perforated) beam. They hang iron washers from opened paper clips hooked to different parts of the beam. They are working out problems written on problem cards. After a while, the teacher says:

> What problem cards of your own can you make? Will your partner understand your directions? If not, try to figure out why.

In an upper-level class pupils want to find out the warmest time of the day. Temperature readings are made on the hour from 10 A.M. until 3 P.M. for 5 days in a row and then averaged. They decide to record their results on a line graph but don't know whether to put the temperature along the side (vertical axis) or the bottom (horizontal axis) of the graph. Is there a "regular" way?

The teacher helps them to see how graphs are arranged in their mathematics text. The change being tested, called the manipulated variable by scientists—in this case, time—is usually placed along the bottom axis. The change that results from the test, called the responding variable—in this case, temperature—is usually placed along the vertical axis.

Defining Operationally

Defining operationally is a sub-process of communicating, usually introduced after the primary grades. To define a word operationally is to describe it by an action (operation) rather than just by other words. Maybe you recall the example in Chapter 3 (page 60) in which some children classified rocks according to hardness. The test for "very soft" was, "Can be scratched with your fingernail." This action, then, is the operational definition of "very soft," at least for those children. This definition is clearer than saying, "very soft means not hard," for instance. Here is another example.

Suppose you invite some pupils to hold an evaporation contest: Who can dry water-soaked paper towels fastest? They begin to speculate excitedly. But there is just one thing they will have to agree on before the fun begins. How will everyone know when a towel is "dry"? This stumps them, so you pose another open question that hints at *actions* they could take: What are some things they could *do to the towel* to tell if it is dry? Now, they start coming up with operations (actions) to try:

Squeeze the towel into a ball and see if water comes out.

Rub it on the chalkboard; see if it makes a wet mark.

Tear it and compare the sound to a dry towel you tear.

Hold it up to the light and compare its color to an unsoaked towel.

See if it can be set on fire as fast as an unsoaked towel.

Put an unsoaked towel on one end of a balance beam; see if the other towel balances it.

The children agree that the last operation is easiest to observe and least arguable. It is stated as an operational definition: "A towel is dry if it balances an unsoaked towel from the same package." Activity begins.

Had the open question not worked, one or two narrow questions (How would squeezing the towel show if it is dry? etc.) could have been posed, followed later with a broad question (What else could you do to the towel to tell if it is dry besides squeezing it?)

When operational definitions are not used, it is easy to fall into the trap of circular reasoning: What is the condition of a *dry* towel? It contains no moisture. What is the condition of a towel that *contains no moisture*? It is dry. Or, to borrow from children's humor, consider this example:

He is the best scientist we've ever had.

Who is?

He is.

Who is "He"?

The best scientist we've ever had.

There are some predictable times when the need for operational definitions will come up. Watch children's use of relative terms such as tall, short (How tall? Short?), light, heavy, fast, slow, good, bad (What is "bad" luck?), and so on.

Recording Activities

This is another sub-process of communicating. When activities require time to gather data (e.g., growing plants over many weeks), or when there are many data to consider (e.g., discovering how much vitamin C many juices contain), it is often sensible to make a record of what is happening. Without a record, it is harder to remember what has happened and draw conclusions. In a way, recording can be considered communicating with oneself, besides others. Many teachers ask their pupils to make records in a notebook or *data log*. Records can be in picture or graph form as well as in writing. But whatever way the data are recorded, they should be clear.

In a primary-level class some children are recording the growth of their plants with strips of colored paper. Every other day, they hold a new strip of paper next to their plant and tear off a bit to match the plant's height. They date the strips and paste them in order on large paper sheets. A growth record of the plants is clearly visible to all.

Other children in the class have drawn pictures of their plants at different stages, from seed to mature plant. These they make into record booklets at the teacher's suggestion. They describe each picture for the teacher, who swiftly writes their short statements on paper slips. The children paste these beneath their pictures. The result is a "My Plant Story Book" for each child, who can proudly read it—unassisted—before impressed parents.

In a middle-level class there are five groups at work with narrow strips of litmus paper. (This chemically treated paper changes color when dipped into acidic or basic liquids.) The children want to find out which of five "mystery" liquids in numbered jars are acidic, basic, or neutral. Each group has a recorder, who records the findings on a data sheet. At the end of the work session, the teacher asks how the results of all the groups should be recorded on the chalkboard. It is decided as outlined in Table 4-1. Notice that by having a code (A: Acid, and so on) written to one side, the teacher cuts down on the time needed to record the findings. The data are now compared, differences noted, and possible reasons discussed. Careful retesting is planned to straighten out the differences.

In an upper-level class some children want to find out if there is a pattern to the clouds passing over the city in the spring. They have made a chart that has three columns, one each for March, April, and May. In each

TABLE 4-1
Acidity of mystery liquids.

GROUP	1	2	3	4	5	
Jane	A	B	N	B	A	
Bill	A	B	N	B	A	A: Acid
Kathy	A	A	N	A	A	B: Base
Robin	A	B	N	A	A	N: Neutral
Joe	B	B	N	B	B	

column is a numbered space for each day of that month. Next to about half of the days the children have drawn the weather bureau cloud symbols for the main cloud cover, if any, on those days. Even though the record chart is only partly completed, a sequential pattern is taking shape. After the chart is completed, the children will compare it to data gathered by the local weather bureau office for the same months in previous years.

For some examples of *communicating* applied in investigations, see:

A Bottle Xylophone (p. 196)

The Properties of Leaves (p. 210)

How Practice Improves Learning (p. 216)

Evaporation (p. 223)

INFERRING AND PREDICTING

The usual meaning of inferring is to interpret or *explain* what we observe. If Carol smiles when she greets us (observation), we may infer that she is pleased to see us (explanation). The accuracy of our inferences usually improves with more chances to observe. Several like observations may also lead us to *predict* that the next time we see her she will smile (observation) because she will be pleased to see us (explanation). For convenience, then, view the process of inferring as having two forms: We may make an *inference* from what we observe, and we may predict an *observation* from what we infer (observation ⟶ inference, inference ⟶ observation). Let's now look at children *explaining* observations, then later, in another section, *predicting* them.

Inferring as Explaining

There are at least three common ways we can help children to infer properly from observations. However, expect intuitive-level pupils to have very limited overall understanding of this process.

First, we can get them to distinguish between their observation and inference.

In a middle-level class two children are looking at a picture of shoeprints in the snow. One set of prints is much smaller than the other (observation). One child says, "One of these sets of shoeprints must have been made by a man and the other by a boy" (an inference). The other child says, "That's true" (another inference). Hearing this, the teacher asks an open question to make them aware of other possibilities:

In what other ways could these prints have been made?

They think for a moment and come up with other inferences: Perhaps two children made the prints—one wore his father's shoes; or maybe it was a girl and her mother; or it could have been a girl and her older brother; and so on.

The teacher points out that what they observe is still the same. But there is more than one way to explain the observation. If the children look at the tracks closely, they may *conclude* that one of their inferences is likelier than the others. A *conclusion* is simply an inference in which one has the most confidence after considering all the evidence.

A second way to help children infer is to let them interpret their observed or recorded data. In the preceding section on recording data, recall that pupils used litmus paper to identify mystery liquids. When the several groups recorded their data, they noticed that some data were inconsistent. Some liquids were labeled both acidic and basic. The children inferred from this that the litmus test was done incorrectly by some group. After the tests were redone, all the data became consistent. So the children inferred that their final labeling of the mystery liquids was probably correct.

Also in the section on recording was the cloud data study. The sequential pattern the children saw, when they examined their data, was an inferred pattern. Later, when they compare their pattern with the weather bureau's, they will be able to evaluate the quality of their inference.

A third way to help children infer is to let them observe and interpret only indirect evidence or clues. Scientists must often depend on clues rather than clear evidence in forming possible inferences. For example, no scientist has visited the middle of the earth, yet earth scientists have inferred much about its properties.

In the everyday world we, too, often use clues to infer about objects or events. Sometimes we go wrong. When the boss at long last praises us, we may be quick to infer that the superior quality of our work has finally been recognized—until we are asked to work late that night. When the headwaiter calls us by name at a fancy restaurant, we may infer that we're special—until we observe everyone else getting the same treatment. We need to be cautious when we infer, as do scientists.

Children can learn to make inferences from incomplete or indirect evidence and also learn to become wary of hasty conclusions.

In a primary-level class some pupils are working with two closed shoe boxes. One box contains a round (cylindrical) pencil. In the other box is a usual, six-sided pencil. The children's problem is, which box has which kind of pencil?

They tip the boxes back and forth and listen intently. They then infer correctly the contents of the two boxes. When the teacher asks them what made them decide as they did, one child says, "You could feel which one was the bumpy pencil when it rolled." The other child says, "The bumpy one made more noise."

Later, the teacher puts into the boxes two pencils that are identical except for length. The pupils now find that correct inferring is harder, so they become more cautious. What observations must they rely on now?

In the middle and upper grades children can do an excellent job of inferring the identity or interactions of hidden objects from indirect observational clues. In science this way of inferring is called *model building*. (The investigation described on page 7, under the heading "Parsimony," is mainly devoted to model building.)

For some examples of *inferring* in which children basically make explanations, see these investigations:

The Makeup of Colored Liquids (p. 192)

The Properties of Leaves (p. 210)

How Practice Improves Learning (p. 216)

How Water Sinks into Different Soils (p. 219)

Predicting

To *predict* is to forecast a future observation by inferring from data. As with regular inferring, the more data that are available the more confidence we can have in the prediction; the reverse is also true. We can be very confident that spring will follow winter, but not at all confident that spring fashions this year will be exactly like those of a year ago. Without *some* data, we can only guess about future observations; to predict is impossible.

When pupils put their data in graph form, there are usually many chances to predict.

Upper-level children measure and record on a graph the time candles burn under inverted glass jars. After they have recorded the times for a 100-, 200-, and 300-milliliter jar, the teacher says:

> *How long do you think the candle will burn under a 250-milliliter jar?*

Notice that predicting the time for a 250-milliliter jar would require pupils to read the graph *within* the present data—they have the times for a 200- and a 300-milliliter jar. This is called *interpolating*. If the teacher asked pupils to predict the candle-burning time of a 400-milliliter jar, the children would need to go *beyond* the present data. This is called *extrapolating* from data. Even though a straight-line graph won't result in this case, using these data to predict is likelier to be more accurate than guessing.

Going much beyond observed data when extrapolating can be misleading. If you are measuring how far a spring or rubber band stretches each time you add a uniform weight, eventually you'll reach its elastic limit. Whatever reading you get beyond that point will be out-of-line with previous results. Likewise, a marathon runner who cuts his finishing time in half in the first year of training can't realistically expect to keep doing so year after year.

Children often need assistance when predicting. Simple diagrams can help them to reason through data. Also, if they cannot calculate precise predictions, just asking them to predict the direction of change is useful. Primary-level pupils might be asked, Will *more* or *less* water evaporate when the wind blows? Middle-level children might be asked, Will a *higher, lower,* or the *same* temperature result when these two water samples of different temperatures are mixed? You can see next in detail how all of these techniques can be applied.

For some examples of *predicting* applied in investigations, see:

How to Make a Bulb Light (p. 198)

Wheel-Belt Systems (p. 201)

Pendulums (p. 204)

Evaporation (p. 223)

EXPERIMENTING

To a child, experimenting means "doing something to see what happens." While this is overly simple, it does capture the difference between experimenting and the other six science processes. In experimenting, we *change* objects or events to learn how nature changes them. Objects and events are usually left unchanged when we use the other process skills. This section is about how children can discover the various conditions of change. You may recall that open-ended investigations, in which pupils explore condition variables, were introduced in the last chapter. Now we'll take up some refinements.

Experimenting is often called an "integrated" process, because it may require us to use some or all of the others: observing, classifying, inferring and predicting, measuring, and communicating. That is one reason some curriculum writers reserve this combined process for upper-grade activities. But experimental investigations, like others, can vary in difficulty. With guidance, even intuitive thinkers can do some limited experiments.

This does not mean any hands-on investigation can properly be called experimenting. Many educators say that two criteria must be met:

1. Children should have an idea they want to test. That is, they should vary the object or event for some reason. The act of forming an idea to test is called *hypothesizing*.

2. Children should vary only one condition at a time. When needed, they should also compare the varied object with a matching object that is left unchanged. This is called *controlling variables*.

How strictly we interpret the two criteria determines how hard it is to do an experiment "properly." To many educators almost any investigation is experimenting *if the child changes an object for a purpose and can compare its changed state to the original one.* This is also the position taken in this book. The stricter view of other educators means that only children near or in the stage of formal operations can properly do experimenting. More on this shortly.

Hypothesizing

How do we get pupils to form ideas they want to test—to hypothesize—before they manipulate objects? Perhaps you realize that a section of the last chapter ("How to Develop Open-Ended Investigations with Questions," page 55) addresses that question. This and the next section will extend the earlier information.

You saw there several ways of getting children to state operations that they wanted to try. For elementary pupils, stating operations as questions—Will dropping a magnet make it weaker? Does adding salt to water make things float higher?—is a clear and easy way for them to state hypotheses. It makes them focus on what they want to do to produce some effect, or on what effect to observe to connect it to a cause.

In adult science, a hypothesis is often stated in an if-then manner: *If* I do this, *then* I believe so and so will happen. Or, stated impersonally: *If* a magnet is dropped, *then* it will get weaker. *If* the acid content of rain increases, *then* more plant species will die. You may want to use the if-then form with older pupils. But for most children, stating a hypothesis as an operational question is easier and more understandable.

As you saw before, letting pupils explore the properties of real objects stimulates them to suggest their own ideas for changing them. Their curiosity usually prompts them to state operations they want to try, or to be receptive to broad and narrow questions you ask for that purpose. Notice how this happens next.

In a primary-level class some children have been making and playing with toy parachutes. They tie the four corners of a handkerchief with strings and attach these to a sewing spool. Some release their parachutes while standing on top of the play slide and watch them fall slowly to the ground. Others simply wad the cloth around the spool and throw their parachutes up into the air.

A few children have made their parachutes from *different* materials. They are quick to notice that some parachutes stay in the air longer than others. After they go back to the classroom, they discuss their experiences. Then, the teacher says:

We have plenty of materials to make more parachutes on the science table. How can you make a parachute that will fall slower than the one you have now?

The children respond in different ways: "Make it bigger," "Smaller," "Use a lighter spool," "Make it like Martha's," and so on. These are the children's hypotheses. Some children say nothing, but peer intently at the materials. They are hypothesizing also— nonverbally. The children's ideas need testing, so what works can be found out. Now the children have purposes for doing further work with parachutes.

Where did the children's hypotheses come from? When the children first observed their parachutes in action, they did much inferring ("Jimmy's parachute is bigger than mine. It stays up longer." "Corinne has a big spool. Her chute falls fast," and so on.) It is natural for people to be curious about the quality of their inferences. *Hypotheses are simply inferences that people want to test.*

Exploring the properties of concrete materials provides the background that most children need to think. They cannot offer broad explanatory hypotheses to test concepts or theories. This calls for the deeper background and concept-seeking mind of the formal operational thinker. This is the reason some "why" questions are hard for children to handle: Why does dew form on the grass? Why does a ship float? Why are there earthquakes? Instead of broad, generalizable hypotheses, concrete thinkers are likely to offer limited hypotheses, best phrased as operational questions, that are tied to the objects they have observed or manipulated.

Intuitive thinkers also do this, as you saw in the foregoing example. But they are far more limited in this ability than concrete thinkers. Their teacher wisely provided more real materials to think about during their discussion instead of relying on talk alone. Even so, many children will need the teacher's personal attention to follow through in a meaningful way. Most intuitive thinkers can only think about one variable at a time. This limits the experimenting they can do, because they are un-

likely to control other variables that might affect the outcome. *So primary-level investigations usually lean more heavily on the other six science processes.*

Controlling Variables

To find out exactly what condition makes a difference in an experiment, we must change or vary that condition alone. Other conditions must not vary. In other words, they must be controlled during the experiment.

Suppose you think that varying the size of a parachute will affect its falling rate. A good way to test the variable would be to build two parachutes that are identical in every way except for size. These could then be released at the same time from the same height. After repeated trials, you could infer if size did make a difference in your test.

But don't expect intuitive thinkers or early concrete thinkers to reason in this way. They will not think of the many variables (conditions) that can influence their experiment. They may unwittingly change several variables at the same time—thickness *and* the length of string, for example. Their intent is simply to make a parachute that will fall slower than another, not to isolate variable conditions. On the other hand, young children will grasp the need to control some variables. Typically, they will insist on releasing their parachutes from the same height and at the same time. Otherwise, "it won't be fair," they will tell you. (Are they applying here schemata constructed from play experiences, such as foot races?)

The parachute experiment is more than just a trial-and-error activity. The children have observed parachutes and have done some inferring about their observations. The changes they try will reflect thinking we can call hypothesizing. And although they may not think of controlling all the possible variables, they are conscious of some. This is the nature of experimenting with children. How well they do and how fast they progress are influenced by how skillful we are in helping them. Here are more examples of teachers helping their pupils to experiment.

In a middle-level class the children have worked with seeds and plants for about two weeks. The teacher says:

We've done well in getting our plants started. But suppose we didn't want our seeds to sprout and grow. Sometimes in nature seeds get damaged, or conditions are not right for seeds to grow. What could you do to keep seeds from sprouting and growing?

The children begin suggesting operations to try, as shown in Table 4-2. These are their hypotheses; at this point they need not be framed as operational questions. The teacher writes them on the chalkboard, silly or not. The teacher then gets them to screen the hypotheses for those that may have possibilities:

With which conditions might the seed have some chance to live? Suppose Jimmy squashed his seed just a little. Would the seed sprout? Would the plant look squashed? Would this happen with any kind of a seed? How about some of the rest of these conditions?

This mixture of broad and narrow questions is posed slowly to give the children time to think. The pupils discuss a number of possibilities. After a while, the teacher says:

How can we test our ideas?

It soon becomes obvious that some children are going to do several things at one time to their seeds, so the teacher says:

Suppose Beth squashes her seed and also freezes it. How will she know which one stopped the seed from growing?

The children decide to change just one condition at a time. Pairs of pupils quickly form operational questions from hypotheses they want to test: Will squashing a bean seed keep it from sprouting? Will cutting a bean seed in half keep it from sprouting? and so on. Interest is high as experimenting begins.

In an upper-level class the children are working in pairs. They are testing their reaction time by catching dropped rulers. In each pair, one child holds the ruler just above his partner's hand. When he releases the ruler, the partner catches the ruler (the flat part—not the edges) between his thumb and forefinger. The ruler number closest to the top of his pinched fingers is recorded. This is his "reaction time number." After a few minutes of this activity, the teacher asks the pupils to give their reaction times. He writes these on the board as shown in Table 4-3. Table 4-3 is a histogram, a type of graph. It is used to classify data in a way that encourages thinking about the differences in the data.

After a few moments to discuss with the children how the scores are distributed, the teacher says:

Suppose everything and everyone were the same in our experiment. How would the histogram look? Well, what differences were there that may have given us these results? What conditions might affect reaction time?

The children start forming hypotheses: "Not everybody did it the same way," "Some

TABLE 4-2
Things that may keep a seed from growing.

Squashing it	Cutting it in half
Chewing it	Not watering it
Freezing it	Watering it with salt water
Boiling it	

TABLE 4-3
Reaction time numbers.

				X							
				X							
				X							
			X	X							
				X	X	X	X				
		X		X	X	X	X				
		X		X	X	X	X	X	X		
X		X		X	X	X	X	X	X		X
1	2	3	4	5	6	7	8	9	10	11	12

people have faster reaction times," "Some kids have more practice," "I was tired today," and so on. After a discussion to narrow down and clarify different ideas, the teacher says:

How are you going to test your ideas?

The children state their ideas as operational questions. Will people have the same reaction time if they do the experiment in exactly the same way? Does practice give you a faster reaction time? Do people who feel "tired" (defined as having less than 8 hours of sleep) have slower times than when they don't feel tired? and so on. Everybody agrees that they must do the experiment in the same way each time to control the test variables. Then, each question is tested separately under the controlled conditions.

For some opportunities for *experimenting* in investigations, see:

A String Telephone (p. 194)

How to Make a Bulb Light (p. 198)

The Growth of Seeds (p. 207)

Mealworms and What They Do (p. 212)

The Need to Consult Authority

It's important to realize that children will seldom be able to consider and control *all* of the relevant variables in an experiment. Nor will they always want to do so. People who still believe in the tooth fairy or who cross their fingers for luck while taking a test are not likely to fully appreciate scientific methods. Failure to control variables, of course, may lead to faulty conclusions. Even research scientists will sometimes err in controlling significant variables. A continual source of argument at science conventions is the quality of experimental design.

So guide pupils to limit their conclusions. Let them verify and extend their findings by checking authority in some form: textbook, encyclopedia, film, and the like. This can be done gracefully, without diminishing child-ren's efforts: Let's see if scientists agree with us. . . . What have scientists found out about . . . ?

If verifying results is necessary, you may say, why even bother with experiments? Our teaching purpose gives an answer. Few elementary school pupils can design and conduct scientifically defensible experiments. Yet they can be taught some investigative methods with good results. Children's experiments are an effective teaching tool to improve their thinking and have them gain some solid knowledge through concrete experiences.

Pros and Cons of Class Data

Consider getting data from the entire class when experimenting and using the other science processes. Individuals or small groups can all work on the same investigation, pooling and cross-checking their data. This gives the pupils more to go on when making inferences. In contrast, the individual experimenter or small group that works alone often must repeat experiments before getting enough data to infer properly about what is being tested. This can take much time. Also, the individual experimenter or small group may keep repeating mistakes, unless you are watchful. Another benefit from the whole class investigation is that a greater variety of ideas will arise for children to mull over when data differences are analyzed.

But we must also be careful with the whole-class approach. Perhaps the most serious problem is that we may think of the children as a class, rather than a collection of individual persons. In designing an experiment, for example, we may get comments here and there from class members. We may then put these comments together ourselves, or lead one child to do so, and then assume everyone knows what is going on. We can be fooled into thinking that what the child can do as a member of a class, he can do independently. This is one reason why many teachers today use individual and small-group experiences besides working with the whole class.

TEXTBOOK EXPERIMENTS

In many elementary schools a children's textbook series makes up the science program. Such books contain many activities for children to work with. Their usual purpose is to illustrate in concrete ways ideas presented in the books. Teachers sometimes call the worst of these activities "cookbook experiments." That is, because the problem, materials, directions, and even conclusions at times are furnished, there is little chance for children to think. All that needs to be done by them is to follow the recipe. Criticism of this kind is waning, because today's books are better than ever before. More authors now use activities that require thinking. And conclusions for activities are now usually tucked safely into the accompanying teacher's manual, rather than right there on a page of the pupils' textbook for all to see.

But authors are restricted by the book format. Working well with children in an experiment typically calls for an interactive process. What we do or say depends much on what the children do or say. If we simply follow the book, there may be little chance for interaction. Yet a good textbook—and there are many—contains much material we can use to begin and move along the interactive process.

In examining a textbook experiment, especially notice the way in which the author leads into the activity and the comments following it. Usually, a question is posed just before the experiment, with extending information following the experiment. This means you can use the author's questions to introduce the experiment and the book's information to extend the children's learning after the experiment is completed. The activity may be done with individuals, small groups, or the whole class. (Ideas about individualizing instruction are dealt with mainly in Chapter 6.)

But start the experiment with the pupils' books closed. The time for reading is after the experiment is finished or at least planned. The book, rather than the children, should serve as the checkup source. "It's fun to find out the book agrees with me," a little girl once said to me. And it's also far more thought-provoking, one might add.

Now consider a contrasting example of two ways to use a text experiment. We begin with an unimaginative method.

Today, we will have a chance to do the experiment on page 161. Let's read the directions carefully so we will know exactly how to set it up.

The pupils follow in their books silently while someone reads orally:

Activity Does planting seeds in different positions change how roots grow?

Materials Ink blotter; wide-mouth glass jar; paper towel; water; bean seeds.

What to Do Place the blotter around the inside of the jar. Wad the towel and stuff it into the jar. This will hold the blotter against the glass. Put seeds in different positions between the blotter and glass. Add an inch of water to the jar to keep the blotter wet, and as needed later to keep about the same water level. Observe for two weeks.

What Did You Find Out? Did all the roots grow downward? Roots grow in this way no matter how seeds are turned. This is because they, like you, are attracted by gravity.

The teacher selects from a thicket of waving hands two volunteers to set up the activity. Daily observations are made to see if the results are like those in the book.

In another class, the same activity comes up. This teacher says:

No need for our books yet, people. We'll be starting with experiments again. Has anyone ever seen some plant roots that were dug up? Which way did the roots seem to grow? What might happen if they didn't grow that way? Well, here's a problem, then. If you plant seeds in different positions, in which direction or directions will the roots grow?

The children respond. The teacher then asks:

How can we test these ideas?

Pupils suggest planting seeds in different positions in soil. Various soil containers are mentioned—paper cups, small milk cartons, quart milk cartons with one side cut out for planting several seeds in a row, and so on. Because the teacher has a box of bean seeds bought at a supermarket, everyone can do the activity. The planning includes procedures to water and then to dig up groups of seeds at staggered times. The teacher says:

It would help to actually see the roots while they are growing. What are some ways this could be done?

Pupils divide into groups to "brainstorm" ideas, but they get nowhere. Seeing this, the teacher places on a table the materials described in the book and says:

Maybe these materials can give you some ideas.

Several suggestions are made by pupils. These are evaluated: How will they tell if the water, rather than gravity, affects the roots? Someone suggests planting a sprouted seed at one end of a cut open quart milk carton placed on its side and watering only the opposite end. Will the roots grow toward the water or straight down, "the way they're supposed to"? Will it work with other seeds? and so on.

Later, the teacher asks the children to compare their findings with those of the scientists, as found in the text. They are pleased with the comparison but find a variable (soil) they forgot to control. Next time, they vow, they will be more careful.

NARROW AND BROAD QUESTIONS FOR SCIENCE PROCESSES

By now, you've seen many examples of teachers asking broad and narrow questions for children to use the science processes. Perhaps you're wondering, Where did the questions come from?

Notice that following this section is a summary of the processes. Each is operationally defined. This means you can see children do the operations listed within each process. Each operation can trigger broad or narrow questions. Let's use "observing" for our example and consider, one by one, each of its three listed operations. Children are observing when they

Identify properties of objects such as color, size, and shape by using any or all of their senses.

A broad question such as, "What do you notice about these objects?" should get this operation from the children. If it does not, you can shift down and ask a narrow question that focuses on a single variable: "What *color* do you see?" or "How *big* are they?" or "What *shape* is it?" and so on. After one or two of these questions, you can shift back to the broad question, "What else do you notice about . . . ?"

State noticeable changes in objects or events.

"What changes do you notice?" can serve here as a broad question. If narrow questions are needed, just focus on a specific change: "How has the *water* changed? How have the polliwogs' *gills* changed?" and so on. Later, "What other changes do you notice?" will serve as a broad question to shift the burden back to your pupils.

State noticeable similarities and differences in objects and events.

"How are they alike? different?" are appropriate broad questions. "How do their *sizes* compare? *shapes* compare? *colors* compare?" are possible narrow questions. "In what other ways are they alike? different?" gets you back again to the broad category.

Knowing how to ask process questions, then, is largely a matter of knowing what operations pupils can do in each process. You'll find a broad question suggested for every listed operation within the processes summary. Narrow questions are not given for the most part because their exact nature depends on the subject matter studied. The best place to see narrow questions used in this book, in combination with broad questions, is in Appendix A. Consult the summary for operations and turn them into questions, like those suggested, as you work with children. Applying them often in your teaching will enable you to soon learn the operations.

SUMMARY OF THE SCIENCE PROCESSES

The following summary of science processes, with pupil operations you can observe, is the basis for every broad and narrow process question found in Appendix A. Further operations could be added to each of the listed processes, since they are open-ended. But if your pupils act in any of the ways summarized here, you can be reasonably sure they are doing process thinking.

Observing. Children are observing when they

■ Identify properties of objects such as color, size, and shape by using any or all of the senses. (What do you notice about these objects?)

■ State noticeable changes in objects or events. (What changes do you notice?)

■ State noticeable similarities and differences in objects or events. (How are they alike? Different?)

Classifying. Children are classifying when they

■ Group objects or events by their properties or functions. (In what ways could we group these objects?)

■ Arrange objects or events in order by some property or value. (How could we put these objects in order?)

Measuring. Children are measuring when they

■ Use standard tools such as the meter stick, yardstick, ruler, clock, balance, and protractor to find quantity. (What standard measuring tools could you use to measure this?)

■ Use familiar objects as arbitrary units to find quantity. (What everyday things could you use to measure this?)

■ Make scale drawings or models. (How could you make a scale drawing or model of this?)

■ Use simple sampling and estimating techniques. (How could we get a good sample or estimate of this?)

Communicating. Children are communicating when they

■ Define words operationally—through some action—when needed. (What needs to be defined here?)

■ Describe objects or events. (How can you describe this . . . so someone else knows what you mean?)

■ Make charts and graphs. (How can you make a chart or graph to show your findings?)

- Record data as needed. (How can we keep track of our observations?)

- Construct exhibits and models. (How can we show someone how this works?)

- Draw diagrams, pictures, and maps. (What can we draw to explain what happens? What map can you draw so someone else can find the place?)

Inferring.   Children are inferring when they

- Distinguish between an observation and an inference. (What do you observe, and what does this tell you about . . . ?)

- Interpret recorded data. (What findings go together?)

- Interpret data received indirectly. (How can you tell what's inside?)

- Hypothesize from data. (What do you think makes this happen?)

- Draw conclusions from data. (From this information, what have you found out about . . . ?)

- Predict events from data. (What do you think will happen?)

Experimenting.   Children are experimenting when they

- State a hypothesis or operational question to test. (What do you think makes this happen? or, Will fanning the water make it evaporate faster? Remember that an operational question—the second question here—is typically narrow and describes an observable action.)

- Design a procedure in which variables are controlled. (How can we find out?)

Remember that many teachers will accept a less rigorous definition for experimenting: A child changes an object for some purpose and compares the changed condition to the original one.

When shown a list like the foregoing, one teacher said, "How on earth am I going to remember *and* get my kids to do all of those processes?" The reaction is common and understandable, but the job is easier than it first appears. For one thing, the science curriculum carries the main load in developing process thinking, as it usually does in developing concepts. Also, the list sums up in one place most of the processes that might be present in a modern science program. Probably only a few advanced pupils could demonstrate all of them well.

While the listed processes are typical of those in modern programs, they may not be identical. How people think can be organized in many ways. The important thing is for you to find the science processes meaningful. If so, you should have little trouble with teaching processes in any modern curriculum. You should be able to shift from one program to another, as school needs may require.

The teacher who understands and appreciates science processes has far more capacity to help children think than one who does not, even when both use the same curriculum guide. Following a curriculum guide can take us only so far. Teaching for process is often done best through the flexible, immediate tactics used in "teachable moments." *These times come up continually if children are allowed to think for themselves.*

An acronym (COMIC-E) can help you remember the science processes during these and other times:

Classifying

Observing

Measuring

Inferring and predicting

Communicating

Experimenting

A mental picture can also jog your memory. Figure 4-1 may help you to remember two things: the acronym itself and that experimenting is supported and complemented by the other processes.

Another way to remember the processes is through practice in recognizing them. All of the investigations in Appendix A of this book have marginal notes that identify the science processes used. You might cover the notes with a narrow slip of paper as you read questions in an investigation. Try to identify the process used in each case and then move the paper down to reveal the note. See if we agree. You can get some idea of how much practice you need by doing the following exercises.

FIGURE 4-1
Experimenting (E) is supported and complemented by classifying, observing, measuring, inferring and predicting, and communicating (COMIC).

EXERCISES
4-1 to 4-5

How Well Do You Know the Science Processes?

Try the following exercises. They are designed to help you practice what you may have learned so far in this chapter. You'll need paper and pencil. Compare your ideas with the comments that appear after each exercise. Also, refer to the summary of processes on page 90 as needed.

4-1 You can ask questions to start children thinking about any of the processes. Notice the accompanying list of processes and seven clusters of questions. Each question cluster goes with one of the processes, but the clusters are now out of order. Are you able to match each question cluster with the proper process?

Process	Question Clusters
[a] Observing	[1] Which soap did the better job? What did you find out? What story do the smaller footprints tell?
[b] Classifying	[2] How could you find out? In what ways could you test your idea? What could you do to be more sure the wind is responsible?
[c] Measuring	[3] How could you put these objects together? In what groups do they belong? How could these things be put into some order?
[d] Communicating	[4] What do you notice? How are these objects alike? Different? How does this compare to how it was before?
[e] Inferring	[5] How heavy (light, fast, slow, tall, etc.) is it? What could you use instead of a meter stick? How can you estimate how many peas are in the jar?
[f] Predicting	[6] What do you mean by "blond" hair? How can you show your findings on a chart? How could you keep a record of your plant work?
[g] Experimenting	[7] Where do you expect the most erosion to take place? If we do this, should the mixture get cooler or warmer? What do you think will happen, judging from your graph?

Comments

Process (a) goes with question cluster (4), (b) with (3), (c) with (5), (d) with (6), (e) with (1), (f) with (7), and (g) with (2). If some questions seem misplaced, please review the summary of science processes.

4-2   The teacher's guide for a program may not identify the processes to be taught in different lessons. If you do not have time to teach everything (a usual problem), you need to choose your lessons carefully. Of course, you can choose more wisely if you are aware of what processes are developed in suggested lessons. Following are some passages from a teacher's guide. Are you able to tell what process needs to be used in each quoted passage? A sample answer is given for the first passage to help you start.

Activity	Process Used
[a] Have the children use the line or bar graphs to roughly tell how high the plants might be on the weekend.	Predicting
[b] Because at least a week may be needed for definite findings, help the children write and attach to their experiments the purpose of each.	

Activity	Process Used
[c] Encourage pupils to think of ways to test the effect of temperature on the bean plants.	_____
[d] Invite them to inspect the plant parts carefully and point out similarities and differences.	_____
[e] Have the children line up the sprouted plants according to size, if possible at this time.	_____
[f] Leave the materials on the table. The children may be able to invent several ways to tell how much larger the leaves have grown.	_____
[g] Let the children check their findings. What makes it seem likely that the light was responsible?	_____
[h] This would be a good time to ask the pupils: How could the materials be used to find out if plants grow toward the light?	_____
[i] The seeds could be divided according to how they travel—water, air, by land animals, and so on.	_____
[j] Suggest that each child make a map for his partner that shows where he found the weed. Will his partner be able to find the weed in that place?	_____

Comments

The process needed in activity (b) is communicating; in (c) experimenting; in (d) observing; in (e) classifying; in (f) measuring; in (g) inferring; in (h) experimenting; in (i) classifying; and in (j) communicating. If some process labels seem misplaced, please review appropriate sections in this chapter, as well as the summary of the processes on page 90. Remember, you will also find it helpful to examine the investigations in Appendix A of this book. The processes used in each are identified in the margins.

4-3 Operational definitions are often needed when language is unclear. If you define a word by what someone or something does—an observable operation—it usually becomes clear. Please underline the word(s) in each sentence that most needs to be operationally defined. Then complete the second sentence to include the operational definition. An example:

You will need a <u>powerful</u> hand lens to see the insect's eyes. By <u>powerful</u> I mean <u>a lens that magnifies three or more times normal size.</u>

1. What is the least distance it takes you to stop when riding a fast-moving bicycle?
   By _____ I mean _____ .

2. Will this detergent get clothes clean?
   By _____ I mean _____ .

3. Add water until the sponge is saturated.
   By _____ I mean _____ .

4. From these, pick out only the truly hard rocks.
   By _____ I mean _____ .

5. Becky is 10 years old, weighs 70 pounds, and has long hair.
   By _____ I mean _____ .

6. Remove the leaf from the pot soon after the water boils.
   By _____ I mean _____ .

Comments

Acceptable answers will be generally like the following:

1. By <u>fast moving</u> I mean <u>more than 10 miles per hour.</u>

2. By <u>clean</u> I mean <u>remove coffee stains from a white cloth napkin, so I cannot see them, after a normal wash cycle in my washing machine.</u>

3. By <u>saturated</u> I mean <u>cannot hold any more water without dripping.</u>

4. By <u>truly hard</u> I mean <u>cannot be scratched by an iron nail.</u>

5. By <u>long hair</u> I mean <u>grown below shoulder length.</u>

6. By <u>soon after</u> I mean <u>before 10 seconds have passed on our classroom clock.</u>

4-4   The purpose of a broad question is to open up a discussion to a variety of responses. But you may get only a yes/no or other limited response if you unintentionally state the question in a narrow form. An example:

What differences can you find? should draw many answers.

Can you find differences? might draw only a yes or no answer.

Sometimes children will sense that you want multiple responses even when a broad question is narrowly stated. When they do not, a follow-up question must be asked. You can learn to avoid this inefficient method with a little practice on how to state broad questions.

How can the following questions with yes/no or limited answers be changed to broad questions with multiple answers?

1. Are the two objects alike?

2. Is there anything you notice about this?

3. Can you think of how this might happen?

4. Do you remember anything else from the chart?

5. Are there other ways to do it?

6. Has it changed? (Assuming observable changes have occurred.)

7. Can you put these objects in order?

8. Do you think something else could make a change here?

Comments

Acceptable answers will generally be like the following:

1. How are the two objects alike? (Or, In what ways . . .)

2. What do you notice about this?

3. How do you think this might happen?

4. What else do you remember from the chart?

5. In what other ways can you do it?

6. How has it changed? (Or, In what ways . . .)

7. How can you put these objects in order? (Or, In what ways . . .)

8. What else do you think could make a change here?

4-5 In investigations, broad and narrow process questions are best used in combination. Narrow questions typically build background in pupils, which allows them to respond successfully to the broad questions. Examine the investigations in Appendix A of the text whose discovery problems begin on pages 195, 199, 202, 205, 211, and 224. Read each discovery problem. Notice where broad questions are used to open up possibilities for exploring many variables. Find where narrow questions are used to focus on single variables. *Please consider all the questions and information that may be contained within each discovery problem, then decide whether the overall problem is broad or narrow in its intent.*

You may find this a convenient way to record your decisions:

p. 000   N   B
  A   _____   _____
  B   _____   _____
  C   _____   _____
  D   _____   _____

Comments

Page 195: A is narrow; B, C, D broad.

Page 199: A is broad; B calls for narrow, either-or-responses; C, D are broad.

Page 202: A is narrow because it refers to the limited choices in the figure. B, C are broad because several possibilities exist.

Page 205: A, B, C, D are narrow because each focuses on one variable. E, F, G are broader because each introduces a problem.

Page 211: A, B, C are broad because each may bring up a large array of variable properties in the child's thinking. The more properties the child describes, the more open-ended the investigation becomes.

Page 224: A, C, D, E are narrow because each suggests limited or single variables to try. B, F, G are broad.

Teaching for process development is serious business. The science processes are vital in learning new concepts, how to attack new problems, and how to construct new knowledge—in learning how to learn, we might say. No wonder all the modern programs include experiences to promote children's thinking.

SCIENTIFIC ATTITUDES

"I can't talk to him. He's closed minded." How often have you heard this said about someone who is unwilling to consider or accept new ideas? This attitude can be annoying when shown by a friend. But it would be a colossal setback to science if scientists were to feel that way.

The processes of science work best when the adults or children who use them are disposed to act in harmony with the processes. Since dispositions are rooted in feelings, they are called attitudes. What favorable attitudes should we look for and encourage as we teach science? The developers of one widely respected program, the Science Curriculum Improvement Study, say this[2]

We have identified four major attitude areas that are part of scientific literacy. The four areas are (a) curiosity, (b) inventiveness, (c) critical thinking, and (d) persistence. Here are definitions and examples of various kinds of behaviors associated with the four areas.

(a) Curiosity. Children who pay particular attention to an object or event and spontaneously wish to learn more about it are being curious. They may give evidence of curiosity by

■ Using several senses to explore organisms and materials.

■ Asking questions about objects and events.

■ Showing interest in the outcomes of experiments.

(b) Inventiveness. Children who generate new ideas are being inventive. These children exhibit original thinking in their interpretations. They may give evidence of inventiveness through verbal statements or actions by

■ Using equipment in unusual and constructive ways.

■ Suggesting new experiments.

■ Describing novel conclusions from their observations.

(c) Critical Thinking. Children who base suggestions and conclusions on evidence are thinking critically. They may exhibit critical thinking largely through verbal statements by

■ Using evidence to justify their conclusions.

■ Pointing out contradictions in reports by their classmates.

■ Changing their ideas in response to evidence.

[2]Reprinted with permission from *Organisms Evaluation Supplement,* written and published by the Science Curriculum Improvement Study. Copyright © 1972 by The Regents of the University of California.

(d) Persistence. Children who maintain an active interest in a problem or event for a longer period than their classmates are being persistent. They are not easily distracted from their activity. They may give evidence of persistence by

- Continuing to investigate materials after their novelty has worn off.
- Repeating an experiment in spite of apparent failure.
- Completing an activity even though their classmates have finished earlier.

Can you imagine the state of science research if scientists did not continually show curiosity, inventiveness, critical thinking, and persistence?

We are dealing here, though, with the teaching of children. Maybe your reaction to the foregoing list of attitude behaviors is like that of a beginning teacher who said, "It's good to know some attitudes to work toward. But *recognizing* positive attitudes isn't my problem. How to *develop* these attitudes is."

What do you do to develop positive attitudes within the four areas as you teach science?

I've often put this question to teachers who do a good job with attitudes. Their responses vary widely, of course, but an interesting thing happens when you boil down their answers. Most use at least one common approach within each of the four areas. Each of these four approaches seems essential. Let's see what they are.

Curiosity

"To be a child is to touch, smell, taste, and hear everything you can between the time you get up and when your parents make you go to bed. I don't have to *teach* curiosity. It's there already."

The kindergarten teacher who said that echoes many of her elementary school colleagues. Yet in some classes it's possible to see girls and boys who lack interest in science. What kills this natural disposition in children?

For an eye-opening answer, walk into two adjoining classrooms, one with a hands-on science program and another where pupils just read and do worksheets during science time. Handing concrete materials to children is like giving catnip to a kitten, rowing downstream, cycling with the wind at your back. Making children sit still and be quiet for long periods is like caging an eagle, rowing upstream, riding into the wind. You can do the latter things, but they are best avoided. Children will lose a lot of their curiosity—at least in school—unless they are allowed to do what comes naturally.

How much time should you give to hands-on experiences? About 40 to 50 percent of the science period seems right to many teachers. This leaves enough time for discussions, explanations, and getting things organized. The exact percentage will vary with the subject.

Teachers who maintain or spark pupils' curiosity also do other things. Most apply science learnings to everyday life as often as possible. Most use textbook experiments, but they often start them with the book closed. Children read the book later to compare their ideas and findings with those in the book. These teachers also use at least several open-ended investigations during a teaching unit—which brings us to the next attitude area.

Inventiveness

To be inventive is to solve problems in creative or novel ways. This contrasts with simply taking a known solution and applying it to a problem at hand: It's good to apply what you know about a car jack to change a flat tire, but what do you do when there's no jack? Inventive people may apply their knowledge to solve problems much as other persons do. But they are more likely to show *fluency, flexibility,* and *originality* in their thinking.[3]

Fluency refers to the number of ideas a child gives when challenged with a problem.

---

[3]John A. Glover and Roger H. Bruning. *Educational Psychology* (Boston: Little, Brown, 1987), pp. 261–64.

We can promote fluency by asking open-ended questions such as

In what ways can you prevent this nail from rusting?

What objects can be charged with static electricity?

What conditions might make orange juice lose its vitamin C?

Creative persons produce a *larger number* of hypotheses (or operational questions) in such cases. It's helpful for all children to consider a number of possibilities before they try to solve a problem.

Flexibility is the inclination to shift one's focus from the usual—to get out of a rut. Suppose children respond to the rust question with

Paint it with silver paint.

Paint it with red paint.

Paint it with green paint.

And so on, in that vein.

Primary-level children, in particular, are prone to this. To promote flexibility, you can simply ask, In *what other ways* besides painting the nail can you prevent it from rusting?

Chances abound for flexible thinking when there is a need to improvise or substitute different materials. Questions such as

What can we use in place of . . . ?

What else can we find to do this . . . ?

How could you use _____ to . . . ?

will prompt children to think of substitutions. To be flexible when substituting one object for another pupils should think more about the present *properties* of the objects, rather than their present *functions*. That's exactly what children do when they convert drinking straws into peashooters.

Originality is shown when pupils generate ideas that are new to them. We can promote it by encouraging them to use their imagination, to combine others' ideas in new ways

(most inventors do this), and by withholding evaluative comments until all ideas are in. Pupils need a psychologically safe environment to be original.

Children who are challenged to demonstrate fluency and flexibility will often—but not always—be original. So encourage them, when needed, to give their own ideas as well.

Precisely how creative persons get to be that way is still debatable.[4] Regardless, children can profit much if you expose them to a wide variety of possibilities in problem solving. You probably realize by now that most of the material in Chapter 3 on open-ended activities can do just that. Experiences like these are a sure-fire way to involve your pupils in creative problem solving. The teachers I know who do the most with inventiveness are convinced of this.

Critical Thinking

Ask two people to define "critical thinking" and you're likely to get divergent and uncomfortable replies. Few terms beg more for clarification.

To think critically is to evaluate or judge whether something is adequate, correct, useful, or desirable. A judge does this when she decides if there is adequate evidence of guilt. An editor does this when he determines the correctness of a writer's grammar. Exasperated parents do this at the dinner table when they yell, "Mind your manners!" at Junior or Sis. In each of these cases someone has a *standard* in mind against which a judgment is made. This, then, is a key to critical thinking: Know the accepted standard of behavior and decide whether or to what degree it is being met.

A problem we face as teachers of elementary-age children is that there are nu-

---

[4]Robert Weisberg, *Creativity: Genius and Other Myths* (New York: W. H. Freeman, 1986), pp. 51–69; and Ellen D. Gagné, *The Cognitive Psychology of School Learning* (Boston: Little, Brown, 1985), p. 144.

merous standards of behavior in science. And many are highly sophisticated. Let's see if we can reduce them to a manageable few and restate them on a level that makes sense to young minds.

There are three overall standards for critical thinking in science that most children can gradually understand and learn to make decisions about: *open-mindedness, objectivity, and willingness to suspend judgment until enough facts are known.*

The open-minded person listens to others and is willing to change his or her mind if warranted. An objective person tries to be free of bias, considers both sides in arguments, and realizes that strong personal preferences may interfere with the proper collecting and processing of data. Someone who suspends judgment understands that additional data may confirm or deny what first appears. So looking for further data improves chances for drawing proper conclusions. Children can learn to judge when they themselves, as well as others, do and do not demonstrate the three standards of behaviors.

It's easy to set up such situations. Just have several groups work on the same activity, then report and compare findings. When data from several sources are being considered, it soon becomes obvious when people refuse to listen to others, push their own ideas, and jump to conclusions before all groups have their say.

Frequently, it is also possible in such discussions for you to detect correlation without causation, anthropomorphism, and the need for operational definitions. Once in a while you may even have need to apply the principle of parsimony. This is most likely when older or gifted children give their theories about how something works but cannot directly observe the action.

Critical and creative thinking go hand in hand. It's artificial to keep them separate. When problem solving or experimenting, for example, children should be encouraged to generate a number of possibilities (fluency), rather than just consider the first idea suggested. You also want them to critically appraise all the ideas at one time so that they can immediately tackle what looks most promising. Controlling variables in experimenting gives pupils another chance to generate many suggestions. But they must also think: Will these controls do the job? Later, if groups come up with different findings, critical thinking is again needed to answer why. Perhaps one or more variables were not controlled after all. You can see that creative and critical thinking are different sides of the same coin.

When pupils seek information, there are really *only two sources* available to them: they themselves—in the form of personal observations and experiments; and authority—in the form of printed matter, audiovisual materials, and knowledgeable persons.

Don't be discouraged if it seems hard for children to appraise the merits of authority used in schools. There are several reasons for this.

Perhaps an obvious reason is that elementary-school children just do not know enough yet. Also, they have less logical ability than they will have later. Another reason is that materials used in the schools are likely to be reasonably accurate and reliable. After all, instructional materials must usually run the gamut of editorial supervision, numerous selection committees of educators, and other sources of appraisal. What survives is likely to be quite acceptable. If not, it is hardly likely that children will have the skill and knowledge to detect error or otherwise evaluate critically.

Certainly, children can be cautioned to check copyright dates and agreement with what is known, to consult more than one source, to note the occasional conflict in fact, and the like. But the possibilities for critical appraisal of authority are relatively few, largely because of children's lack of background, limited logical capacity, and few appropriate materials. Therefore, we typically spend little time on critical analysis of materials. Instead, we help children learn the sources of authority that exist, ways to consult these sources efficiently, and to understand what the sources say.

There are many more chances to teach critical thinking in the experiments and observations that children themselves make during science study. These activities are close to the raw, unadulterated facts—information minus the "editorial filter" already supplied when the usual school resources are consulted. Pupils must provide their own intellectual filter, with our guidance when needed, if the data are to be trustworthy.

Persistence

Most elementary science activities can be completed within a short time. But some require a sustained and vigorous effort. This can be a problem when you are dealing with children.

To do our best work—the product we look to with pride, the memory of achievement that motivates us to try even harder on future occasions—often takes persistence. You and I know this, but children lack the background of experience that continually impels adults to stick with a worthwhile goal.

Primary-level pupils, especially, want instant results. Their short attention span and need for physical activity can easily convert into impatience. Some older children are not much better. How do many experienced teachers combat this natural inclination of children? They arouse or use children's *interests*.

What we've considered already, hands-on, open-ended investigations, are powerful vehicles you can use. They allow you to offer pupils a broad array of choices to investigate and the freedom to choose. They also can bring up the need for pupils to commit to specific operations or observations as part of a group effort. Learning centers and personal

projects, which we'll take up in Chapter 6, give other ways to spark and lock onto interests.

When things don't go as desired in long-range activities, pupils may become discouraged and give up. This is the time to help them figure out why and to explain the scientist's positive approach to failure. Then they, too, may view such results as bringing them closer to their goals.

Early learning of attitudes begins with imitation and later comes from experiencing the consequences of having or not having the attitudes. This means that your pupils will probably look to you as a model as they begin to learn scientific attitudes. And they may learn even more from the experiences you provide.

People continually furnish models for our behavior. The more we like and respect them, the more likely we are to model our behavior after theirs. The open-minded, accepting, nonthreatening teacher who reflects positive attitudes is more likely to influence pupils in positive ways than one who lacks these qualities.

But even more important, in a science program where children use science processes, attitudes can develop as they do with scientists. You simply help pupils compare the consequences of having or not having scientific attitudes. The activities—especially those that are open-ended—bring out the consequences at every turn. Success is very much bound up with curiosity, inventiveness, critical thinking, and persistence. So children learn, in a more limited way, the same habits of mind as scientists and other reflective people. Their self-esteem grows as they continue to successfully practice these attitudes.

Such practice is best continued throughout all subjects of the curriculum. Attitudes are the broadest of all learnings, and they are mostly well learned over the long haul. They can be valuable whenever we tackle a problem or make a decision. Educated people use them in every subject, and so can your pupils. The advantage of introducing such attitudes through *science* comes from the many consequences that pupils can literally see for themselves. Just remember,

- For curiosity—use hands-on experiences.
- For inventiveness—use open-ended investigations.
- For critical thinking—use standards.
- For persistence—use interests.

And, best of all, use them in combination as often as you can.

SUMMARY

Science processes are tools that enable children to gather and think about data for themselves. They include observing, classifying, inferring and predicting, measuring, communicating, and experimenting. To teach the processes, we have pupils investigate a variety of subject-matter contexts with concrete materials and guide their thinking with broad and narrow questions pointed to each process.

In *observing*, pupils learn to use all of their senses, note similarities and differences in objects, and be aware of change.

In *classifying*, pupils group things by properties or functions; they may also arrange them in order of value.

Measuring teaches them to use nonstandard and standard units to find or estimate quantity. Measurement is often applied in combination with skills introduced in the mathematics program.

Communicating teaches pupils to put observed information into some clear form that another person can understand.

In *inferring*, children interpret or explain what they observe. When pupils infer from data that something will happen, usually the term *predicting* is used. When people state an

inference they want to test, usually the term *hypothesizing* is used. So predicting and hypothesizing are special forms of inferring.

In *experimenting*, we often guide pupils to state their hypotheses as operational (testable) questions and help them to control variables within their understanding.

The processes of science work best when the persons who use them have attitudes that harmonize with the processes. Four major attitude areas that are part of science literacy are curiosity, inventiveness, critical thinking, and persistence. Teachers can effectively promote curiosity through hands-on experiences, inventiveness through open-ended investigations, critical thinking through use of accepted standards, and persistence through pupil interests.

SUGGESTED READINGS

Beyer, Barry K. *Practical Strategies for the Teaching of Thinking.* Boston: Allyn and Bacon, 1987. (Comprehensive array of methods to teach thinking skills in most school subjects.)

Funk, H. James, et al. *Learning Science Process Skills.* Dubuque, Iowa: Kendall/Hunt, 1985. (Sixteen skills are developed step by step in a workbook format.)

Kyle, Jr., William C., et al. "What Research Says About Hands-on Science." *Science and Children,* April, 1988, 39–40, 52. (Science attitudes of Texas schoolchildren improved far more in a hands-on program than in a book-centered science program.)

Ostlund, Karen L. *Science Process Skills.* Menlo Park, CA: Addison-Wesley, 1992. (Ways to assess each of the science processes, with material lists and reproducible worksheets.)

Ross, John A. "Learning to Control Variables." *Journal of Research in Science Teaching* 27 (6): 523–39 (September, 1990). (Two methods to improve the ability of upper-grade pupils to control variables in experiments.)

Weisberg, Robert W. *Creativity: Genius and Other Myths.* New York: W. H. Freeman, 1986. (Separates research from popular but shaky education folklore on creative problem solving. An absorbing eye-opener.)

5

How to Use Different Resources to Teach Science

The kind of science program you have in your classroom will much depend on what materials you have to teach with. Some school districts or schools furnish total packaged programs. These may include detailed lessons and the equipment and materials needed for each lesson. (Several such programs are described in Chapter 7.) However, in other situations a set of texts is the program and few, if any, materials are purchased to go with the text.

Will this be a big problem for you? Not likely. Most school districts have a variety of resources teachers can draw from to teach science, even though the resources may not be specifically tied to the science text or other programs adopted in the district. This chapter should help you learn many sources of materials commonly available and ways to use them.

GETTING EQUIPMENT AND SUPPLIES

Despite inadequate funds for science supplies, some teachers seem to have no trouble getting many materials to teach science. Often they achieve this happy condition just by turning loose sixty or more volunteers eager to help—pupils and their parents. They then supplement these materials with a few others from commercial sources. Let's see how these methods can help you to get supplies.

Children and Parents As Resources

Most of the materials used in elementary science programs are simple and easy to get—the kind found around the home, school, in local stores, or other convenient places. Pupils themselves often can get what is needed for hands-on learning experiences. It's a good idea to let them do so.

When everyday materials are brought to school and used by children, they can continue the experience at home if necessary. That is common with open-ended investigations. Also, pupils are likely to have a hand in planning the experience. This usually makes its purpose clear and develops in them a commitment to follow through. And by having more materials, more children can participate.

Of course, not all pupils are equally resourceful or reliable. Many primary-level children (and older ones, too) quickly forget what they so eagerly volunteered to bring the day before. So give them notes, remind them of what they will bring the next day, and let several children volunteer for the same item. It is also good for public relations to let parents know that nothing is *required,* to counter the children who may say to them, "We *have* to bring . . ."

The best materials to request are reusable or no-cost items: foam cups, empty shoe boxes, old string, wire hangers, small boxes of soil, and so on. Children should clearly understand that permission of parents is required before any items are brought to school.

Parents can be especially helpful in acquiring materials if you contact them directly. One of the best times to request their help is at the beginning of the year during Parents' Night or some other introductory meeting. Consider passing out a photocopied list of inexpensive or no-cost items needed for the year.

How to get such a list? It is probably already prepared by the publisher of your science program. If so, just duplicate it. Check the teacher's edition of your grade-level guide. Many publishers make two lists of things needed for each chapter or instructional unit: materials supplied by the publisher in kit form, and a list of low-cost or discardable materials usually found around the home and school. Parents are concerned about the quality of education for their children. Most respond well to specific and reasonable requests for commonly found materials. In economically disadvantaged neighborhoods, parents may be able to donate only a few throwaway items. Look for federal and state supplemental funds in these cases.

Parents' Night is also a good time to ask for qualified parent (and grandparent) volunteers who might give special help in one or more instructional units. Be specific. You might want someone to help set up a photo-developing center or a classroom garden; to give an eyewitness account of an earthquake or some other natural phenomenon; or to share information about a science-related occupation, such as laboratory technician, airplane pilot, electrician, meteorologist, and so on.

Commercial Sources

It would be hard for us to rely on children or parents for everything needed in a science program. Commercial sources need to be used: science supply houses, hardware stores, drugstores, and department stores, for example. Many school principals keep a petty cash fund for small purchases or will do so if you ask. The more expensive items can be bought through a science supply house.

Science supply houses provide catalogs that describe available materials and how to order them. A usual practice among several school districts is to circulate periodically to teachers and administrators an equipment and supply list that is at least partly based on the items found in supply house catalogs. After items on the list are checked, the district representative then orders for everyone at one time. All benefit from the usual price discount that accompanies large orders.

Some general supply companies have developed special elementary school catalogs. These make it easier to select materials suit-able for children from the innumerable items intended for research or education at more advanced levels.

You can find information about general equipment and materials for elementary science in Appendix C.

Science Kits

What kind of science kit should you have if given a choice? Some elementary schools provide self-contained science kits. These consist of a durable box or chest with a teacher's manual and a wide array of materials stored inside. The science kit provides for many activities without most of the storage and distribution problems that accompany the ordering of individual supplies.

The gain in convenience, though, is offset by several disadvantages. The kit is likely to be more expensive than items gathered separately. Also, there is the natural tendency to want to use fully what has been bought. The materials tend to dictate the program, rather than the other way around. Finally, the program is likely to consist more of demonstrations, with materials for only one person, than inquiry experiences.

Many publishers have also developed kits, sometimes called "science labs." These contain equipment and supplies to accompany their science text series or other program. Some labs contain basic materials for all the activities at a given grade level. Others may provide materials for a specific unit of instruction or module (Figure 5-1). Publishers' kits hold several advantages over the general variety. They contain multiple items for hands-on experiences, and so they allow most of your pupils to participate individually or in small groups. Another advantage of the publisher's kit is that it is correlated with a curriculum. You can more easily extend and enrich the concepts taken up because the materials and program go hand in hand.

FIGURE 5-1
This science lab contains materials for a specific module.

Some teachers also make *shoe box kits* to hold materials. These usually complement, rather than take the place of, the publisher's kit. Each shoe box contains one or more sets of materials for a single activity or lesson. Materials inside are listed on the box for quick reference. A collection of shoe box kits is a handy way to package materials for whole-class instruction, learning centers, and individual or group projects.

READING MATERIALS

If you believe that children need to explore many materials firsthand to learn science, you have plenty of company. Most educators do. But some topics and questions that come up in science programs are hard or impossible to handle that way:

What makes a volcano erupt?

Where do comets come from?

How do scientists know about the dinosaurs?

Also, it takes far too much time to sample firsthand all the things pupils need to know. So educators see a need to teach some science through indirect sources, including books and other printed materials. At the same time, they want pupils to apply their reading skills to continually become better all-around readers.

Let's look at some reading materials you are likely to find in your classroom and see how to work with them. Science education offers four main sources for reading:

■ Textbooks

■ Trade books

■ Reference materials

■ Language experience charts

Textbooks

In many schools, a coordinated series of textbooks is the science program. Table 5-1 details some of the differences that exist between these science books and reading books through which children learn to read.

Observe how the properties of science textbooks all point to reading as a thinking process. When reading a reader, the child who does not recognize certain words can usually proceed with understanding after decoding and pronouncing them. But with the science textbook, the real problem with many words may be not knowing their meaning *after* they have been recognized. You can see how this is with the following example:[1]

> The batsmen were merciless against the bowlers. The bowlers placed their men in slips and covers. But to no avail. The batsmen hit one four after another with an occasional six. Not once did a ball look like it would hit their stumps or be caught.

Did you find the meaning of this paragraph hazy at best? If so, you have probably never experienced the British sport of cricket. But note that the lack of meaning does not come from the strangeness of the words. Nearly all are simple and quite recognizable when considered in isolation. Instead, the problem comes from *the unfamiliarity of the context*. Recalling the section in Chapter 2 on information processing, it can be said that you lack a suitable schema to which you can refer.

This is one reason you cannot depend on reading formulas when you check the difficulty level of a science or social studies textbook. Most formulas have you count the lengths of words and sentences, and some-times the number of words that appear on familiar-word lists. While of some help, these measures do not go far enough.

A more valid estimate of readability in the content areas raises questions that require judgments about things a reading formula might miss:

- How abstract are the ideas for intuitive-level or concrete-level pupils?
- How heavy is the load of abstractions presented?
- How familiar to children are the contexts in which the ideas are presented?
- How clear is the syntax—the ways in which the words are put together?

Probably the best way to estimate clarity is to give a *Cloze* (derived from "closure") test. Here, children typically read a typed 250-word passage from the beginning of a chapter. Every fifth word is deleted—every tenth word for a smaller primary-level passage—and its space left blank. Pupils write a word in each blank that makes the most sense to them as they read the passage. A score above 55 percent correct usually indicates that the reading material is at an instructable level.

Vocabulary and Meaning. Take care not to rush into reading activities. The ability to understand words relates directly to our experiences. When children explore problems and the environment before they read, they begin to acquire percepts, ideas, and a vocabulary. All are needed to understand the printed material. In other words, when needed, we should provide concrete experiences first, then the words to label them. This practice is especially helpful for slow readers and pupils with limited English-speaking ability.

The difficulty of words can fool you. Consider this question, for instance. Which is harder for a child to read: "tyrannosaurus rex" or "energy?" If you chose the first item, by "read" perhaps you mean being able to

---

[1]Robert J. Tierney and P. David Pearson. "Learning to Learn from Text: A Framework for Improving Practice." In *Reading in the Content Areas,* edited by Ernest K. Dishner, et al. Dubuque, Iowa: Kendall/Hunt, 1981, p. 56.

TABLE 5-1
Differences between reading books and science texts.

Reading Books	Science Textbooks
Purpose—learn to read	Purpose—read to learn
Stories in narrative form	Information in expository form
Mostly common words	Many technical words
Everyday references	More remote references
Simpler concepts	More complex concepts
Graphic aids simple	Graphics more complex
Readability at grade level or lower	Readability harder than it seems

decode and pronounce words. A choice of the second word may mean that to read is to comprehend. You can easily supply the first term to a child, and he may never forget it. What child wouldn't like to go around the neighborhood babbling "tyrannosaurus rex?" It is much more impressive than "king of the dinosaurs" or "terrible lizard." On the other hand, "energy" is an elusive, difficult concept that builds slowly in the child's mind only after many firsthand experiences. To read in the full sense of the term, of course, a child needs to decode *and* comprehend. Still, it is important to understand the distinction.

It is easy to equate glibness with understanding. Pupils who rattle off big words and memorized definitions may be only hazily aware of what they are reading or talking about. Ironically, pupils who "read" less well may have minds that are well stocked with intuitive concepts. They may simply lack verbal labels to pin to what they already understand.

Remember that the names of objects are much easier to learn than concepts. Identify the *Celsius thermometer* in your classroom by its proper name right away and children will quickly do the same. But they may need a sequence of planned experiences to truly understand the differences between the concepts of *temperature* and *heat*.

You'll generally run into three kinds of vocabulary problems when children see a key word in print that they do not recognize. (1) The word is not recognized, but it is in the children's oral vocabulary and is understandable. (2) The word is not in the children's sight or oral vocabulary, but they understand the concept. (3) The word is not in their sight or oral vocabulary, nor do they grasp the concept. You can handle the first two problems through discussion. But the third may require your pupils to have some firsthand experiences before they can understand the word (concept).

Reading for Meaning.   Just as you may need help to get more meaning from the paragraph on cricket, children often need help to understand what they read in science textbooks. You can give such aid before, during, and after they read. Here's how.

Before Reading [about 5 minutes, excluding item 1]

1. Furnish real or vicarious experiences before reading, with vocabulary, if your pupils have little or no background with the concepts to be learned. Experiments, demonstrations, a study trip, displays of real objects, and audio-visual materials will lay the foundation for successful reading. (Chapter 7 gives details.)

2. Relate what your pupils are about to read to what they have studied or otherwise experienced before. This assists them in link-

ing ideas presented in the textbook to the mental schemata they already have. ("Who remembers what a food chain is? That sums it up nicely, Rosa. Well, today we're going to see how living things in several food chains may be connected in a *food web*. How do you think that might happen?")

3. State some clear purposes for reading. ("Your ideas are interesting! You'll find out more about them as we read. Also look for answers to these two questions I've put on the chalkboard as we read pages 105 to 110 in our science books: What is the difference between a food chain and a food web? and, What kinds of food webs might you find in and around our town lake? Be ready to use some facts from the book to back up what you say.")

4. Briefly introduce a few vocabulary words you have selected from the text, to help pupils recognize them in print. Write each word on the chalkboard, pronounce and define it, and use each word in a sentence that parallels its use in the text. ("Before we read, let's take a quick look at these two words on the chalkboard that you'll also see in your book. *Predator.* What does it mean? Good try, Nancy. A predator is an animal that eats another animal. A hawk is a predator that feeds on mice and other small animals. *Prey.* What's that? Almost, Jason. *Prey* is an animal that is eaten by another animal. A mouse may be the prey of a predator, such as a hawk. Let's read now. If you finish early, remember to use your library books to look up some other examples of food webs, especially in and around a freshwater lake.")

During Reading [about 5 to 15 minutes]

1. Have pupils read silently and adjust their pace to suit their purposes. They might skim when looking for specific facts, for example, but slow down when attention to detail is important to understand a process or idea.

2. Move around the room to aid pupils as needed, but instruct them to use self-help first when they meet unknown words, as follows:

   a. Pass over the word and finish the sentence; use context clues and any accompanying graphics to grasp the meaning.

   b. If needed, analyze the word for familiar roots, prefixes, and suffixes.

   c. If needed, use the text's glossary or a dictionary, being careful to select the definition—if several are given—that makes the most sense.

   d. If needed, ask for your aid.

3. Have pupils who finish early switch to self-selected library books on the topic, or reference books, to find additional information on the questions raised.

What to do if pupils cannot read the textbook independently? Read to them aloud as they follow in their books, but do it in an *interactive* way. That is, have them participate enough for you to check whether they can keep up with you and understand what is being read.

Check whether your pacing is all right by occasionally omitting an easy word and having a child supply it *without breaking your rhythm*, if possible. Move around as you read and signal who will supply the word by lightly tapping someone on the arm a second or so before you omit the word. Or check your pacing by noting how children move down a colored marker (a strip of 1-inch by 6-inch paper) under each line as you read.

To monitor understanding, every paragraph or so ask a low-level factual question and invite brief responses. (Which living thing is eaten first? Which animal is the last predator in this food web?) A few such questions might already be in the text. Some textbook authors routinely write in low-level questions to keep the reader's mind active and so promote comprehension from one paragraph to the next. You want pupils now to understand the details as they go along. Later, they will recall and put together this information to answer the one or two main questions you posed at the beginning of the reading session. Pupils will feel encouraged if you periodically remind them through appreciative comments that *they understand well what they are reading*. Interactive reading can change a frustrating failure experience into an encouraging success experience.

Instead of your "live" reading, you could tape the passage for later playback on a cassette player. But pupils are likely to learn more when you interact with them. You can also help less able readers by pairing them with compatible partners who read well.

Above all, avoid round-robin reading, in which children routinely take turns reading aloud sections of the text while the others supposedly follow along. This is boring and ineffective, for several reasons. Children typically read—and should practice reading—much faster silently than orally. Few children read well orally unless they are familiar with the material. Also, the oral reader, preoccupied with the mechanics of the job, understands less than when she reads silently. The situation differs when you read orally because you are likely to do it smoothly, interact with pupils as you go along, maintain a pace that children will follow, and limit the practice to times when children cannot go it alone.

After Reading [10 to 15 minutes, excluding item 2]

1. Have pupils respond to the main purposes or questions first posed. (What is the difference between a food chain and a food web? What food webs might be in and around our town lake?) They may silently skim or reread some sections to find information that supports their responses. If needed, this may be a good time to have a few children read aloud informative excerpts of one or two sentences. If the chapter ends where the present reading assignment ends, you might also have pupils answer the text's chapter-summary questions to find out more about what they have learned.

2. Many text programs supply activity worksheets, for children to extend and apply their learning, at the ends of sections or chapters. You might want to distribute these now. This can also be a good time to invite pupils to do independent or small group projects on activities suggested by the teacher's manual or on topics of children's personal interest.

Summary of Text Reading for Meaning.

Children will usually understand well what they read in their textbook if you do the following before, during, and after they read:

Before

1. If pupils have no background on the subject, do something concrete first.

2. If they have background, relate it to what they will read now.

3. State one or two clear purposes or questions for the reading.

4. Briefly introduce a few unfamiliar vocabulary words, if needed.

During

1. Have pupils read silently with purpose(s) in mind.

2. Help them with words only if they first cannot help themselves through ways you have taught.

3. Have pupils who finish early switch to further references.

4. Read aloud in an interactive way with children who cannot read independently.

After

1. Have *all* pupils—able and less-able readers alike—respond to the purpose(s) or question(s) first posed.

2. Extend the learning through follow-up activities, if warranted.

More Textbook Uses. As you'll find in Chapter 7, treating the text as an important tool within a unit of instruction will offer the most possibilities for a variety of worthwhile uses. Here are some extra ways you can profitably use a science text and its accompanying teacher's manual:

- *As a source of investigations, activities, problems, and basic science principles.* ("Before we open our books for help, can you figure out the answer to this problem on the chalkboard?") When used for these purposes, the children's books may be closed at first; the textbook author's ideas are used by the teacher.

- *As a check-up source for experiments and ideas.* ("Let's see if the scientists agree with us.") In these cases, the book may serve as a check for the children to compare the completeness and accuracy of their ideas and activities with those in the book. The book is opened for verification or comparison only after the initial thinking and doing have taken place. Slow readers are helped individually or in small groups.

- *As an information source.* ("You'll find answers to some of your questions in our science book.") Now the book may be consulted for details to address children's questions or purposes. In a primary text consisting mostly of pictures, the pictures may be examined in detail.

- *As a source of additional examples to reinforce a previous activity.* ("For more examples of mammals, let's open our books to page 74.") Study of open-ended experiments, principles, or concepts can be enhanced by learning of additional examples. Frequently, such examples are either mentioned or illustrated in the text.

- *As a summary of important ideas in units of instruction.* ("See if you can sum up the three main ways rocks are formed after you read pages 55–60.") The clear, careful organization of subject matter typical in modern texts is ideal to summarize firsthand experiences within important segments of a unit or even the entire unit itself. The additional filling in of detail and seeing previously studied material in a new context through summary reading provide reinforcement and more completeness in learning.

Trade Books

Even the best of textbooks cannot always do an ideal job in each of the five uses just mentioned. They would soon grow too heavy to carry and too expensive to buy. However, you can turn to other printed materials for help. Children's *trade books,* commonly called library books, are excellent for additional detail. Trade books were so named because, intended for general readership, they are sold through retail trade outlets, such as bookstores, which is not so with textbooks. Often developed around one topic, such as simple machines, weather, soil, or electricity, trade books give richness in depth difficult to put into a textbook chapter. Most schools now have instructional resource centers that contain good collections of trade books. (For examples of titles in different content areas, walk through the science section.)

Some school districts prepare collections of books, or at least bibliographies, to accompany scheduled instructional units. Local libraries may permit up to 30 or more trade books to be checked out to teachers for a limited period. Children can go to the local library, also, and find books that can help them investigate problems or topics. An advantage in self-selection is that children usually choose books that they can read.

Trade books are probably the best means we have of providing for individual differences in reading. If a variety is available, it almost ensures that able readers will have challenging materials. Less-able readers, also, will usually have at their disposal books that are both interesting and within their more limited capabilities.

Children's trade books are not just limited to interesting expository treatments of science topics. They also include biographies, autobiographies, diaries, reports of major scientific events, and science fiction. Children often find these books inspirational and exciting. They are also an excellent means to stimulate creative writing.

Creative Writing. Here are some ideas for creative writing that you can use repeatedly with different trade books.

Diary. Write an entry from an event in the life of George Washington Carver, Marie Curie, and so on. ("February 18, 1897. Is it impossible? I have now tried dozens of ways to . . .")

Letter to a Famous Scientist from the Past or Present. ("Dear Dr. Einstein:")

Interview with a Famous Person. (" 'What was it like being an astronaut, Mr. Glenn?' 'It had its up and downs, Sally,' he said with a grin.")

Future Autobiography. ("An exciting page from your life in the field of _____ !")

TV or Radio Script: "You Are There!" Reenactment and report of the first landing on Mars, first colony on the moon, development of the first human clone, first successful brain transplant, peaceful visit to earth by creatures from another planet, discovery by junior scientists from Room 6 of the languages used by dolphins, chimps, dogs, and so on, and what they have been waiting so long to "tell" us.

Finding the Best Trade Books. Many trade books and other books are printed every year. It could be a continual problem just to keep up with what is published, much less pick out quality material. Fortunately, we have several places to which we can turn for help. Among the more useful sources is the annotated bibliography "Outstanding Science Trade Books for Children" prepared annually by the National Science Teachers Association and the Children's Book Council. The listing is published in the March issue of *Science and Children,* a practical magazine for elementary school teachers. For details, write to *Science and Children,* 1742 Connecticut Avenue, N.W., Washington, DC 20009.

Another carefully screened review is "Science Books and Films," published by the American Association for the Advancement of Science, 1776 Massachusetts Avenue, N.W., Washington, DC 20036.

Also very helpful is "Appraisal: Children's Science Books," Children's Book Review Committee, Boston University, 36 Cummington Street, Boston, MA 02215. This publication uses specialists to independently appraise the literary quality of the trade books as well as their scientific validity.

Reference Books and Other Reading Matter

How useful are *encyclopedias* for children? They do provide additional information. But most are hard for younger children to read without some help. Above all, discourage the usual practice of simply copying information out of the encyclopedia. When this happens, comprehension may reach the vanishing point. Help the children interpret information when necessary. If needed, read short segments aloud so individual pupils can jot down in their own words facts they wish to report or know.

Encyclopedias are best used when pupils want to find an answer to a specific question, rather than to see what they contain about some general topic. For the second purpose, try trade books.

"What's this bug?" "Is that bird a robin?" Children like to name and find out more about what they observe. From time to time you might need to use *identification books* in the classroom. These references classify, name, and usually give interesting information about living and non-living things. It is important to have books that are well illustrated. Most pupils rely more on matching pictures than on the use of keys for identification. An excellent and inexpensive shelf of books with color illustrations is the *Golden Guides* series. It is available in inexpensive paperback or cloth editions at many bookstores and from the publisher, Western Publishing Company, 1220 Mound Avenue, Racine, WI 53404. Titles include *Birds, Flowers, Trees, Insects, Stars, Reptiles and Amphibians, Rocks and Minerals, Fishes,* and *Seashores.*

Besides reference, trade, and text reading materials, many teachers discover that magazines, newspapers, charts, workbooks, catalogs, almanacs, bulletins, and the like are worthwhile for seeking information. You'll find that using a variety of reading matter often has double benefits. Not only do children get better at locating and learning science information, but they also improve their ability to find and learn information in other curriculum areas.

Language Experience Charts

"How can children read *science* material if they can barely read at all?" This lament is a familiar one in some schools. But rather than overwhelm beginning readers, science can readily be made to serve their needs.

It is natural for young children to learn new vocabulary words when they have first-hand experiences in science. At the same time, they are more likely to organize and remember these experiences if they summarize and record what they have learned. The making of a language experience chart prompts them to describe their experiences in a form that can be written down. This steps up their oral language development, science learning, and ability to read. The technique is well suited to primary-level pupils, or to older children who read poorly or not at all.

In a first-grade room, the teacher suggests that the class make a chart to tell parents about a just-finished chick-hatching activity. A general discussion follows about the events and their sequence to aid pupils' recall of events and vocabulary. The teacher lists some key words on the chalkboard as they come up: Mr. Simpson, incubator, turned over, hatched, shells, fluffy.

At this point, many experienced teachers refer to the key words to establish a sequence: What happened first? Next? and so on. Once the sequence is determined, individual pupils are then invited to dictate what happened. Some primary teachers *also* feel the need at this time to better control what the children say. They believe, quite correctly, that they are now acting like a text author who is writing something that all the class—not just one child who is contributing a sentence—should be able to read. They claim better results when they state narrow questions to which individual pupils respond: Who gave us the six chicken eggs? What did we do with them? How often did we turn them? and so on. Depending on the teacher's method, then, each child called on in our first-grade example either describes one event or responds to one narrow question about an event.

The teacher now carefully writes what is said on a sheet of large lined paper but tries to keep each sentence short and clear, so everyone can read it. He says each word aloud as he writes, then reads the whole sentence aloud, has the dictating child do so, and then the whole class in unison orally reads the sentence. He moves his hand from left to right each time to guide pupils' reading. This emerges:

Mr. Simpson gave us six chicken eggs.

We put them in an incubator.

We turned them over every day.

Three chicks hatched after 21 days.

They broke the shells and got out.

They were wet.

Then they got dry and fluffy.

The class next reads aloud the entire chart in unison, paced by the teacher's moving hand. Then, individual volunteers each read a line in response to some questions: "Which line tells how the chicks got out of their shells?" "Which line tells who gave us the eggs?" and so on. A title is agreed on—"Our Three Chicks"—and written above the first line.

Being aware of individual differences, the teacher asks the children to copy as few as four to as many as all seven lines of the story on lined paper and circulates to help as needed. Pupils also copy several words of their own choosing onto their individual word lists, for later use.

Children with sparse prereading and early reading backgrounds probably would find the preceding language experience chart too hard. To make it easier, ask narrow questions, keep the chart message limited to fewer lines at first, use shorter sentences, more word repetition, and furnish beginning sentence patterns, when you can, as follows:

"How many eggs did we get?"
　　We got six eggs.
"Where did we put the eggs?"
　　We put the eggs in an incubator.
"What did we do with the eggs every day?"
　　We turned over the eggs.
"How many chicks hatched?"
　　Three chicks hatched.
"What is this story about? What short title can we give to this story?"
　　Our Three Chicks

Regularly summarizing pupils' experiences on charts rapidly improves their sight vocabulary of commonly spoken words. So it becomes easier for them to read longer sentences and focus on new science words as successive charts are read. This also makes them more able to write and read their own charts about their science experiences. These individual writings usually have longer sentences than group-made charts and embody each child's unique style. Since each is read mainly by the author and a few adults, readability for other children is of less concern.

NONREADING MATERIALS

What nonreading resources can you expect to find in most schools today? They may include:

still pictures

films and filmstrips

slides

models and constructions

microscopes and microprojectors

televisions

videocassettes

microcomputers and related equipment

Strictly speaking, even these materials may require some reading—captions in films, descriptions of pictures, directions for using a microcomputer program, and the like. (We'll consider in Chapter 6 how to use microcomputers and related equipment in science instruction.) As with books, you'll do better if you select and use each resource for a specific purpose.

Pictorial Materials

Let's begin with pictures, films, filmstrips, and television. You can use each of these resources in three general ways:

1. To introduce or overview lessons and raise problems.

2. To help answer questions or explain difficult ideas.

3. To summarize or extend with more examples what has been studied.

Illustrations, or pictures, are probably among the most common aids used in elementary science, perhaps because their sources are so accessible. There are many magazines in which suitable illustrations may be found. Let children help locate these pictures. Books also may contain numerous helpful photographs or drawings. Sometimes you can get valuable pictures from old or discarded books. District and local libraries frequently furnish collections of pictures to interested teachers. A large supply is also obtainable from free and inexpensive commercial sources. These are listed later in this section.

After only a short time of collecting illustrations, the need for a handy way to file them becomes obvious. You can solve this problem by first mounting the pictures on tagboard or stiff paper backing of uniform size, and then filing the pictures upright in an orange crate or a cardboard box of the right dimensions. Almost any careful system of cataloging should assist in retrieving desired illustrations. A system that seems to work well is to file illustrations first by unit titles and then according to specific concepts or ideas within units. Be sure to use cross-filing notations on any pictures that can be used with more than one topic.

Motion pictures can make available in the classroom vicarious experiences that are otherwise difficult, hazardous, or impossible to realize firsthand. Through the technique of animation, motions of bodies in space are seen and understood better in dynamic form. Microphotography enables children to see cell division, rare and active microscopic life, and body defenses reacting to invading germs. Time-lapse sequences enable the movements of developing plants to be recorded. Slow motion permits the leisurely analysis of swift and complex movements. Photography also makes possible the repeatable, safe viewing of solar eclipses, volcanoes, and other natural events. These are just a few examples of techniques and applications available in educational films.

Filmstrips are helpful in that they can show a process or develop an idea in a sequential step-by-step way. In addition, you can stop at specific frames and discuss them as long as needed. *Slides* enable you to do all of this and also arrange the order of presentation.

Growing numbers of teachers are using *videodiscs* (Figure 6-9) in place of still pictures, films, filmstrips, and slides. Even so, the large inventory of these latter materials in many schools, and their continued worth, means they are unlikely to vanish anytime soon.

Television programs in science are now regularly scheduled in many school districts, sometimes over a closed circuit arrangement and sometimes over a public broadcasting station. Schedules and teaching guides are distributed to teachers. The teacher typically presents an overview of the lesson, raises some questions or points to consider with the pupils, and acts as a discussion leader after the telecast is over.

When a *videocassette recorder* (VCR) is available, programs may be taped for showing at convenient times.

Teachers often prefer videocassettes over films, even though the pictures displayed are slightly less sharp and limited to the size of the TV monitor at hand. The cassettes are easily inserted into the VCR, machine noise is absent, and you can more easily rewind or advance the tape to find a scene that needs to be reviewed. Videocassettes also cost less than films, so the present trend toward declining use of films should continue.

Many elementary science TV programs are now available on videocassettes. The nation's largest disseminator of instructional television, the Corporation for Public Broadcasting, allows schools limited copying privileges for numerous shows. One of its best programs for elementary science, *3-2-1 Contact*, includes more than 140 30-minute broadcasts on a broad variety of topics. It's likely that your county, regional, or state instructional television authority has this series and many more.

For a free comprehensive listing of CPB programs correlated with the most used elementary science programs, write to: Corporation for Public Broadcasting, Office of Education, 1111 Sixteenth Street NW, Washington, DC 20036.

MICROSCOPES AND MICROPROJECTORS

"Let's see what the grasshopper's mouth looks like!" Sometimes children want to see a small object more clearly than is possible with the naked eye. For the most part, a hand lens or magnifier is sufficient, especially for primary-level children. From about grade three on, a *microscope* may also be helpful.

Children typically want to see the highest possible magnification of a specimen. The result is usually unsatisfactory. It may be hard to focus the instrument properly. The field of observation may be too narrow to locate the desired area on the specimen. Minor movement or shifting of the slide is greatly exaggerated when viewed through an eyepiece. It is also possible that children will not understand what they are observing. For these reasons, well-built microscopes of lower power—and lower cost—are satisfactory for elementary schools. (See Figure 5-2 for an example of an inexpensive model.)

Because we can seldom be sure of what children are viewing, and since it is likely that only one or a few microscopes can be available for use at one time, many teachers prefer the *microprojector* (see Figure 5-3). With this instrument, it is possible to project an enlarged image of the specimen onto a screen, much like other visual projectors. It is convenient when instructing a whole class because everyone can view together what is taking place. Some science supply houses sell an inexpensive microscope that can quickly be converted into a microprojector, with a filmstrip or slide projector as the light source. (See Appendix D to request science catalogs.) Although the quality is less than that of

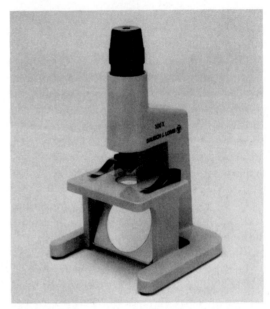

FIGURE 5-2
A suitable microscope for elementary schools.

the more expensive models, elementary school teachers are often pleased with the results. When microscopes and a microprojector are available, you may find microscopes more convenient for individual viewing projects.

Here are some examples of things children are likely to view with microscopes or microprojectors: compound eyes of the housefly, various other insect eyes; fiber structure of wool, cotton, and other cloth materials; penetration of inks and dyes into several materials; newly laid insect, frog, and snail eggs; anatomy of the mosquito and bee; composition of human hair, several kinds of body cells; crystals of salt and sugar; algae, freshwater protozoa; effects of disinfectants on protozoa; composition of mold growth, bacterial colonies; parts of a flower, leaf, seed; onion, root, stem, leaf cells; root hairs; capillary action with colored water; circulation of blood in the tail of a goldfish; heartbeat of a water flea; mouthparts of harmful insects; fiber structures of various kinds of paper.

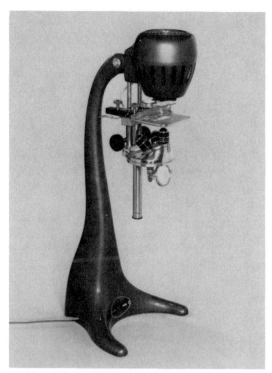

FIGURE 5-3
A microprojector.

Constructions and Models

School and district instructional media centers often have models you may borrow for instruction. These may range from the familiar globe model of the earth to a model skeleton that may be taken apart and assembled again.

In many classrooms, time is also given to constructing models and apparatus. The best kinds of constructions are *functional;* that is, they work by teaching an idea, a process, or helping to gather data. Working constructions such as telegraphs, weather instruments, electric circuit boards, and so forth usually involve thoughtful planning on the part of children.

Less useful are constructions that might be called props—materials that are more decorative and atmospheric than functional: a spaceship made out of cardboard, a paper glacier, a chicken wire and papier-mâché di-

nosaur, a model volcano that shoots up sparks and ash when a chemical is ignited, and so on.

This is not to say that such materials are useless. They may have a worthwhile purpose in dramatic play or art-centered activities, for example. But weigh whether the limited time for investigating basic ideas and processes should be largely used up in this way.

Free and Inexpensive Materials

You can borrow or permanently get many instructional aids from commercial and institutional sources through request only or at low cost. Films, filmstrips, slides, charts, pictures, booklets, samples of raw or processed materials, models, posters, recordings—all these and more are available to supplement science programs.

But before you write for these aids, check the policy of your school district about such materials. Many commercial, institutional, and other donors in the past have used free and inexpensive materials as an advertising or propaganda medium. Educators have been forced to restrict their use.

The supply of donated materials you get by mail is notoriously unreliable. It is wise to use current and reliable listings in making requests. The following compilations of sources are revised yearly. Efforts are made to edit out those sources that either have misrepresented their materials or have otherwise proved unsatisfactory.

Educators Guide to Free Science Materials (films, filmstrips, slides, tapes, transcriptions, pamphlets, and printed materials)

Elementary Teachers Guide to Free Curriculum Materials (pamphlet, picture, and chart materials for elementary and middle school levels)

Guide to Free Computer Materials (films, videotapes, pamphlets, charts, disks, and more)

The guides are often found in university and school district curriculum libraries. All are available at reasonable cost from Educators Progress Service, 214 Center Street, Randolph, WI 53956.

Be sure to use school stationery whenever you request free supplementary materials from sources in the guides. You are more likely to receive them.

SCHOOL AND COMMUNITY RESOURCES

It is possible to get so engrossed in acquiring materials for first-hand experiences, books, and other instructional aids that we forget there is an out-of-class environment for science exploration. The school building itself is a good place to start.

School and Surroundings

Objects and events introduced in science programs become more understandable when they show up as real-life examples in familiar places: Why are there cracks in the masonry and plaster? How do the automatic fire sprinklers work? Why are the stairs worn in the middle and not at the sides? What is making some of the paint outside peel? How is the school heated? How many simple machines does the school custodian use?

Things are also happening on the school grounds. Why are they planting ground cover on the hill? What makes the hot asphalt on the playground "steam" after the cloudburst? How does the seesaw work? What are the names of the birds around the schoolyard, and where do they nest? What makes the shrubs planted on the north side grow more slowly than those on the south side? Why is snow still on the roof of the main building when it has melted on the other roofs? What makes shadows longer in the afternoon?

Study Trips

Where can your pupils see science-related objects and events in their community? There might be many places to explore: a zoo, wooded area, garden, nursery, greenhouse, pond or brook, pet store, bird refuge, observatory, natural history museum, road cut, stone quarry, vacant lot, construction site, waterworks, sewage treatment plant, dairy, airport, and weather bureau. All these and more are rewarding places for elementary school pupils to visit.

Before you take a study trip, some preparation will help make it worthwhile. A school district catalog of suggested places to visit in the community may be available. This can furnish the necessary details for educational trips. In general, however, you will want to keep the following points in mind:

1. Be clear about the purpose for leaving the classroom. A common reason is to stimulate interest and problems at the beginning of a unit of study. Sometimes a study trip is helpful to give additional topical information or see applications of principles.

2. Check with the principal for school policies. Chances are, several procedures will need to be followed—notification and permission of parents, a phone call to the site to be visited, a transportation request, and so forth.

3. Visit the site yourself. It is much easier to make plans when you actually know what conditions are present.

4. Plan with the children what to look for. A list of questions or purposes, and some background, may be needed to enable them to observe intelligently.

5. Develop with the class some behavior and safety standards to be remembered. A buddy system can be used in which each child helps to keep track of another. Less reliable children can be placed at the head of the line. Several parents or moni-

tors at the end of the line can prevent straggling.

6. At the site, make sure everyone can see and hear adequately and ask questions if desired. If the class is large, it may be necessary to divide it into smaller groups.

7. After returning to the classroom, help pupils evaluate the trip. Did they achieve their purposes? Were safety and behavior standards observed?

When it is impossible to arrange visits away from the school, resource persons from the community may be able to visit your classroom. Many districts compile lists of informed persons who are willing to volunteer some of their time and talent for the education of children. As with study trips, maximum benefits from a classroom visit are likelier to happen if there has been some preplanning.

RESOURCES FOR TEACHING PUPILS WITH SPECIAL NEEDS

Stand outside almost any urban school today at dismissal time and watch diversity stream out the doors: girls and boys of different colors, ethnic and cultural origins, religions, economic levels, and abilities—physical and mental. Such differences have always been present in the schools, but never to the degree we see today. What's more, some pupil conditions once thought to require a special education are now expected to be handled in the regular classroom. How do you teach children who need some special provisions in your science teaching? What help can you expect?

Working with Handicapped Pupils

Once, handicapped children were routinely placed in special classrooms. Now federal law requires that handicapped pupils in schools be assigned to the "least restrictive environment" that seems best for their development. This means that some handicapped children who were formerly placed only in special education classrooms may spend some or all of their time in regular classrooms—the "mainstream" of education.

Mainstreaming presents both opportunities and challenges to people in schools. Mainstreamed children learn to live and work in settings that are more likely to develop their potentials to the fullest. The other children profit from a heightened sensitivity and a greater capacity to live and work with individual differences.

The challenges largely come from the diversity of handicaps found in special education. It's natural to ask the question, "How do I deal with them?" On examination, the situation is less difficult than it seems at first. For one thing, each handicapped child is likely to be much more like other girls and boys than unlike them. Each who comes to your classroom is identified as a teachable child. To help ensure this, you share in the placement decision.

The disabled who require the most change in the science curriculum—totally blind or deaf children, for example—are rare. *For most handicapped pupils, a solid hands-on program gives the multisensory experiences they need to learn science well.* So much of what you know and can do now will serve nicely.

Also, realize that an Individualized Education Plan (IEP) is developed for each child by a *team* of persons. Included on the team is at least one person qualified in special education. With a team, you are able to draw on more skills, information, and ideas than by working alone. Responsibility for the child's progress is shared by the team. In many states, the IEP is also accompanied by whatever special instructional media and materials the team believes are essential to meet objectives.

What kinds of handicapped pupils are you likely to teach? What are some of their characteristics? How can you generally help them?

What resources can you draw on that apply specifically to science?

There are many kinds of handicapped children. For our purposes we'll limit the review to four: the visually impaired, hearing impaired, orthopedically impaired, and mentally handicapped.

The Visually Impaired.[2] The problems of visually impaired children may range from poor eyesight to total blindness. Nearly all mainstreamed pupils will have partial sight. A basic problem with the pupils is a lack of firsthand experience with many objects, which is reflected in their language. Vocabulary and descriptive capacity therefore need considerable strengthening.

Some ways to help a child are

1. Use concrete, multisensory experiences to build a greater store of needed percepts.

2. Give plenty of time to explore and encourage the use of descriptive language during explorations.

3. Tell the child what you are doing as you do it.

4. Use tactile cues with materials, such as a knotted string for measuring.

5. Walk the child through spaces to demonstrate barriers and tactile clues.

6. Encourage the use of any remaining vision.

7. Avoid vague phrases, such as "over there," "like that one," or any descriptions that require vision.

8. Be tolerant of, and prepared for, spilled or scattered material.

9. Use oral language or a recorder for instructions and information.

10. Pair the child with a tactful, sighted partner.

---

[2]Many of the suggestions in this section are based on information supplied by Gilda Servetter and Anne McComiskey, Department of Education, San Diego County, CA.

The American Printing House for the Blind (see page 122 for address) produces several current elementary science series in large print and braille. Illustrations and graphs are often in the form of touchable raised-line drawings.

The Hearing Impaired. The hearing of these children may range from poor to total deafness. Most wear a hearing aid and have partial hearing. Communication is aided when the child can read lips and certain facial movements, and when sign language is used. Retarded language development is common.

Some ways to help a child are

1. Use concrete objects, pictures, sketches, signs, and the like to get across ideas.

2. Seat the child close to you.

3. Give clear directions and face the child as you speak.

4. Speak with usual volume and speed.

5. Model, rather than correct, pronunciations for the partially deaf child.

6. Wait longer than usual for responses.

7. Make sure you have the child's attention; use direct eye contact.

8. Use gestures and body language, but don't exaggerate these.

9. Avoid speaking for the child.

10. Talk with the child frequently about what she is doing.

The Orthopedically Impaired. Orthopedically impaired children typically have gross or fine motor malfunctions that cause problems in locomotion, coordination, balance, and dexterity. One of the most common impairments is cerebral palsy. Orthopedically handicapped pupils may use walkers, wheelchairs, crutches, braces, or other aids. Like the visually and hearing impaired, they often do about as well academically as the nonhandicapped when proper conditions are present.

Some ways to help a child are

1. Encourage some participation in all activities.
2. Modify activities to avoid frustrations.
3. Encourage the use of limbs to the fullest ability.
4. Find alternative methods to manipulate things.
5. Allow alternative methods for the child to respond.
6. Keep traffic lanes clear in the classroom.
7. Acknowledge and deal openly with feelings of frustration.
8. Have someone ready to help the child move to where the next activity is if needed.
9. Promote the child's confidence and independence whenever possible.
10. Use activities that foster problem solving and growth in thinking skills.

The Mentally Handicapped.   Mentally handicapped pupils show significantly subaverage abilities in thinking and often in motor development. They are likely to have problems in learning, remembering, problem solving, and everyday skills. Other frequent characteristics are short attention span, confusion, and minimal ability to make choices.

Some ways to help a child are

1. Use direct, closed-ended, concrete teaching methods and materials.
2. Be sure you have the child's attention before you give directions.
3. Demonstrate and model as you give simple directions; speak slowly.
4. Break tasks down to simple, step-by-step parts.
5. Outline expectations clearly for the child before work begins.
6. Review and summarize ideas and procedures frequently; let the child repeat experiences.

7. Give positive reinforcement immediately after each small success.
8. Give responsibility within the child's limits; let the child observe and assist in a role before giving her responsibility.
9. Apply learnings frequently to everyday experiences.
10. Begin instruction with what the child knows and build on that.

Additional Considerations.

Helping.   Disabled children are much more likely to have a poor self-concept than other children. Many adults realize this but overprotect the disabled in order to compensate. Unfortunately, this inhibits development and confidence. Disabled children, in turn, often learn and accept overdependence, so a cycle develops that feeds on itself. What to do?

1. Consider when help is necessary, rather than convenient.
2. Except for obvious need, get consent from the child before giving help.
3. Don't persist if the child declines help; let the child discover if help is needed.
4. Offer help matter-of-factly.

The Disabled as Individuals.   There are many other kinds of disabilities found in mainstreaming: the learning disabled (children with neurological and emotional handicaps that interfere with learning); the speech/language impaired; the health impaired; the multiply handicapped; and so on. Be aware that entire books are devoted to each one of these and the previously described handicaps. Fortunately, there is no need to become an overall expert in special education to help a specific mainstreamed child. Although it is nice to have some general knowledge about a handicap, *it is far more important to know how that handicap affects a particular child.* You learn this by working with the child.

Disabled girls and boys are individuals, with as many personalities and variables as other children. Making an Individualized Education Plan with the IEP team soon after you receive a disabled child will give you a good start. But be prepared to continually modify the plan as you get to know the child better. By considering and working with handicapped pupils individually, you are most likely to help them learn.

Resources for Science Teaching. There are several sources that offer programs and information to better teach the mainstreamed handicapped child. An excellent and well-tested program is *FOSS,* the *Full Option Science System.* Designed for *both* handicapped and nonhandicapped pupils in grades K–6, it was developed at the Lawrence Hall of Science, University of California, Berkeley. FOSS is an outgrowth of earlier projects at Lawrence to improve science education for visually impaired and physically disabled pupils. Several modules at each grade level include lesson plans in the earth, life, and physical sciences. Extension activities include work in language, computer, and mathematics applications. The developers worked hard to match activities with pupils' ability to think at different ages. Further work was done to make the program easy to instruct and manage. The commercial distributor of FOSS is the Encyclopedia Britannica Educational Corporation, 310 South Michigan Avenue, Chicago, IL 60604.

Some further sources that can help you plan lessons for children with different disabilities are

Alexander Graham Bell Association for the Deaf, 3417 Volta Place, N.W., Washington, DC 20007.

American Printing House for the Blind, P.O. Box 6085, Louisville, KY 40206.

Center for Multisensory Learning, Lawrence Hall of Science, University of California, Berkeley, CA 94720.

ERIC Clearinghouse on Handicapped and Gifted Children, 1920 Association Drive, Reston, VA 22091.

National Center on Educational Media and Materials for the Handicapped, Ohio State University, 154 West 12th Avenue, Columbus, OH 43210.

Lewis, Rena B., and Doorlag, Donald H. *Teaching Special Students in the Mainstream.* New York: Merrill/Macmillan, 1991.

Shulz, Jane B., *et al. Mainstreaming Exceptional Students.* Boston: Allyn & Bacon, 1991.

Working with Limited English Proficiency Pupils

Not long ago, only a few cities in the United States contained significant numbers of schoolchildren whose native language was other than English. Today they are present in nearly every school. Foreign-born pupils who do not speak English may be placed in bilingual classrooms and taught by someone who is facile in both English and the foreign language. As the pupils acquire some English proficiency, they are mainstreamed for larger parts of the school day. In other schools, they are taught in all-English classrooms. As a regular classroom teacher, expect to have at least some pupils of limited English proficiency (LEP) from time to time. How can you best help them to learn science when their English is still subpar?

Many LEP pupils experience some culture shock, since what they observe now may differ radically from their earlier environment. They may be reluctant to speak because they are afraid to make mistakes. Your warm acceptance and frequent praise will boost their confidence. Whatever you can do to reduce anxiety, to increase meaning of content studied, to model good English, and increase chances to informally interact with English speakers will benefit them. Here are some things that can work for you, based on what many effective teachers have learned from helping LEP pupils.

1. Use a listening–speaking–reading–writing sequence in teaching whenever possible. Listening lays the foundation for the

other language skills. It's easier to speak what we have first heard, read what we have spoken, and write what we have read.

2. Use multisensory, hands-on teaching methods whenever you can. Concrete materials, investigations, demonstrations, audio-visual media, graphs, diagrams and so forth, are more likely to foster meaningful learning than studying printed matter. One great advantage of hands-on science over most other subjects is that the actual doing demands little verbal ability. Most speaking occurs before and after the event.

3. Pair LEP pupils with bilingual partners who can supply brief translations as needed. But coach these partners to focus on teaching English words and phrases for actions taken or objects observed during investigations. For a good pattern, have them say the word or phrase referring to an action or object, and have the LEP child immediately repeat it.

4. Place LEP pupils in cooperative learning groups to increase chances for frequent, low anxiety, informal interactions with other children. (See page 128 for a description of cooperative learning in science.)

5. Speak slowly, use short sentences, and rephrase what you say if a child seems unsure rather than repeat what you have said. Use body language, props, pictures and sketches to clarify your words.

6. Check more specifically whether a child understands by asking questions answerable by yes or no, or by having the child do something you can observe, such as point to an object.

7. Avoid idiomatic expressions; they can be confusing when taken literally: "It's as easy as pie." "Please take your chair."

8. Make whatever you refer to as concrete as possible—what you know the children have done or observed in the past. Give observable examples in the present as

well: "The handle of this pencil sharpener is also a lever."

9. To help pupils build schemata, write key concepts and vocabulary used during a lesson on the chalkboard. Often make a concept map to outline what is to come in a lesson or to summarize the content of a lesson. (See pages 186–87 for concept mapping.)

10. Emphasize and repeat key words of the lesson as you teach. This cues the child about what to remember and how the words sound.

11. For the easiest and most meaningful reading, make language experience charts. Try interactive reading as well. (Pages 109, 113.)

Pupils who are becoming proficient in English require some extra time and attention, but they can also enrich the curriculum by bringing multicultural knowledge and perspectives to what is studied. For many children, bilingualism and bicultural knowledge should enhance their opportunities for academic, social, and economic success throughout life. Others, though, may not be as fortunate.

There is a well-known relationship between socioeconomic status and success in schools.[3] Poverty diminishes the chances for success in a large percentage of immigrant children of minority heritage who come from less-developed countries. This is also true of many native-born children. Pupils from middle- and higher-income homes of all races and ethnic groups are more apt than their poorer classmates to enjoy benefits that help them to achieve at school. Among the benefits are these: (1) They are more likely to have many cultural, travel, and educational experiences outside the school that enrich and extend their knowledge; (2) to have parents who are functional English-speakers and

---

[3]Daniel Levine and Robert Havighurst, *Society and Education,* 6th edition (Boston: Allyn & Bacon, 1984).

able to guide them academically; and (3) to meet or know of a wide variety of persons who may serve as role models in occupations that require higher levels of education.

Curriculum writers are well aware of these advantages and have built into many of the newer science programs factors to enrich the education of all children both at school and home. Besides containing a wealth of materials for hands-on investigations, most published programs offer many multimedia resources you can use to provide vicarious experiences for pupils. For example, choose among videotapes that bring the wonders of barrier reefs, hot air balloons, and giant cave explorations to children. Use videodiscs and bring further sights and sounds into your classroom. Find computer simulations that invite pupils to decide how best to preserve a deer population or plan a town in an earthquake-prone area. You may also discover audiotapes your LEP or other pupils can use to practice saying new words or to review further by themselves what they have studied.

For the home/school connection, look for letters to parents—often in Spanish as well as English—that tell them what science their children will study and how they may help at home. Your program may also include concept summaries and glossaries of key words, printed in some half-dozen languages, that you can send home with pupils. Check to see if science activities are also suggested in which parents and children can explore together concepts being studied at school.

If you leaf through a teacher edition of almost any newer program, you'll probably see places marked to show opportunities for multicultural learnings. You may also find suggestions about how you may locate and invite into your classroom appropriate role models from the community to enrich your instructional units. In the pupil texts, observe how biographies, descriptions, and photos of persons in science and technology reflect diversity in race, ethnicity, gender, and age.

If your school district has a culturally diverse population, chances are it has a long-standing department and materials that can help you to work with LEP pupils. Should more support be needed, sixteen regional resource centers for bilingual education in the United States give training and technical support services to schools. For the center nearest you, call or write The National Clearinghouse for Bilingual Education, 1118 22nd Street, N.W., Washington, DC 20037 (Telephone: 1-800-321-6223). These references from the National Clearinghouse can also further your work with LEP pupils:

Hamayan, Else and Perlman, Ron. *Helping Language Minority Pupils After They Exit from Bilingual/ESL Programs: A Handbook for Teachers,* 1990. ($2.50)

Short, Deborah J. *Integrating Language and Content Instruction: Strategies and Techniques,* 1991. ($2.50)

Working with Gifted Pupils

What can you expect from mainstreamed pupils classified as "gifted" by your district? Gifted children display many of the same developmental qualities as most children. What is different is the greater *degree* to which, and the *speed* with which, these qualities develop. In kindergarten, for example, gifted pupils may perform like second graders. By their senior year in high school, they typically outperform average college seniors on academic tests.[4] From their ranks will come many leaders and most of our future scientists and other high-level professionals.

What are some of their attributes? Compared to other pupils, the gifted child is much more likely to

1. Tolerate ambiguity and complexity.
2. Have a longer attention span.
3. Be a highly curious and sharp-eyed observer.

---

[4]James J. Gallagher, *Teaching the Gifted Child,* 2d ed. (Boston: Allyn and Bacon, 1975), p. 69.

4. Be a top-notch reader who retains what is read.

5. Have a well-developed speaking and listening vocabulary.

6. Have learned well the basic skills.

7. Understand complex directions the first time around.

8. Be imaginative and receptive to new ideas.

9. Be interested in broad concepts and issues.

10. Have one or more hobbies that require thinking.

Gifted pupils who show all or most of these attributes are often placed in a full-time special class or a "pull-out" program for part of the school day. But many are totally mainstreamed. How can we help these children? By working in harmony with their attributes.

A common problem with having gifted children in regular classrooms is that the curriculum is restrictive and unchallenging for them. *One way to "take the lid off," and yet have the gifted manageably working with other children, is to use many open-ended investigations and activities.* This stimulates the kind of creative, divergent thinking gifted pupils need to grow toward their potential. Fortunately for us as teachers, these and other experiences described next also work well for most of the nongifted.

A second important way to help the mainstreamed gifted is to encourage them to build a large knowledge base. This is usually easy because of their broad curiosity, strong ability to locate and understand information, and ability to remember what they find out. A wide variety of open-ended science investigations stimulates them to try multiple observations and experiments and to read for background. Gifted children readily sense how a broad array of knowledge feeds their creative and problem-solving abilities. This motivates them to learn even more.

A third way to help the gifted is to let them manage their own learning through individual *and small group projects, including those done for school science fairs.* (See Chapter 6.) Investigations like those in Appendix A of this book can be valuable here, as well as those found in references at the end of this section. Independent study is also fostered when we show pupils how to locate and use references, trade books, and other instructional materials in the school library.

A fourth way to help gifted pupils is by exposing them to persons in science and other professions who can serve as information sources and future role models. This is particularly important for pupils who come from economically disadvantaged backgrounds. Gifted children have the interest and quickly develop the capacity to correspond with knowledgeable adults, interview them by phone or in person, and understand much of what they see and hear. The adults, in turn, are almost always delighted and stimulated from their interactions with these precocious youngsters. Many schools keep on hand a file of adult professionals in science and technology who live in the community and are willing to meet occasionally with children.

We can also help the gifted by attending to their social skills as they interact with other children. Not only are these skills needed for success in many professions but for personal happiness as well. A central objective for mainstreaming the gifted is to help them communicate and get along with persons of all ability levels.

The following references can help you work with the gifted and the nongifted, too:

Alfred De Vito and Gerald H. Krockover. *Creative Sciencing.* Glenview, IL: Scott Foresman (Goodyear), 1991. (A broad spectrum of creative activities to explore concepts.)

Alfred De Vito. *Creative Wellsprings for Science Teaching.* W. Lafayette, IN: Creative Ventures, 1989. (Imaginative projects and puzzlers.)

Alfred E. Friedl. *Teaching Science to Children: An Integrated Approach.* 2d ed. New York: Random House, 1986. (Activities include many discrepant events—those that are unusual or unexpected—which gifted children find particularly interesting.)

MANAGING HANDS-ON ACTIVITIES

The new science coordinator who strongly praises discovery learning at the district's first in-service session is apt to hear this impatient cry for help: "It's all right for you to talk about discovery because you can put 30 sets of materials in the hands of 30 children. But what about those of us who can't? What I want to know is, how do you get everyone involved when you only have a few things to work with?"

It would be ideal if every child could always manipulate materials individually or with a partner. But for the present, this is something only a few programs have been able to achieve—at substantial cost. We can

often solve the problem through learning experiences that use everyday materials, such as those in Appendix A of this book. But this is not always possible. At these times, what's a teacher to do?

Whole-Class Teaching

One way you can handle the problem of a shortage of materials is to work with the entire class at one time. This is not ideal, but a proper seating arrangement and a mixture of broad and narrow questions addressed to individual children can be fairly effective. The idea is to have everyone close to the action and able to see what is going on. Also, it's important for individual children to have quick access to the materials when called on or when they want to do something to find out what happens.

Figure 5-4 shows how this is done. A low table is placed near a chalkboard, and movable chairs are arranged before it in a semicircle. Half the children sit on chairs, and

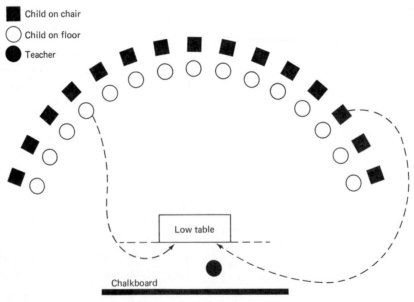

FIGURE 5-4
This arrangement makes it easy to either view or participate in an activity before the whole class.

half sit cross-legged on the floor in front of the chairs. Everyone is close to the table. No one's view is obstructed. There is ready access to the table as individual children are called on to participate. With some reminding, participating pupils will remember to stand *in back of* the table so that everyone can see what is happening. An arrangement of this kind is especially needed with younger children. It is easy for them to lose interest or become distracted when seated some distance away from the activity source. A nearby chart holder or a chalkboard in back of the table can serve for any needed recording.

After the activity is over, put the materials on a science center table so pupils can do the activity on their own during free periods.

The semicircular pattern is also convenient at other times. If a candle flame, hot plate, or other potentially hazardous item is needed in an activity, you can demonstrate the activity in a safe setting. You can also set standards with pupils for small-group activities and assign areas of the room for working. After the several groups or committees have completed their work, you can reassemble them into the initial seating pattern for easier reporting or discussion.

With older children there is less need for this type of seating arrangement. Short attention spans and distractions are less of a problem. The regular grouping of desks and chairs may serve for most occasions, but keep the materials table reasonably close to all the children when experiments and demonstrations are done before the entire class. There is usually no trouble with class control when everyone can see what is happening. If class desks are permanently fixed to the floor, use a higher than usual table for adequate viewing. It may be necessary to let some children change seats or move to a satisfactory location.

Group Teaching

When more materials are available, you can organize the class into smaller groups of two,

four, or six pupils each. Many activities need two people, so even numbers usually work best. Suppose, for example, you have five sets of materials for one activity. This is common when a kit goes with a textbook. You can divide the class into five groups, and have each work with one set. (With primary children, you might have cross-age tutors, parent volunteers, or aides assist the groups.)

You can do much the same thing with one set of materials for each of five activities. Here, the children rotate from one table or learning station to the next after a designated time (Figure 5-5).

When the school provides a kit for every classroom, you may be able to have even more materials by borrowing the kit of another teacher at the same grade level. This is easier to do when units are scheduled at different times and activities don't require consumable supplies. Of course, you'll want to replace all materials well before your colleague needs them, then return the favor.

A further way to stretch materials is to use learning centers, which we'll consider in the next chapter.

Keeping Everyone Involved

Many teachers find that their pupils work better in groups when each has a specific job.

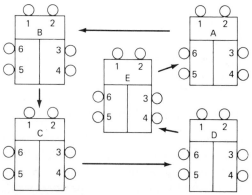

FIGURE 5-5
This arrangement shows how children might move from one learning station to the next after a designated time.

This is easy to arrange, especially from about grade three on. Try the following procedure, which works well in most classrooms.

Cluster the children's tables into islands of two or three each, depending on how many sets of materials you have. Most science kits contain one item for every four to six pupils. Each child sits at a numbered place—one to four or one to six—at the island, which bears the group's letter or name. (See again Figure 5-5.) Children take turns doing the steps of an activity, one step each. All the children in each group take their own notes during the activity, then together at the end they assemble a group report. Each day, a different-numbered child orally gives the report for the group when it's time to discuss results with the whole class. Others in the group add their ideas as well.

A different-numbered child each day picks up and returns the materials. This materials monitor is responsible for making sure everything not consumed is returned, and for reporting in writing what needs to be replaced.

With brief training, group materials monitors can smoothly pick up or return materials set out on a table in *less than* a minute. Notice in Figure 5-6 the inefficiency of *A*. Each monitor waits while the one ahead picks up a materials tray. In *B*, they move almost as one person to a tray, pick it up, and go back to the group. Set a high but realistic performance standard for monitors soon after beginning activities. Stick to it every day, but avoid competitive haste. Children delight in meeting such challenges.

A Class Science Committee

To manage materials, especially if you have a science kit, it will help to appoint a class science committee of about three pupils. (One person for each two groups works well.) Have them prepare trays of materials for the groups, put back the materials where they belong when returned by the group monitors, and check that everything has been

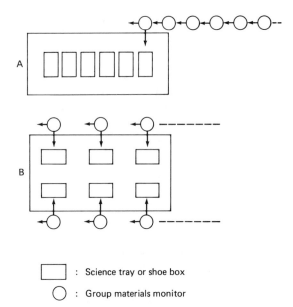

□ : Science tray or shoe box

○ : Group materials monitor

FIGURE 5-6
Arrange science trays or boxes so that group materials monitors can pick them up and return to their groups quickly and efficiently.

returned. Discarded shoe boxes or Styrofoam pizza covers make good trays.

For efficiency, keep the committee small and staffed by children who are rarely absent. Make it a permanent or long-range job, and replace no more than one person at a time. It takes a while to learn where everything goes in a kit, and more than just a few pupils will get in each other's way. Train the committee to collate the daily reports of what, if anything, must be replaced and hand you the list weekly, or as needed.

Cooperative Learning and Managing Group Activities

You may know the story of two stone masons at work. When asked what they were doing, one said, "I'm fitting stones together." The other said, "I'm building a cathedral."

The degree of cooperative behavior, responsibility, and achievement you get from a group is often linked to your outlook—which sooner or later becomes plain to pupils. Some teachers, for instance, view clean-up time at the end of an activity as something to be endured or even dreaded, as room control may get out of hand. Other teachers see it as a chance to develop cooperative skills, build self-esteem, and raise the level of personal responsibility in class members.

Some of the most effective ideas about managing groups stem from the work on cooperative learning by Roger T. Johnson and David W. Johnson.[5] Pupils generally achieve more science learning when they work cooperatively, and learn to better accept one another as well.[6] More and more teachers today are noticing the ability peer groups have to ignite active learning in children. They also see the value of diversity come alive as each child applies unique prior knowledge and perspective to group tasks. In their view, multicultural, racial, socioeconomic, gender, physical and mental differences enrich and broaden education. After all, these teachers say, for what society are we preparing children? Following are six cooperative learning practices I've observed in classrooms that reflect to some degree the Johnson model.

1. *Each group is made up of a cross section of class members.* New groups are chosen by the teacher every few weeks. This insures a balanced spread of talent and exposes pupils to a mix of persons to work with. A group usually consists of two to four members, with as many as six if materials are scarce. Two pairs of pupils work well as a group when enough materials are at hand. One pair consults with the other to iron out problems, share results, and prepare a report. At the primary-grade level, two-person groups are common.

2. *Everyone shares leadership responsibilities.* This includes taking turns doing the steps of an investigation and assuming a specific job for the day. Some useful jobs are *materials monitor,* who gets and returns materials; *checker,* who checks to see if everyone knows what to do, reminds people to stay on task when necessary, and asks the group to decide whether completed work meets expectations; *spokesperson,* who asks the teacher or a spokesperson from another group for help if the group gets stuck, and then conveys the information back to the group; and a *coach,* who notices and praises anyone who uses a newly-introduced social skill, or reminds someone when the skill would be useful. Pupils rotate jobs each day.

3. *Group members depend on each other when doing an assignment.* The group members have a common task, materials are shared, and a group report is prepared. Each group is accountable for working up to a standard rather than having its work compared to that of other groups.

4. *Each person is individually accountable for learning.* It's critical in group work for each person to learn and do his or her fair share. Teachers try to motivate each child to participate and learn in several ways: (a) by randomly picking someone from each group to report group findings at discussion time; (b) by randomly selecting one child's paper or other finished product from each group to represent each group's work; (c) by randomly asking a child in each group to describe what she is learning; (d) by making brief notes periodically about the quality and extent of each child's participation; and (e) by giving tests to individuals on the assigned material.

5. *Each group learns to largely govern its own behavior and learning.* Questions and problems that pupils have are first directed to

[5]See, for example: David W. Johnson and Roger T. Johnson, *Learning Together and Alone: Cooperation, Competition and Individualization* (Englewood Cliffs, N.J.: Prentice-Hall, 1991).
[6]Roger T. Johnson and David W. Johnson. "What Research Says About Student-Student Interactions in Science Classrooms." *Education in the 80's: Science,* Mary B. Rowe, ed. (Washington, DC: National Education Association, 1982), pp. 25–37.

each other, before the spokesperson calls the teacher or confers with another spokesperson. If help is needed, other group members stay at their station and continue to work quietly as well as they can until help arrives.

6. *The children are introduced to and practice a variety of social skills.* Courtesy and the Golden Rule are modeled as much as possible, starting with the teacher. Only one person speaks at a time, with a soft voice. The teacher also teaches group members to share ideas, encourage one another, and to seek agreement by weighing evidence rather than by unsupported argument. Many experienced teachers prefer to observe groups in action before they introduce more than just a few starting skills, to identify needs. Social skills or their lack can make or break cooperative learning, so they are taught as needed along with academic objectives.

Learning experiences can go very smoothly when cooperative learning is given a chance to flourish. Here are some things that effective teachers usually consider when they manage group work. Their planning includes advance preparation for the lesson and what to do at the beginning, middle, and end of the lesson. (We'll focus here on the mechanics of management. Chapter 7 stresses planning for subject-matter and process learning.)

Advance Preparation. Try to select an interesting and worthwhile activity or investigation. What materials are needed that you have on hand or that must be brought in? Are there enough materials for pairs, fours, or sixes? When children work in pairs, it's still desirable to have them consult and form a group report with others at their table cluster.

Some time before the science period—shortly before school, at recess, during free time, for example—have the science committee prepare trays or shoe boxes of materials for each group. At the primary level, this may be done by an aide, a parent volunteer, or a cross-age tutor.

Beginning/Introduction. Look at the situation from the children's viewpoint. You have the "toys." They are itching to get their hands on them. So make the introduction as brief as you can. However, don't hesitate to introduce social skills if needed.

Earlier in the year you may have several times gotten into group work with them in some other subjects as well as science. You may have set such standards as: take turns, speak softly, and only one person in a group speaks at a time. Also, when you give a "stop" signal—bell, piano chord, both hands raised, lights off and on, or the like—everyone stops, is silent, and all eyes are on you.

If you want to introduce a new social skill to the children, now is a good time. Suppose you want to stress the importance of *being a good listener.* Some teachers would begin by role-playing good and bad examples with a child. You could also start by asking,

What do the words "good listener" mean to you? How do you feel when you speak with someone who is a good listener? a bad listener? What does a good listener look and sound like?

After discussing the questions one by one, list on a chart or chalkboard what children reply to the last question; add a few ideas of your own if needed:

A Good Listener

Lets the person speak.
Keeps eyes on the speaker.
May nod head.
May ask questions.

You might briefly model each behavior, to clarify.

Encourage your pupils to especially practice listening today. They can check the list for reminders as needed. Ask them to look for times when the skill is used, to compliment the good listeners, and to remind persons if they forget to use the skill. Tell them you will do that, too.

To summarize, whenever you want to teach a social skill: (1) establish the need, (2) clearly describe and model the skill, (3) provide the practice, and (4) monitor to evaluate, correct, and reinforce the skill.

If the standards are well known in this beginning part of the lesson, you mainly pose the activity problem, rapidly but clearly work out procedures with the pupils, and announce the time period they will work. To avoid distractions, only you have materials at first—to show as needed.

Ask someone to repeat the directions for the class *while* you have the group monitors quickly pick up the materials trays. This prevents dead time. Children go to work immediately on getting the materials. If one or two pupils still have questions, their group tries first to answer them.

It's a good idea to say *everything* you need to say before the whole class gets down to work. Some teachers habitually interrupt the class with further directions and other afterthoughts. This distracts the children, wastes time, and often requires more effort than expected.

Middle/Work Period.   Walk around to different groups to observe how they are doing. Try to spend no more than a minute with one group so you can keep attentively circulating. Stand when possible where you can see all groups as you assist one group. Simple eye contact with a child who starts to get off task quickly stops most misbehavior at the easiest stage. Encourage pupils to help themselves as much as possible. Notice how well they listen, take turns, speak softly, practice courtesy, encourage one another, and do their assigned jobs. Quietly praise helpful behavior as you notice it. If there is a problem, give the group time to work it out and return later. When the lack of a social skill is the trouble, calmly model what to do rather than criticize unhelpful behavior. Make a few brief notes about helpful behavior or any other

matter you may want to bring up later with the whole class.

If your pupils can write, have *everyone* record what's done in the investigation or task. (Use the format of the text activity or one like it. Most published programs now routinely provide individual lab sheets for recording.) This keeps everyone busy and on track. It also allows members to put together a group report in several minutes, and save their own work for personal folders.

If a group finishes early—this seldom happens with *open-ended* investigations—find out how well it did the task before it begins another. Ask broad and narrow questions to learn how well they applied science processes and constructed concepts. If weaknesses show up, most children will readily redo or restudy with purpose. When groups do finish early, have on hand trade books and other references pupils can use to extend their knowledge of the problem or concept being investigated. Children who give interesting new facts in discussions gain status and enrich learning for everyone.

When it is time, give the signal for cleanup alert. Everyone stops and makes eye contact with you. You then tell the class to go ahead. If you prefer, add the time-keeping chore to one of the group job assignments—materials monitor or checker, for example. Be sure, though, that all groups begin and end cleanup at about the same time. Efficient cleanups over the school year can add hours for more hands-on science.

End/Cleanup   and   Discussion.   Everyone pitches in to place materials back on the trays just as received. All stay in their seats and work quietly. This should seldom take more than a minute and can take even less time. The materials monitor makes sure everything is present, then quickly takes the tray back to the materials table. The science committee checks in the materials. (If some things need cleaning, this may be done at a later time.) Meantime, group members at each table cluster quickly compare their notes, using soft voices, and agree on a group report. You might allow about three minutes for this.

Select at random one person from each group to give a report on their work. Help pupils compare findings, resolve disagreements among groups, and make valid inferences.

If you have introduced a social skill, have the reporters mention a few behaviors in their group that reflected the skill. Praise the children for their successes. If they did a super job, have them pat themselves on the back, applaud, shake hands with one another, or give a "high five" to each group member. If a similar behavior problem came up in several groups, ask the group reporters to describe what happened without giving names. Guide the class to suggest effective ways to handle such problems. This is a powerful way to correct and prevent unproductive behavior, especially with older children.

You might now also mention before the whole class several helpful comments or courtesies—whatever positive behaviors you want to reinforce—that you observed in some groups. (Here's where previous note-taking is handy.) There's no need to mention individuals, just the group. Recognize the group before the class, and its members will appreciate and welcome these contributions from their peers even more. Of course, you'll want to tell the helpful child sometime that you are talking about her, if there is any doubt.

The teaching of social skills takes time, particularly when children receive little instruction at home, but experienced teachers know its value. "The time I spend during the first ten weeks or so is more than made up during the rest of the year," one twenty-year veteran recently told me. "And I enjoy teaching the kids a *whole lot* more!"

SUMMARY

The quality of your science program is strongly influenced by the teaching resources you select. Most elementary programs use common, everyday materials. So they are ordinarily easy to gather, especially if you ask others to help. Motivated children can bring to school many free or discardable materials. Parents are also usually willing to help. Other items are best supplied by the school through commercial sources.

Both reading and nonreading classroom materials are needed to teach science. Reading materials include textbooks, trade books, reference materials, and language experience charts. All are more understandable when you provide concrete experiences and develop vocabulary before using them.

Nonreading materials include kits, free and inexpensive items, constructions and models, microscopes and microprojectors, and visual aids—pictures, videotapes, and the like. Each is well suited for particular teaching purposes. Outside the classroom, remember that the school and nearby environment may illustrate concrete examples of objects and events introduced in the science program.

Some special resources and ways to use them are needed for mainstreamed exceptional pupils. A school advisory team is likely to meet with you to compose an individualized educational plan (IEP) for each handicapped pupil. You can best help pupils of limited English proficiency by reducing their anxiety, increasing content meaning, modeling good English, and giving them many chances to informally interact with English speakers. Gifted and talented children thrive on open-ended, divergent investigations and activities.

When few materials are available, hands-on learning experiences require more planning. Arrange the class so it can easily observe several pupils perform activities, then later place the materials where more children can manipulate them at convenient times. You can also divide the class into groups and rotate them among several table clusters that contain materials for single activities.

When you have a class materials kit, have a small committee set out and put back the materials and report what needs to be re-placed.

The handling of materials is easier to manage if you routinely follow the mechanics of what to do before, during, and after the lesson. Try cooperative learning for an effective way to enlist the aid of the whole class in managing first-hand learning experiences.

SUGGESTED READINGS

Brandwein, Paul F. and Harry A. Passow, editors. *Gifted Young in Science.* Washington, DC: National Science Teachers Association, 1989. (Advice from 34 scientists, teachers, and scholars on how to develop learning environments that encourage the precollege gifted at all levels to reach their potential.)

Ellis, Susan S. and Susan F. Whalen. *Cooperative Learning—Getting Started.* New York: Scholastic, 1990. (A small and practical handbook, based on research by D. & R. Johnson.)

McCloskey, Mary Lou, and Lorene Quay. "Effects of Coaching on Handicapped Children's Social Behavior and Teacher Attitudes in Mainstreamed Classrooms." *Elementary School Journal* 87(4):425–35 (March 1987). (Exposes several difficulties in changing social behaviors of some handicapped children in grades one through four.)

Romance, Nancy and Michael R. Vitale. "Sealable Science for Busy Teachers." *Science and Children* 28(5):24–26 (February 1991). (How to efficiently organize and package some science materials.)

Russell, Helen Ross. *Ten-Minute Field Trips.* Washington, DC: National Teachers Association, 1990. (How to take advantage of the immediate environment with quick visits for specific purposes.)

Saul, Wendy and Sybille A. Jagusch, Eds. *Vital Connections: Children, Science, and Books.* Portsmouth, NH: Heinemann, 1992. (A comprehensive look at the place of science literature in the lives of children.)

Scarnati, James T. and Cyril J. Weller. "The Write Stuff." *Science and Children* 29(4):28–29 (January 1992). (Explains four purposes for writing assignments in science.)

6

How to Arrange and Manage Complementary Experiences

Should the children in your class all study the same topics and activities, or should there be some variations among individuals and small groups? A class of 30 or so pupils will display a wide range of abilities and interests. Thoughtful teachers often see a need to complement the basic science program with further, more individualized activities.

Many educators say that children should have some choice in what and how they learn. They find that different children learn best in several ways and through varying interests. Allowing some choices can boost morale and whet lifelong interests. Many teachers use individualized activities to cultivate a more open form of inquiry and independent learning. They use them to enrich a teaching unit, or to permit some pupils to pursue their science interests if science is not scheduled in the school district curriculum throughout the year. They use them to stretch few materials among more pupils. Teachers may also employ individual or small group teaching approaches with computer-assisted instruction.

No child learns science solely from classroom activities. Each brings to school concepts and attitudes that are shaped by home and other influences. How can parents complement what their children learn at school and further support your science teaching?

This chapter shows three ways of using individual or small group experiences to complement basic instruction—learning centers, microcomputer centers, and projects—then suggests ways to enlist parents' aid in enriching what their children learn.

HOW TO MAKE SCIENCE LEARNING CENTERS

A classroom learning center is a place where one or several pupils at a time can do activities independently through materials and directions found at that place. A learning center may be arranged so children may choose the activities they can do, or are interested in, and work at a pace that is right for each person. Some teachers also permit children to select the times they go to a center and partners to work with, if any.

An example of a science learning center for a combination second- and third-grade class is shown in Figure 6-1. The topic is the growth and development of frogs. The center's purpose is enrichment. That is, the center allows children to explore independently an area of high interest and develop a background that they may use in a variety of ways. About four children could use this center satisfactorily at one time.

Notice the stored activity cards and worksheets. The cards suggest different things to do. The worksheets go with some of the cards. Children use these to write down data or make drawings as suggested on some cards. Completed worksheets are placed in the left pocket on the background board for later examination by the teacher. Just below that spot is a record booklet in which each child records completed activities.

Observe some other features of this center. An attractive background shows the topic and invites children's attention. Simple overall directions tell how to work at the center. A large aquarium containing frogs' eggs and tadpoles allows firsthand observation of their growth and development. Stories with pictures are available for reading by able children. Those who cannot read may hear these stories through earphones connected to a tape recorder.

Notice the teacher-made game in the foreground called "Ribbet." The title, chosen by the children, mimics the sound made by frogs. Each lily pad on which a player lands contains a question about frogs' stages of development. To advance, a player must be able to answer the question correctly. Contro-

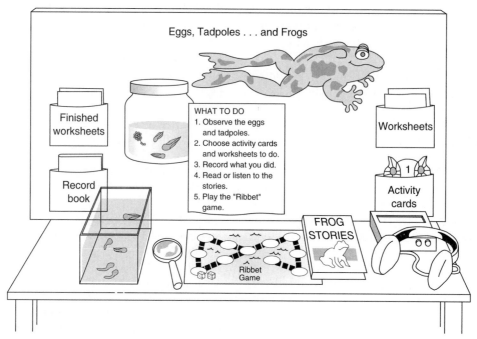

FIGURE 6-1
A science learning center.

versies are resolved by observing the aquarium's contents and looking up information in the stories.

To construct this center, the teacher considered these matters:

- Purpose and objectives.
- Activity cards and worksheets.
- Materials and their resupply.
- Record keeping and evaluation.
- The physical setup.

See now how each of these matters affects the making of a learning center.

Deciding Purpose and Objectives

The first thing in making a science learning center is to decide its purpose. Do you want it for general enrichment? While this is the most common purpose, center activities may also be used to complement an instructional unit[1] or present an entire unit when materials are few. For instance, unit activities may require microscopes, but only several may be handy. The best way to teach the unit, or at least furnish some complementary activities, might be to schedule several children at a time into the science learning center at staggered intervals.

Some topics are best left for whole-class unit instruction. For example, you may want considerable group interaction with overall class data before children generalize about their work. This is particularly important in biology, because variations in organisms—plant and animal—are always present. Also, some topics may call for children to work mostly outdoors. Other areas of investigation may require room darkening. Some activities

---

[1]An instructional unit is a series of related lessons, usually organized around a topic, problem, or set of objectives.

may be quite noisy or involve much movement. In these cases, judge whether a learning-center approach is appropriate. Center activities must be compatible with everything else going on in your classroom.

As a rule, avoid activities whose outcomes take more time to happen than you assign pupils to be at the center. Children want action and they want it *now.* There are, though, occasional exceptions to the rule. In the activity shown in Figure 6-2, taken from a "Things That Change" learning center, pupils start a "changes" jar. They put in materials they believe will deteriorate and will view these slow changes (away from the center) over the course of a month or longer. But the other change activities at this center happen much faster: Ice cubes melt, liquids evaporate, mixtures fizz, and so on.

When center activities are unit related, you can state objectives for knowledge and process as you do with a unit.

Developing Activity Cards and Worksheets

How can you communicate activities in the most understandable and appealing ways? The directions on activity cards must be simple—what to get and what to do—so independent work is possible. Use short sentences and easy words. Draw pictures beside key words if the cards are intended for less able readers (see Figure 6-2).

Despite your best efforts, some children may not be able to read your directions. What to do? Pairing the child with a good reader will help. In some schools, the policy is to have multiage grouping for classes. Other schools have active cross-age tutoring programs in which older pupils may volunteer to assist younger ones. In such schools, it is relatively easy to help the slow reader or nonreader. Of course, in schools where teacher aides or volunteer parents are available, they can give assistance.

A few teachers find that recording directions on a tape recorder works satisfactorily. However, the children must learn how to use the machine. Teachers of primary-level children usually find that they must briefly introduce each new activity to the entire class before most children can do the activity by themselves.

Try to make the design of your activity cards appealing and different for each topic. To do this, you might design the cards to go with the topic. For example, with the topic "The Melting of Ice Cubes" make each card look like an ice cube. For "Air and Weather" make cloud-shaped cards. Above all, make the cards as childproof as possible. Cut them from heavy paper or tagboard. Avoid having

FIGURE 6-2
A "changes" jar begun at a center allows children to continually observe, away from the center, slow changes.

thin, easily bendable parts, and laminate the cards, or cover them with transparent contact paper.

Include as many open-ended activities as you can that have possibilities for process-skill development. These will also make it more possible for children to suggest additional activities, which they enjoy doing.

Worksheets are a convenient way to know what the child has done, if you cannot directly observe the child at work. A worksheet may be simply a plain sheet of paper on which the child has made a drawing or recorded some data after an activity-card suggestion.

Some teachers like to have a worksheet for every activity. Other teachers reserve worksheets only for activities in which data recording is necessary for the activity to make sense—graphing temperature or other changes, keeping track of results from testing different materials, drawing a conclusion from a number of facts, and so on. Sometimes worksheets are called "laboratory sheets," or "data sheets," along with other titles. See Figure 6-3 for an example of an activity card and its accompanying worksheet.

Several published science programs have activity booklets designed to go with the texts. Usually, these are for grade three and beyond. The detachable activity sheets in these booklets may serve as both activity cards and worksheets for a science learning center.

Providing, Storing, and Resupplying Materials

In your center it is good to have activities that can be done with everyday materials. The children may be able to bring in most of what

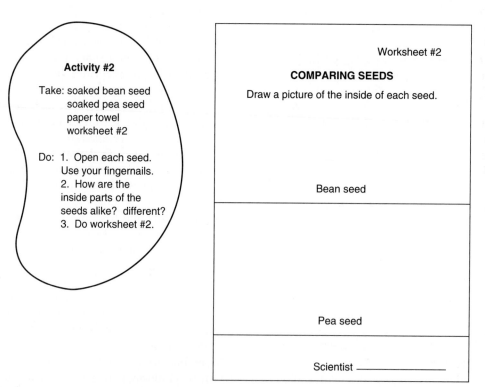

Activity #2

Take: soaked bean seed
     soaked pea seed
     paper towel
     worksheet #2

Do: 1. Open each seed. Use your fingernails.
    2. How are the inside parts of the seeds alike? different?
    3. Do worksheet #2.

Worksheet #2

COMPARING SEEDS

Draw a picture of the inside of each seed.

Bean seed

Pea seed

Scientist _____

FIGURE 6-3
An activity card and its accompanying worksheet.

is needed. Also, this may dispel the idea of some children that science is a strange enterprise conducted with expensive and mysterious objects.

Use printed and audiovisual materials as well as experiments. Items loaned by museums and collections can be a real help. And motivated children have been known to cut out, mount, and organize extensive picture collections in an hour or less.

How can you package and store your materials? Shoe boxes numbered for each activity card can work well. Tape a list of the contents of each box on the front end. Number both the box and its lid. Some teachers tape one activity card to each shoe box lid so a separate list of contents is not needed. This is fine when one activity requires one box of materials, but sometimes it may be more convenient to have one shoe box of materials for several activities.

You may set up shelves for storing materials from wooden boxes obtained free at some food stores. Or arranging shelves from boards supported by cement blocks may be more convenient.

If your activities require consumable materials, a list should be made of things that must be replaced. It can be displayed by the materials shelves. Beyond the primary grades, materials monitors can be appointed to keep track of such needs.

Record Keeping and Evaluation

Observing children in action is the best way to learn what they need help with and what they can do. Yet if many activities are going on, it's hard to keep track of everything each person has tried.

One way to record pupil progress is to have a master list of all the center's activities or objectives with the children's names written to one side. If each activity has a worksheet, these can be filed by the child in a folder at the center. Check the worksheet against your master list. The worksheet will show what activity was performed. It will also reveal something about the quality of the performance. Develop your own code system for recording the quality of the work and indicating what is incomplete, what should be done over, and so on.

It may be impractical to have a worksheet for each activity. A record booklet of the center can be used by the children to check off the activities they have completed. However, this may cause a few children to make critical comparisons between their work and that of others. ("Ramon did four activities. I only did two.") So it may be better to have a record system in which the child refers only to his own work.

To do this, some teachers give each child who uses a center a record sheet containing only activity numbers. (See Figure 6-4.) A space is left at the top for any center title to be written in. A line is drawn under the last

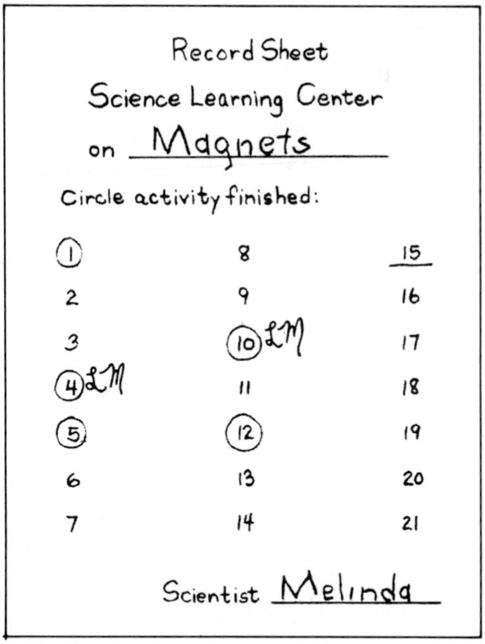

Record Sheet

Science Learning Center

on ___Magnets___

Circle activity finished:

①	8	15
2	9	16
3	⑩ LM	17
④ LM	11	18
⑤	⑫	19
6	13	20
7	14	21

Scientist ___Melinda___

FIGURE 6-4

A record system in which each child refers only to his own work prevents children from making critical comparisons of each other.

number that equals the named center's total activities. On completing an activity, the child circles the activity number on her or his sheet. This record sheet is kept handy for the teacher to review during informal or scheduled conferences. The teacher's initials may be written next to selected activity numbers if the child appears to have accomplished the appropriate objectives. To save time, only the more important objectives may be sampled. The record sheet is filed in the child's science folder along with worksheets and other work products.

Keep an eye on how successful your center is in meeting your objectives and holding the children's interest. What is there about the activities that appeals to the children and gets the job done? Why are pupils avoiding or doing poorly with other activities? Ask the children to give their views, also. Together you can continually improve the quality of your different centers' learning opportunities.

Schedule individual conferences periodically to learn more about each child's accomplishments. Make some brief notes for future reference as needed. Ask questions when you want to evaluate concepts or principles. Invite the child's reactions to the activities performed.

Can the child profit from further, deeper study in the form of an independent project? (See page 153 for details.) Such a project can be particularly valuable with the able and older child. This may be the time to set up a "contract" between you and the child. Or, the child may make a preliminary study before deciding with you on the exact topic, time, and goals for the contract. A worthwhile project may be shared with the class in a report or exhibit. Older children might even construct a simple learning center based on a limited topic or problem.

Arranging the Physical Setup

Where is the best place to put a science learning center? How should it look? What are some ways to cut down the work in setting up new centers? These are some things worth thinking about.

Rule number one, if you listen to experienced teachers, is put the center where you can always keep an eye on it. This alone can do more than anything else to ensure that it gets used properly.

Some science topics require water. In these cases, consider placing the learning center next to a water source and sink. Carrying water to and from a distant sink can be messy, especially with young children. If audiovisual equipment is required, there should be an electrical outlet handy.

How will children move into and out of the center? Locate the center where it will not interfere with other activities. Or, establish a traffic pattern so children working on other activities won't be bothered. Will wall space be needed? Take this into account also.

It is helpful to make a rough sketch of a proposed center. As you draw the sketch, think about where you will put the things that have been mentioned in the preceding paragraphs. Try to have a colorful and eyecatching background that reflects the center's topic.

You can draw enlarged background pictures by using an opaque projector (or make a transparency by putting a picture through a copying machine and then projecting the transparency with an overhead projector). This is a help to anyone and an indispensable tool for the artistically untalented. With it, you can enliven your center's background (or classroom bulletin boards) with familiar comic strip or story characters for child appeal: Dr. Doolittle, Peanuts, Snoopy, and Dr. Seuss' menagerie. It's also interesting to use mystery, surprise, oddities, contrast, and drama in captions or pictures.

For durability, many teachers use a pegboard background as shown in Figure 6-5. The two pieces of pegboard are painted to match the wall color and are joined by sturdy

FIGURE 6-5

One easy, versatile way to assemble a learning center is with two or three pieces of pegboard.

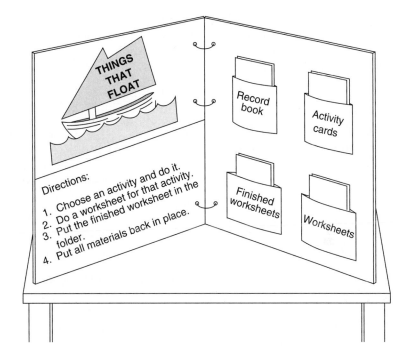

duct tape or metal rings. A three-panel pegboard set also works well. Extra-long paper fasteners are used to secure the four folded-paper pockets, directions chart, and the theme-setting picture.

What if the teacher wants to change the topic of this learning center? The boat is quickly replaced by another theme-setting cutout, and new activity cards and worksheets are placed in the pockets. Everything else is permanent. If the center is no longer needed, the pegboard background is easily folded and stored.

A disadvantage of pegboard is its heaviness. Matte board, chipboard, and corrugated cardboard cut from large cartons are less durable but also work well. Poster board is too flimsy and is best avoided.

Colored matte board is the most convenient of these substitute materials to use for the background. It does not need to be hinged, painted, or covered, and can last for years. A 36-inch by 42-inch sheet (sold in art supply stores) will make two centers that are compact and easily fitted into many smaller, underused spaces. To construct a center:

1. Cut the longer dimension into two equal parts with a sharp knife. This will give you 2 background pieces, each 21 inches high and 36 inches wide. For stability, a background board should be wider than it is tall.

2. Consider one piece now. It needs a fold in the middle, so it can stand without toppling. Score it lightly down the middle of the back or uncolored side with an ice pick or nail. Now it should fold easily. Each side of the fold will be 18 inches wide when open and standing.

3. To reinforce the folding part, first completely fold the board. Then stick a wide strip of masking tape evenly down the length of the fold.

4. Open the board and attach a picture, directions, and pockets as with a pegboard-type background. Make holes with an ice pick or nail, and secure the items with ½-inch-long paper fasteners.

If you use extra-large pockets for holding paper or cards, only two may fit on the right front panel. If so, just fasten one or two additional pockets for finished worksheets and record booklet on the *back* of the panel.

Timesaving Shortcuts: Converting Investigations into Centers

Probably the easiest way to make a learning center is to convert one or more of the open-ended learning experiences described in this book. Most of the investigations in Appendix A can be readily changed into centers, as well as some of the more open-ended activities found there. To select them, use the criteria suggested on page 146, especially the following:

Can children work inside the classroom?

Can children work without interfering with others?

Do activity outcomes happen at the center during the allotted times?

Are most of the learning experiences open-ended?

Examples of investigations that meet the criteria are

Makeup of colored liquids, 192.

Wheel-belt systems, 201.

The properties of leaves, 210.

How practice improves learning, 216.

Examples of those that do *not* meet the criteria are

A string telephone, 194.

A bottle xylophone, 196.

The growth of seeds, 207.

How water sinks into different soils, 219.

Can you see why the last four investigations do not belong in a learning center? The first is distracting to other pupils, the next two take much time, and the last needs to be done outdoors.

Figure 6-6 shows a center made by a teacher from an investigation in Appendix A,

FIGURE 6-6
Many science investigations can be readily made into learning centers.

on page 216. Table 6-1 shows where the parts come from.

Instead of having a separate "Try This" section, some teachers make this feature the first activity card. To save more time, you can photocopy the discovery problem section as a whole and glue it to a card rather than copy it one problem to a card. Make duplicate cards if more than two children use the center at one time.

Some teachers save further time by not tying the center title and drawing to a specific topic. You can, for example, simply entitle the center, "Science Center," and attach an appropriate picture (child inspecting some object with a hand lens, or holding up a test tube, or netting a butterfly, for example). Now all you need to change are the activity cards and hands-on materials as you change to further learning experiences. While a "generic" center like this may not look as fresh and interesting to your pupils as one whose theme frequently changes, you may feel that the time saved is worth the trade-off.

To introduce the center to a class, simply use the introduction to the investigation. For sample objectives, background, and so on, see the "Teaching Comments" section of the investigation.

Even converting an Appendix A investigation into a center takes some time. But because it is simple and straightforward, an aide, a volunteer parent, or an older pupil can do much or all of the task with some supervision.

Seek ways for pupils to help you plan, gather, and prepare materials for centers. It will mean more to them than if you do everything yourself. Also, your centers may be set up in less time with more and better materials. A well-organized teacher who enlists the aid of pupils is usually far ahead of one who does not. This is likely at all levels, but especially so beyond the primary level. Pupils then are more skillful at cutting out things, applying contact paper, writing contents cards for shoe boxes, and so on.

Parents, too, are usually eager to contribute many ready-to-discard but usable items, as well as occasional volunteer service. Volunteer work is more likely to be offered by parents of primary-level children.

MANAGING THE SCIENCE LEARNING CENTER

How will you schedule children into the center? How can you introduce the center and keep things running smoothly? It's hard to describe precisely what will be instantly useful in every situation. Schools and individual classrooms vary so much.

In many schools, there is an instructional materials resource center to complement materials and activities in the classroom. In some classrooms, several persons work together as a team—a teacher, a student teacher, teacher's aide, one of several volunteer parents, and an older child from another class who

TABLE 6-1

Parts of a center may be derived from an investigation.

Center	(Comes from)	Investigation
Leading question		Exploratory problem
Try this		Try this section
Picture		Traced from page 216
Activity-card problems		Discovery problems

serves as a cross-age tutor. An open-space classroom may contain 70 to 100 or more children, with a team of 3 to 5 teachers working together. However, in most instances, a single teacher still works with about 30 children in a self-contained classroom. Let's assume this is your situation.

Scheduling the Center

If you have never worked with learning centers, start with a modest plan within a familiar topic. After you learn the ropes, you can become more creative.

Reserve a large block of time from which a segment can be used for work at a learning center. For example, many teachers reserve a two-hour block daily for the language arts. Suppose you have 32 pupils divided into 4 groups: A, B, C, and D. You rotate these groups daily through several different language arts activities. Table 6-2 shows how you can adapt this organization to schedule a science center.

The block is divided into four half-hour segments. In the first half hour of the block, group A works with you in the literature book. Meanwhile, group B does creative writing. Group C does individualized spelling activities.

During the same half hour, the eight pupils of group D are evenly divided between a language assignment and a science learning center. Four pupils work on activities such as poetry writing, vocabulary development, dictionary use, alphabetizing games, and punc-

tuation practice. (This can be done at their desks or a language development center.) The other four pupils of group D are at the science center doing different open-ended activities of their choice. Both sets of four pupils in D switch assignments after two days. On Friday, all eight pupils of group D work on language activities during the first half-hour period. No one is assigned to the science center.

During half-hour periods two, three, and four, each group rotates into a new assignment as shown. At the end of each daily two-hour block, all four groups will have experienced four different assignments. Usually by Thursday, all the children will have had one hour of work at the science learning center.

If you want more time for science, consider skipping the language center for a while. That way, everyone will have two hours a week at the science center by Thursday. On Friday, reserve some time to summarize and evaluate as a class what has been learned at the center.

Here is a second plan you may want to try. Start with a free period that all the children receive at the same time, for example, 30 minutes. During this time, the children are free to go to the school library or materials resource center, do recreational reading in the classroom, play educational games, and so forth. Of course, some pupils could go to the science center at that time. How about the rest? Each time you plan to teach the class anything that has a follow-up seatwork assignment of about 30 minutes, schedule 4 or more pupils into (or let them choose) the science center. To serve more pupils, add more centers. The seatwork assignment is made up in the next free time period. This is a trade-off most children are delighted to make for science activities.

Free periods also give you time to confer with pupils. Here is where children's records of what they did, and completed worksheets, can be used to extra advantage.

TABLE 6-2
Rotating schedule for small groups.

1	2	3	4	Daily Two-Hour Block
A	D	C	B	Literature book (teacher)
B	A	D	C	Creative writing
C	B	A	D	Individualized spelling
D	C	B	A	Language or science center

Chances are your experience with science learning centers will be as successful and rewarding as that of many teachers. If so, consider a more flexible arrangement that uses additional centers in several subjects. Some teachers reserve mornings for the three Rs and unit teaching. Afternoons are for individualized enrichment and skill-building activities at different learning centers, such as the following:

Science or social studies center

Fine arts center

Hobby center

Literature center

Writing center

Speaking and listening center

Math center

Work at the centers may be either assigned or optional. This setup allows you freedom to vary time and other considerations, and to assist and confer with individuals. You and each child can cooperatively decide on ways to pursue interests, knowledge, and skills. The best learning usually happens when children themselves take an active part in planning their learning.

Introducing Science Learning Centers

Give your pupils a thorough introduction to the science learning center. It will prevent most problems from arising. Describe carefully:

What to do at the center.

How to get and return materials.

Where to put completed work.

How to get help, if needed.

Also show them a general directions chart containing this information displayed at the center. After a while, the chart will no longer be needed.

Introduce one or two activities to whet their interest. The most practical activities will be open-ended ones. At the primary level, you may need to introduce one or two new activities a day. Most young children will not be able to read activity cards satisfactorily.

During the first few days, try to have a parent volunteer or an older child present at the center to help with the activities. If that is not possible, start off with a few of your most able pupils and let the other children consult these able pupils if help is needed. Of course, if you have independent work going on, or several centers operating, you'll be free to give such help yourself. You may try taping some directions, but this can become complicated for young children if multiple activities are involved, and it may require a lot of your time.

How much is "too much" noise? Be sure to work out some obvious signal to alert pupils at the center if their noise level interferes with the work of others. Also, discuss the least-disturbing traffic pattern for going to and departing from the center.

Show the schedule, if any, for using the centers. You might use a pocket chart with pupil's names and times on it. If you start with the rotating schedule described earlier, you can announce to the class when to shift assignments.

To make sure your class understands the setup, take a few minutes to "walk through" the pattern. After a few trials, most children should learn what they need to do.

HOW WELL CAN YOU CONSTRUCT AND MANAGE SCIENCE LEARNING CENTERS?

As with most teaching, actually making and managing a science learning center is a surer way to become able than by merely reading about it. If you do go ahead, it will help to have some guidelines by which you can judge the adequacy of your plan. Following are some questions you might use for the job. They are organized under the same categories used in this chapter and reflect most of the points mentioned. Parenthetical remarks are used to help you recall these points. Look over the list carefully. You may want to omit some questions and add some of your own. You may also want to arrange some order of priority among the questions. Concentrate at first on what you think is most important. In revisions, work on other points. It takes a lot of practice to do *everything* well.

Choosing the Right Topic

1. What is the purpose of the center? (Enrichment, support of text, complement unit, whole unit.)
2. What are the objectives? (Performance, especially if unit connected.)
3. Can children work inside the classroom?
4. Will children be able to work without interfering with others? (Room darkening, noise, movement.)
5. Do activity outcomes happen at the center during the allotted times? (Some activities with long-range outcomes could be started at the center.)

Activity Cards and Worksheets

1. Are most of the learning experiences open-ended? (For process development, individual differences, children's possible contributions.)
2. Do the cards give simple directions? (Materials needed, what to do.)
3. Are the cards interesting? (Design reflects topic, large size, colorful.)
4. Can the cards be read easily? (Simple words, short sentences, drawings, pair

child with a good reader, taped directions.)
5. Are they reasonably childproof? (Laminate or contact paper, sturdy design.)
6. What, if any, worksheets are needed?

Materials, Storage, and Resupply

1. What local materials are available that go with the activities? (Also, printed materials, audiovisual materials, museum loans, collections.)
2. What is a good way to package and store the materials? (Shoe boxes, wooden-box shelves, cement-block and board shelves.)
3. How will you know when to resupply? (List, inventory monitors.)

Record Keeping and Evaluation

1. Do you have a master list of activities and objectives on which you can record pupil progress?
2. Does the child have a record sheet or record book to keep track of progress?
3. Can you observe center activities on a regular basis?
4. Are you able to have informal and scheduled conferences with the children?
5. Are you able to view children's work products? (Worksheets, constructions, reports, drawings, child's science folder.)

Arranging the Physical Setup

1. Where is the best spot to locate the center? (Water and sink, electric outlet, wall space, traffic flow.)
2. How can you make it attractive? (Cartoon character background, color, furniture arrangement, fabrics.)
3. How will the center look? (Sketch, materials needed.)

Managing the Center

1. Who will use the center and at what times? (Rotational assignments, need basis, optional signups.)
2. What do the children need to know to work at the center? (Schedule, what to do, how to get and store materials, where to leave completed work, behavior standards.)
3. What can be done to avoid problems when a new center is introduced? (General directions chart, walkthrough practice, use able pupils as consultants, cross-age or parent or other helpers.)

MICROCOMPUTER CENTERS

"I've never seen kids or parents so excited about an innovation," a principal told me a decade ago, after a successful schoolwide drive to buy a single microcomputer. How times change. More recently her school had two in every classroom and thirty more in the school's instructional materials center. What *hasn't* changed is children's enthusiasm for computer-assisted instruction (Figure 6-7).

At their beginning, school microcomputers served mostly for drill and practice in math and language. But now they are also being used to teach broader applications, simple programming languages, and aspects of the content subjects. With more machines has come improved chances for us to apply them in complementary science activities and for occasional whole-class teaching.

Setting up a microcomputer center for science study, whether in your classroom or school instructional materials center, raises some of the same questions that arise with other learning centers: What do you want to accomplish? Are other means of instruction better? Who will use the center and when?

FIGURE 6-7
Students are enthusiastic about computer-assisted instruction.

What will they need to know? How can you best introduce the center? Answers here parallel those with regular centers.

And there are more matters to weigh. What kinds of programs and computer-directed materials are available? How can you best use them? Consider now the three broad kinds of programs you are likely to see in your school.

Different Kinds of Programs

Microcomputer programs, called *software,* usually appear on small plastic disks that are inserted into the machine. Pictures or words are stored magnetically on the disks. The pictures show on the screen of a TV-like monitor when coded instructions are typed on an accompanying keyboard. Software is available to teach both science processes and knowledge in three loosely defined formats: *tutorials, educational games,* and *simulations.*

Tutorials may teach vocabulary, facts, topical information, or skills—usually in small bite sizes. Questions follow each chunk of presented information, and pupil responses trigger what appears next. The computer may also record responses for evaluation. Tutorial materials and subjects vary widely. Topics include simple machines and their applications, why the oceans are important for survival, how the human heart works, how to classify animals, common constellations, and properties of rocks, to name just a few.

Educational games employ an appealing chancy setting as a device for drill and practice, or to teach processes and knowledge. Programs are designed to sift pupil responses, keep score, and sometimes compete to spur pupil effort. Increased learning may enable children to row a cartoon-style boat farther, climb higher on a mystical mountain, or receive screen-flashed token awards and a rousing musical salute. With reinforcers like these, who wouldn't get excited? This is why some sort of game is often integrated into tutorials.

Simulations give pupils roles in situations that can approximate real events and squeeze years into minutes. The players decide what to do when given certain data, and the computer instantly feeds back good or bad news. In one program (*Geology Search,* McGraw-Hill), small teams compete to find the best places to drill for oil. Success is linked to how well they learn mapping skills and geologic features. In another program, *SimAnt* (Broderbund/Maxis), pupils take on roles of ants. They learn ant behaviors, including how to communicate with one another and how to avoid being done in by fierce red ants, ravenous spiders, and heavy human feet. Using scientific information, pupils develop strategies to survive, increase the size of their colony, and finally reach the ultimate reward—a nearby home with a lavish food supply.

Simulations are excellent to present science phenomena that otherwise are too remote, dangerous, complex, costly, or time consuming. They teach the consequences of real-life decisions yet allow pupils to escape from actually bearing them. Who could ask for anything more?

Computers as Research Tools

How do scientists use microcomputers? Can children use these machines in similar ways? Science educators and computer specialists are digging deeply into both questions. The software and other materials coming from their efforts get children into the heart of science: the gathering, organizing, and sharing of real data.

The software of several programs for pupils have accompanying hardware called *probes.* These are sensing devices that are connected through a cable to the computer. When used with the proper software, probes can measure temperature, light, sound, heart rate, acidity of substances, motion, force, pressure, and other properties of objects.

Several probe-type lab programs (also called microcomputer-based labs) have had much use in elementary schools from about grade three on. The *Bank Street Laboratory* (Holt, Rinehart and Winston) gives pupils chances to record and analyze graphs of temperature, light, and sound data. *Science Toolkit* (Broderbund) has rugged, easy-to-use probes for measuring light, temperature, time, and distance. Data can be organized into tables, charts, and graphs. Probe labs make it easy to gather much data over short or long time periods and then instantly convert the data into analyzable forms.

Further software has been developed that allows pupils to share their information with others through a huge computer network. Children in variously placed schools gather data, transmit the data to a central computer, and share findings with other schools.

In one unit of a popular science program, children in schools scattered around the nation measure the acidity of rain in their local areas and send the data by modem—a telephone/computer linkage—to a scientist collaborating with the program. The data are then pooled through a central computer, organized on charts and maps, and sent back to the pupils. (For more on this project-developed program and others, please see the *National Geographic Kids Network* in Appendix C.)

Accessing Multimedia

"A real fish doesn't look like *that!*" says a child seated at a microcomputer. The reaction is understandable. Visual displays of software material are often only a crude version of the real thing. This is one reason teachers may complement some software with video-cassettes, films, and the like. But a big drawback of these aids is the difficulty of interacting with them. Also, they store only a limited amount of material.

The *videodisc* (also called *laserdisc*), solves both problems. This is a thin aluminum plate, usually about the size of an old long-playing record, sandwiched between two layers of plas-

tic (Figure 6-8). Each side may contain thousands of recorded still pictures and numerous film clips with sounds and narration—often in both English and Spanish.

A computer linked to a videodisc player can access the recorded material in any order within a few seconds and display it on the computer monitor. A laser sensor in the player head flits on command from one place to another on the disk and "reads" the material. You can also display the material *without* a computer by connecting the player to a separate video monitor. In this case, you control the material through the player with either a hand-held remote controller or a bar code reader.

How do you know what's on the disk? A teacher's guide usually comes with it. Each photo frame or sequence, organized under topics, is given a number and bar code identification. With the remote controller, you punch in the numbers of your selection to activate the player. Using the bar code reader

FIGURE 6-8
Videodiscs store audio and visual information that can be displayed on a computer screen or video monitor.

is even easier. You lightly rub one end of the reader across the code, point the other end at the player and push a button.

Most nationally-published science programs today employ videodiscs to some degree—from a centerpiece role to enrichment. Teacher guides may include both whole-class lessons with the disk and ways to put it to work in an individual or small group setting, such as your microcomputer learning center. With the center, for example, you might select frames and animated sequences to follow up a lesson on earthquakes, then arrange bar code stickers or numbers in a sequence to guide pupils. Some science programs provide pupil worksheets with bar codes of the extending material already printed on them. In both cases, pupils may also interact with the material in any way they prefer. Older pupils might also search out material by themselves to integrate into small group or individual reports to the class.

The *CD-ROM* (compact disc, read-only memory) is another way to bring a vast amount of computer-controlled audiovisual material into your classroom. About half the size of a videodisc, you insert it into a CD-ROM drive that is connected to a computer. The material is accessed through the keyboard and viewed on the computer screen. The CD-ROM is simply a variation of the familiar audio compact disc. It's been used mostly for storing reference information, as in encyclopedias and dictionaries, but this function is expanding to others as well. One version of Compton's Encyclopedia (Jostens) includes on a single CD-ROM many thousands of photos and other illustrations, sixty minutes of speech, music, and sounds, an interactive world atlas, and many other features besides the entire printed text. You can see how all this could make the material more meaningful, attractive, and quickly accessible to children than the usual bound books.

If you want your pupils to use your classroom computer center for word-processing science reports and the like, consider attach-

ing a *scanner* to your microcomputer. Like a photocopier, it allows the user to copy photos or drawings and incorporate them directly into a written report or other product produced on the printer.

Should you or a pupil want to deliver to the whole class a presentation on the computer screen, it may be hard for all to see what's displayed. Here's how you can project an enlarged display for easy viewing. Place an *LCD* (liquid crystal display) *projection pad* on the lighted bed of an overhead projector, attach the pad to the computer, and project on a large screen what's on the computer monitor. Of course, you can also use this system whenever you want to introduce new software or otherwise instruct the whole class on how to work with the computer. Figure 6-9 shows some of the microcomputer equipment used in schools.

Advantages and Some Problems

You've already seen some ways computer-assisted instruction can benefit you and your pupils in both learning centers or larger settings. Let's look at several more advantages and then address a few concerns.

It takes only brief experience with computer-assisted instruction to see how much children delight in this medium. The immediate feedback to their responses prompts them to learn more quickly and surely. Slow or fast learners can go at their own pace with an infinitely patient teacher. When they respond incorrectly, a good program branches them into a remedial sequence that reteaches the material in simpler steps. When they respond correctly, a good program moves them quickly into harder material. This truly individualizes instruction.

Perhaps the greatest promise for computer-based instruction lies in simulations. The computer-controlled videodisc and other resources offer all kinds of opportunities for making decisions and solving problems in realistic settings. Any airline pilot can tell you that what's seen through the cockpit wind-

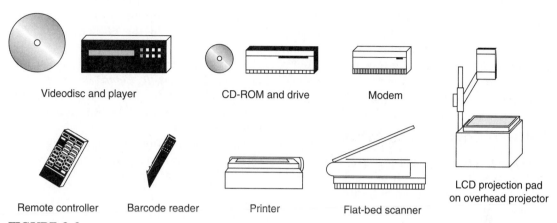

Videodisc and player   CD-ROM and drive   Modem

Remote controller   Barcode reader   Printer   Flat-bed scanner

LCD projection pad
on overhead projector

FIGURE 6-9
Some equipment used with microcomputers in schools.

shield of a flight simulator just after a right or wrong move comes uncannily close to the real thing. Now there are increasing chances for children to experience a huge variety of educative and motivating settings in interactive ways.

There are some problems with computer use too, though most are temporary and solvable. Despite noticeably improved software programs, many you'll find in schools are mediocre. Some neglect science process and present information in bookish ways that slight the computer's potential. And software made for one machine may not work in another. Expense is another concern. What can the school budget afford for the extensive hardware and software now available and soon to be developed?

Another drawback of some elementary science software is a lack of accompanying hands-on experiences. This is more likely with older and stand-alone materials. In contrast, the software now integrated into the comprehensive multimedia science programs of major publishing companies usually provides for concrete activity, often before *and* after computer instruction.

The "magic" that lets us work the microcomputer as a tool—to efficiently find data, to reconstruct and show data in different ways, to produce original or graphic materials—is the greatly simplified software now available. Once written in baffling technical language, the newer software allows us to give directions to the machine in plain English: stop, go, print, and so on. Even so, nearly everyone needs some extra guidance and practice to creatively apply this remarkable tool. If you're new to computing, it's easy to feel overwhelmed by the sheer quantity of unfamiliar technology and methods employed. But the good news is, there's plenty of help around to get you up to speed.

If you are new to a school, ask colleagues and the principal what machines and help are available at the school and district levels. Both in-service workshops and informal, person-to-person arrangements are common. And don't be surprised to meet pupils with considerable expertise at microcomputing. By the sixth grade, some children have had several *thousand* hours of experience with these machines at home and school. They can be invaluable aides to other pupils and you.

Consider, too, joining a computer-user group for your school's brand of machine. Colleagues and computer dealers typically can give details. In many cities, you can find groups composed entirely of teachers. Elsewhere, they may be a section of a larger group. You may find, as I have, that teachers in user groups are among the most enthusiastic and creative appliers of microcomputers in education. It's surprising how many problems, even budgetary ones, yield to their imaginative solutions.

Software Sources and Reviews

How can you learn what is currently available and worthwhile? The supply of usable science software continues to grow. Software publishers are producing more materials that reflect the best thinking in cognitive psychology and science education. Science textbook publishers (today they are more accurately called multimedia science program publishers) are integrating software titles into text units and chapters. Some also develop their own software for that purpose.

There are numerous publishers of software. Rather than contacting each, an easier way to find what's accessible is to inspect the catalog of a distributor of products from many companies. Two large distributors are:

Educational Resources
1550 Executive Drive
Elgin, IL 60123
1-800-624-2926

Cambridge Development Laboratory, Inc.
The Science Shop
214 Third Avenue
Waltham, MA 02154
1-800-637-0047

Comprehensive education software catalogs may also be obtained from the two main manufacturers of school microcomputers:

Apple Computer, Inc.
20525 Mariani Avenue
Cupertino, CA 95014

IBM Corporation
Education Software, Dept. 779
1 Culver Road
Dayton, NJ 08810

You can find in-depth evaluations of educational microcomputer products in *PRO/FILES*, published by the EPIE Institute, P.O. Box 839, Water Mill, NY 11976.

Another comprehensive guide to current software is *Microsift Courseware Evaluation*, published by the Northwest Regional Educational Laboratory, 300 S.W. 6th Avenue, Portland, OR 97204.

Find further reviews and many suggestions for using classroom computers and related materials in these magazines:

The Computing Teacher
University of Oregon
1787 Agate Street
Eugene, OR 97403

Electronic Learning
P.O. Box 3021
Southeastern, PA 19398

Media & Methods
1429 Walnut Street
Philadelphia, PA 19102

Science and Children
1742 Connecticut Ave., N.W.
Washington, DC 20009

Technology & Learning
2451 East River Road
Dayton, OH 45439

Appraising Software: What to Look For

You can do a good job of appraising science software for yourself with just a handful of criteria, posed as questions:

1. Is the program compatible with your objectives? (If not, there is no need to consider it further.)

2. Does the program teach important and transferable knowledge or processes? (Look for basic, durable material that children can apply in their lives.)

3. Can the learning happen better through other means? (Hands-on activities may be

more suitable. The clear, full-color illustrations in videotapes, films, and filmstrips may serve better than the computer's fuzzy graphics. The program may consist largely of reading matter at an inappropriate level.)

4. Does the program make good use of the computer's special features? (The pupil continually interacts with the program by making decisions instead of simply pushing a key to keep it going. Responses regulate the difficulty and speed of learning. Responses are recorded when appropriate.)

5. Is the program "user friendly"? (Look for a supportive, encouraging tone, clear directions, easy operations.)

6. Does a helpful, nontechnical teacher's guide accompany the program? (Look for warm-up suggestions, hints on operating the program, supplementary concrete activities.)

7. Does the program fulfill its stated objectives? (You can find out by consulting others who have tried it with children or by trying it yourself. There are probably no other reliable ways.)

SCIENCE PROJECTS

I once had a withdrawn, listless boy in my fifth-grade class who did not come to life until he built a simple, working model of the human lung. He impressed the class and me with a good oral report and demonstration of his project. It was then that I began to appreciate the possibilities of this kind of experience.

A *project* is an organized search, construction, or task directed toward a specific purpose. It's ordinarily done by one person, or a small team of two or three persons, with minimal guidance from the teacher. A project

may clarify, extend, or apply a concept—and cause children to use science processes along the way. Most projects require a lot of independent effort. So they are less appropriate for primary-level children, who usually lack the skills and perseverance needed to operate largely alone.

The need for projects most often arises during a regular instructional unit. But projects may also begin with interests expressed by pupils or from a desire to have a science fair. Our job is to provide some realistic project choices, give deadlines for completing the projects, tell how they will be presented, and check at times for progress.

Providing the right set of choices is the most demanding of these functions. Children need some background and guidelines to proceed smoothly. How to begin? Probably the easiest way is to use the investigations and activities in Appendix A of this book. With some practice, you can move beyond these experiences into an almost unlimited world of possibilities. Let's get down to specifics.

Using Investigations for Projects

Investigations that you might use with the whole class or in learning centers often present one or two extra open-ended opportunities to go beyond the basic investigation. For example, in "Wheel-Belt Systems," page 202, a follow-up question says, "What wheel-belt systems can you invent?" In "Mealworms and What They Do," page 213, a final question is, "What are some questions about mealworms you'd like to investigate?" In "Evaporation," page 224, the last questions ask, "Who can dry a wet towel faster?" and "What is the longest you can keep a wet paper towel from drying?"

These are the times to either have everyone continue with the investigation or to invite pupils with individual interests to pursue projects. Reports of projects can be presented later to the whole class and the materials placed on a science table for other interested pupils to manipulate. *Since everyone has some background, these further investigations become enriching extensions of familiar concepts and processes.*

You can also use for projects investigations that the class has not seen. Again, make them part of a topic under study in a unit. This makes them more understandable. Because most investigations are broad, let a team of two or three volunteers cooperatively divide the project. Assign a good reader to the team so it is less likely to continually need your help. Just show the team the investigation as printed (minus the "Teaching Comments" section).

Create additional projects by converting closed-ended experiences into open-ended investigations as shown in Chapter 3.

Using Activities for Projects

Activities like those in Appendix A also give possibilities for projects to enrich units or meet pupil interests. But to ensure a good match between pupil and project requires some understanding of your pupils and the kinds of activities that are available.

Some activities are short-range, straightforward demonstrations of concepts or procedures. These are noticeably closed-ended and give exact guidance to pupils. Some examples are

> *What happens to water [pressure] with depth? (p. 221)*
>
> *How high can water flow compared to where it comes from? (p. 221)*
>
> *How can you show that air takes up space? (p. 221)*
>
> *How can you tell if air weighs anything? (p. 222)*

Activities like these make especially suitable projects for less able pupils and those who lack experience.

Some activities give longer-range and more open-ended experiences. They may call for changing some variables or keeping records of observations for a time. Some examples are

> *How can you make a "nerve tester" game? (p. 200)*
>
> *In what places are seeds in soil? (p. 209)*
>
> *How can you measure changes in air pressure? (p. 225)*
>
> *What does the moon look like from day to day? (p. 226)*

Different persons and places are tested in the first pair of activities, and records are kept in the second pair. Such activities make good projects for children who have the interest and patience for a more sustained experience and a willingness to keep good records.

Some concrete activities may be extended and enriched afterward by consulting authority in various forms:

> *How are the colors made in comic strips? (p. 192)*
>
> *What happens when your eyes tire from seeing one color? (p. 194)*
>
> *Which foods have starch? (p. 218)*
>
> *How can you measure changes in air pressure? (p. 225)*

A local newspaper office and an eye doctor are possible authorities in the first pair of activities, along with reference materials. A nutritionist and a local meteorologist, or reference materials, might be suitable for the second pair. Projects like these allow children to extend their interest through applying interviewing and reference skills to answer real needs. Some pupils have poor skills? Pair each with an able one, or give extra help.

Reporting Projects

Children at all elementary levels do better at oral than written reports. But for either kind, some structure aids their understanding of the projects. Here is a form that makes sense to children, with traditional terms stated at the right.

What did I want to find out?	Problem, hypothesis
What materials did I need?	Materials
What did I do?	Procedure
What did I find out?	Findings, conclusions

The first three steps are best stated in the past tense for *reporting* projects, and present tense for *guiding* them. If you want a distinct hypothesis in experimental projects, this might be stated as, "What did I think?"

The simplified form usually works well for *both* observational activities (in which one observes properties of objects and events) and experimental activities (in which one changes the observed properties).

Is the simplified report form really necessary? Probably yes, if the whole class is involved. Remember, there are significant differences in mental abilities in your classroom. So the simplified version is generally easier *for both the givers and receivers* of reports to understand.

As your pupils gain experience, nourish their independence by continually making the projects less directive and more open-ended. At the same time, remain aware that what they are able to do varies greatly among individuals.

Science Fairs and Invention Conventions

With some history of successful projects, consider having a *science fair* to display them. This is exciting to pupils and excellent for public relations. It is wise to keep it modest at first—perhaps for only your classroom or parents' open house. Display projects on tables next to the walls, with written reports behind mounted on a cardboard or chipboard background. Use the simplified form above for the reports.

Instead of prizes, consider presenting a "Certificate of Completion," perhaps with proud parents looking on, to each child who displays a completed project. This formally recognizes everyone's efforts, but downplays invidious comparisons, which elementary school pupils find hard to handle. Other beneficial side effects may be less heavy-handed participation by some parents, and greater class interest in submitting projects. Of course, differences in pupil achievement will still be noticeable to you for educational purposes.

At another time, you may want to work with a fellow teacher for a combined operation, or even organize a schoolwide fair. For details on organizing schoolwide and other science fairs, see:

National Science Teachers Assn., *Science Fairs and Projects for K–8.* Washington, DC: National Science Teachers Association, 1988.

Van Deman, Barry and McDonald, Ed. *Nuts and Bolts: A Matter of Fact Guide to Science Fair Projects.* Harwood Heights, IL: Science Man Press, T.S.M. Marketing, Inc., 1980.

As part of the modern trend to teach science that children can apply to their lives, some science programs today recommend "invention conventions" as well as typical science fairs. Since technology is science applied to solve practical problems, the idea is to give girls and boys chances to develop "technical" solutions to their everyday problems and interests:

I'm tired of feeding my dog. (Maybe an automatic, gravity-driven feeder would come in handy.)

How can I tell how fast the wind is blowing? (A home-made wind gauge, fashioned from cardboard and wood, could fill the bill.)

I'd like to make a weird toy that rolls uphill by itself. (A hidden, twisted rubber band inside an empty salt box may do the job.)

My little brother Corky keeps sneaking into my room. (Perhaps a "burglar" alarm, fashioned from a buzzer, two flashlight batteries and some wire, will give Corky pause.)

I've heard you can make a stool from newspaper that's so strong you can sit on it. (Rolled-up newspaper makes surprisingly sturdy columns.)

For a wealth of fun-filled ideas and ways to stimulate inventiveness in your pupils, see:

Caney, Steven. *Steven Caney's Invention Book.* N.Y.: Workman Publishing, 1985.

Eichelberger, Barbara and Larson, Connie. *Constructions for Children: Projects in Design Technology.* Menlo Park, CA: Dale Seymour, 1993.

McCormack, Alan J. *Inventor's Workshop.* Belmont, Cal.: David S. Lake Publishers, 1981.

If you are interested in a competitive awards program for projects, consider *Invent America!,* a K–8 student contest with yearly cash prizes for students, teachers, schools, districts, and state departments of education. This is a national program, formed after needs were expressed by the U.S. Patent Office, and U.S. Education and Commerce departments. It aims to stimulate creativity and invention in young people as part of a broad effort to keep the nation competitive in science and technology. The award money is donated by American business and industry, and the program is run by a private, nonprofit foundation.

Teachers get sample lesson plans, examples of how to manage the program, ideas for working with parents and community, suggestions for displaying the inventions, and examples of how schools have benefited from using invention programs.

Free materials are available from the U.S. Patent Foundation, 1331 Pennsylvania Avenue N.W., Suite 903, Washington, DC 20004.

HOME/SCHOOL COOPERATION

Common sense and research tell us that pupils do better in school when their parents take an active interest in their studies.[2] While parents want to help their children succeed, they may not know how to go about it, especially when the subject is science. How can you help parents nurture their children's efforts, and how can they support your science teaching?

Recall that in the last chapter I mentioned that your school's science program might include copy masters of letters to parents, concept summaries, and activities that parents and children could do together. Many newer programs include such materials. The letters periodically announce a new unit of instruction, briefly describe it, and state some things parents might do to complement lessons. The concept summaries, often in several languages, inform parents about ideas they might discuss with their children and reinforce with experiences outside of school. The activities usually relate to the unit being studied and feature everyday materials.

Doing and discussing concrete activities with their children is a good way for parents to cultivate science interests and achievement. To further these objectives, some teachers keep at hand fifteen to thirty shoe box kits containing activities that pupils can check out and take home. Kits are easy to prepare when you get parents to help. Here's a way to do so.

Inspect Appendix A of this book and science source books for activities and investigations that might enrich your regular science program. Be sure that only free or very low cost materials are needed. Select any number of these and make one copy of each. (Activities usually work better than investigations for parents because they are shorter and less likely to need teaching expertise.) Write a different identification number on each sheet, from one to whatever total you have. Pick one activity, get the materials, and put

---

[2]N. L. Gage and David C. Berliner, *Educational Psychology,* 3d ed. (Boston: Houghton Mifflin, 1984), p. 117.

them in a shoe box. Trim the margins of the activity sheet with scissors and tape it to the *inside lid* of the shoe box. Boldly mark with crayon or felt pen the activity number on top of the lid and both ends of the box.

During Parents' Night or similar meetings early in the school year, briefly introduce your science program—what topics pupils will study, some materials they'll work with, and so on—then show your shoe box kit and give its purpose. Pass out the duplicated activity sheets, have parents examine them, and then ask for volunteers to make the kits. Encourage the volunteers to do the activities with their children, discuss the results together, and have these pupils bring the completed kits to school for checkout by others.

Some teachers like to have parents experience first hand a few children's activities across the curriculum. This puts them in better touch with their children's work than talk alone, and sets up a delightfully informal and enthusiastic meeting. For a science activity that is a good icebreaker, try "How Useful Are Your Thumbs?" on page 215 in this text. A former student teacher of mine did this activity with parents just before requesting shoe box kits from them. Her score: 27 parents, 27 kits.

As mentioned in Chapter 5, remember that parents are also typically willing to supplement your science supplies with discardable items from around the home and with very low-cost materials. Some will volunteer to assist at science learning centers, especially at the primary-grade level. Others may volunteer their expertise in science or technology as tied to what your pupils are studying. But for these things to happen, parents need to hear details from you about what's needed.

Parents are usually more concerned about their children's progress in reading than in any other subject. Point out to them that research consistently underscores the value of parents reading aloud with their children, sharing books, and discussing concepts that

come up in the reading.[3] Show them several kinds of science trade books available— biographies, diaries, expositions, and so on— that correlate with upcoming units. Pupils may check out these books from several sources—school or district or public library. If your school has a newer multimedia science program, yet another source is the supply of science-related literature books that typically accompanies these programs.

Show parents examples of useful articles from a newspaper, news magazine, *National Geographic,* or other sources they might share with their children who, in turn, might share the information at school. Explain that this material is easier to understand and remember when it relates to topics and concepts being studied at school. Stress the need to discuss the articles with the children, since they are seldom written in an age-appropriate style. When articles are from a morning newspaper, harried parents who commute to work may not have time to immediately discuss them. Suggest that these be clipped and discussed later. When this happens, pupils are more likely to share at school news that makes sense to them and their classmates. Mention, too, some titles of science periodicals for children. (See listing on page 229.) They contain excellent current material, are more age-appropriate, and will help pupils learn what to look for when scanning newspapers and other publications.

Mindless television-watching is a sore subject with parents, but the fact is that some of the best science programs ever produced are available to children on TV. Ask parents about science programs they have liked sharing with their children. *National Geographic* specials, *Wild Kingdom, Nova* (some subjects), and *3-2-1-Contact* are examples of shows that grownups and kids can enjoy together and discuss to some degree. If program hours are inconvenient, they might be taped and

[3] *What Works—Research About Teaching and Learning* (Washington, DC: U.S. Department of Education, 1986).

viewed at another time. Also, encourage your pupils to watch for upcoming shows and announce them to classmates.

Probably some parents and children already will have visited a local natural history museum, zoo, observatory, bird refuge, botanical garden, and so on. Ask parents about these experiences and suggest additional places recommended by seasoned colleagues and school district publications. A school catalog may describe and list places for families to visit at different grade levels or for certain units of instruction. And if *you* intend to take your class on study trips to these places, a parents' meeting is a good time to drum up volunteers to accompany the class.

You probably realize that I've mentioned more things to inform parents about than you'll have time for in one introductory meeting, especially if you discuss other subjects. Periodic newsletters, a classroom newspaper, individual conferences, and further parent–teacher meetings all present more chances to reach them. The content of your message is far more important than its forum. However it's delivered, please remember this: When you give parents specific ways to help their children study science and support your efforts, everyone gains.

SUMMARY

Teachers often complement their whole-class teaching with individual and small group experiences to meet the wide range of abilities and interests in their classes. Three common ways to do this are to use learning centers, microcomputer centers, and projects.

A classroom learning center is a place where one or several pupils at a time can do activities independently through materials and directions found at the center. The center may be organized so pupils can choose at least some of the activities they do and work at their own pace and learning level. Open-ended experiences usually serve best for these purposes. Many of the investigations in this book can be directly converted into learning centers.

A microcomputer center can be set up and run much like a regular learning center. Microcomputer programs are available in three broad instructional formats: tutorials, which teach small chunks of material in sequential lessons; games, which use a chance-taking setting and appealing reinforcers for pupil responses; and simulations, in which pupils respond to situations that approximate real events. Videodiscs, controlled by either the computer or hand-held remote controls, greatly expand the range of audio-visual materials available for instruction. Computer-assisted instruction is ideally suited for individualizing instruction in science, but may neglect hands-on experiences. This problem is remedied in several ways.

A science project is an organized search, construction, or task directed toward a specific purpose and ordinarily carried out by one to three pupils. The need for projects often arises in instructional units through interests expressed by pupils. Both investigations and activities like those in this book may be converted into science projects. However, some are more demanding than others. Knowing a pupil's abilities and what the project demands are important in arranging a suitable match.

Parents can complement what their children learn about science at school by participating with them in various out-of-school experiences. These might include doing science activities at home, reading and discussing trade books, viewing selected TV programs, and visiting museums or other community resources. Parents are also frequently willing to volunteer their assistance at learning centers, to make shoe box kits, to provide some low cost materials, and share science-related expertise.

SUGGESTED READINGS

DeBruin, Jerry. *Science Fairs with Style.* Carthage, IL: Good Apple, 1991. (A comprehensive guide for upper-grade projects.)

Dockterman, David. *Teaching in the One-Computer Classroom.* Cambridge, MA: Tom Snyder, 1990. (Describes a variety of ways one to several microcomputers can be effectively used in a classroom.)

Linn, Marcia C. "An Apple a Day." *Science and Children,* Nov./Dec. 1987, 15–18. (Describes a probe-type lab in which pupils learn the difference between heat and temperature using real-time data and graphing.)

Paulu, Nancy and Margery Martin. *Helping Your Child Learn Science.* Washington, DC: U.S. Department of Education, Office of Educational Research and Improvement, 1991. (How parents can whet their children's science interests through home activities. One of a series on different school subjects. Available at $3.25 from OERI Outreach Office, 555 New Jersey Ave. NW, Washington, DC 20208-5570.)

Pearlman, Susan and Kathleen Pericak-Spector. "Helping Hands from Home." *Science and Children* 29(7):12–14 (April 1992). (Parent volunteers make active science more manageable.)

Stone, George K. *More Science Projects You Can Do.* Englewood Cliffs, N.J.: Prentice-Hall, 1981. (A paperback book of many interesting projects for upper elementary and middle school pupils.)

7

How to Organize and Assess Science Teaching

How do you effectively plan and assess science teaching? This chapter aims to enable you to answer that question for yourself. If it does its job, you'll probably preface your answer with the words, "It depends." Here's why.

The teaching conditions for science education can be quite different from one school district to another. One district will put into your hands an activity-centered program with a kit brim-full of materials for everyone in class. Another might supply a multimedia program, with all the materials and hardware you need to teach science seven days a week. At a third site your school principal may just point to a pile of old textbooks and discretely back out of the door.

Naturally, such diverse conditions require different planning. Further considerations include the teaching and cooperative practices you are able to fashion, given your particular pupils and unique background. As you go through this chapter, you'll see a wide array of practices often displayed by top-notch teachers. How many can you immediately expect to handle, especially if you are new to the game? In baseball talk, a realistic aim for you now may be to hit a string of solid singles and an occasional double. Later, with more chances for practice, you can go for home runs.

To take up these matters and more, we'll begin with descriptions of exemplary activity-centered programs, old and new. Next, we'll consider modern multimedia programs and what help to expect from school district curriculum guides. Finally, you'll see ways to construct and assess your own "multimedia" program, using a science textbook and local resources.

ACTIVITY-CENTERED PROGRAMS

Some science programs center on what children can learn through concrete, hands-on experiences. Textbooks, videotapes, and other secondary sources for learning have little or no place in them. Hands-on science programs got a big boost in the 1960s, when national concern for improved science and mathematics teaching led to many federally supported curriculum projects. More recently, a second wave of major curriculum projects featuring hands-on experiences has moved into the limelight. Let's look at the intentions behind these programs and how they might affect your teaching.

The Old and the New Activity Programs

Many professional scientists of the 1960s saw the science teaching going on then as a shallow and bookish perversion of the disciplines they knew. So a number of them recruited teachers, learning psychologists, and science educators, and went to work on curriculum projects. Three major programs in elementary science emerged after almost 10 years of effort: *Science—A Process Approach* (SAPA), the *Science Curriculum Improvement Study* (SCIS), and the *Elementary Science Study* (ESS). Though each differs in format and stresses different things, the three have much in common:

- Learning begins and proceeds through work with concrete materials from specially designed kits.
- Scope of study is narrower but deeper than in book programs.
- Learning activities are more open-ended than in book programs.
- Pupils use a variety of science processes as they work.
- Each program is supported by recognized learning theory.
- Basic science principles are stressed, with little or no technology.
- Mathematics is often integrated into learning activities.

Most measures show that the three programs well met their objectives.[1] Yet even during their period of greatest use, the three major project programs were only adopted by a minority of school districts. And their use as full-scale packaged programs continues to wane today, though many districts and teachers happily keep some parts to supplement text programs.[2] The weight of tradition, the programs' high costs, extensive in-service requirements for teachers, the back-to-basics movement of the seventies, and other things combined to keep down their adoption.

Today, a fresh lineup of activity-centered programs, most government-aided to some degree, are drawing national attention. Among them are *Science for Life and Living, Full Option Science System, EDC Insights, Science and Technology for Children,* and *The National Geographic Kids Network.* (For individual descriptions of these and other project-developed science programs, please see Appendix C)

These curricula retain many of the strong features of the earlier programs, build onto others, and introduce new features:[3]

▪ Topics and activities have far more personal and social applications.

▪ More subjects, particularly language arts, are integrated. (Printed materials, or even books, may be used.)

▪ Activities challenge pupils' misconceptions and allow time for pupils to rethink their own ideas (schemata).

▪ Teachers and administrators have more say in the design of the programs.

▪ Ways to help teachers teach the program, and manage the materials, are more prominently featured.

If your school district uses one of these or earlier hands-on programs, you'll find that almost everything you've learned so far in this book will apply. That is because the principles that formed the projects are much like those that guided this writing. What's more, this chapter should further help you fine-tune the program to your exact needs. This should make it easier for you to teach with skill and confidence, once you learn the program's details.

Importance of Science Curriculum Projects

Will more schools adopt the newer hands-on curricula than was done with the older programs? It seems likely, but the impact of government-aided projects goes far beyond the specific programs that come out. Innovations in education are risky business. Few commercial publishers can afford to initiate changes in education. Yet competition makes them eager to take on what is accepted.

Good results from science curriculum projects influence nearly everyone in science education, especially textbook and curriculum writers. This noticeably upgrades the quality of what they produce. How far can this go? In the long run, perhaps the only limits to innovation will be the money and time that schools can commit to the products.

▉ MULTIMEDIA PROGRAMS

For more than fifty years textbooks have dominated science teaching in elementary schools. But accelerating evolution has transformed what was once a read-about-science series of books with few activities, into an integrated multimedia program with many

[1] James A. Shymansky, William C. Kyle, Jr., and Jennifer M. Alport. "How Effective Were the Hands-on Programs of Yesterday?" *Science and Children* 20(5):14–15 (Nov./Dec. 1982).
[2] An updated version of *SCIS,* Delta Education's *SCIS3,* is stimulating new interest and support for this landmark program.
[3] Nancy M. Landes, et al. "What Research Says About the New Science Curricula." *Science and Children* 25(8):35 (May 1988).

activities, videodiscs, software, printed materials, and much more. While printed materials form the center of most multimedia programs, it's also possible to find core instruction focused on the videodisc.

For example, *Windows on Science* (Optical Data Corporation) offers a comprehensive program in the earth, life, and physical sciences on a series of videodiscs with integrated support materials. Lessons begin with a videodisc presentation followed by a pertinent hands-on activity. Pupils next study a leaflet designed and written to further build the concept under study, then write and do extending activities that develop thinking.

Multimedia programs are likely to contain a wide array of products for teaching science:

- Pupil books (several forms)
- Teacher guides
- Activity material kits
- Activity logs (for recordings)
- Videodiscs (applying concepts)
- Videotapes (vicarious field trips)
- Software (problem-solving simulations)
- Concept summaries/glossaries (in several languages)
- Audio tapes (for ESL pupils, concept reviews)
- Teacher anthologies (literature selections)
- Blackline masters
- Posters
- Trade books
- OHP transparencies
- Activity cards (for learning centers and projects)
- Assessment package (detailed evaluation materials)

Even more items could be added to this list, but by now you have the idea: modern publishers offer comprehensive, integrated multimedia programs, not simply textbooks. If you have the chance to teach a complete multimedia program, your biggest challenge may be to learn how to use its many options within the time you have to teach science. You might want to start small—with whatever basic material you can comfortably handle—and then add options one at a time.

How much of a complete multimedia program is adopted by a school district usually comes down to what it can afford and what usable teaching materials are already on hand. Many schools can only buy the core printed materials, which may be found in two forms: pupil books and booklets. The booklets, called *modules* or *units,* are like separately published parts of a whole book—each equivalent to a large chapter or section. Why use them? They make it easier for a school district to customize its curriculum, by choosing from about fifty modules or units that may be available for all the elementary grades. Activity materials are separately packaged by units, to fit whatever titles are selected.

Let's assume that you'll only have pupil books and the teacher edition to work with. Most of the following pages will show you how to work with that condition. Once you learn how to operate successfully within lean times, anything extra that comes your way should make it even easier to do a good job.

An instructional unit in a textbook is often a chapter that the authors write from a framework of generalizations, such as

1. Weathering and erosion wear down the earth's surface.
2. Topsoil is made up of mineral, vegetable, and animal matter.
3. Lava flows and crustal movements build up the earth's surface.
4. Three kinds of rocks are formed as the earth's surface wears down and builds up.

Each of the generalizations may be developed in a separate section of the chapter that is headed by a topical title or question:

1. Weathering and Erosion/What is weathering and erosion?
2. Topsoil/What is in topsoil?

3. The Earth's Changing Surface/How does the earth's surface change?

4. How Rocks Form/How are rocks made?

The authors will also usually write one or more objectives for each section, such as the following.
Pupils will

1. *Define* weathering and erosion and give examples of each.

2. *Infer* the three parts of soil after examining soil samples.

3. *Describe* how lava flows and crustal movements build up the earth's surface.

4. *Explain* how igneous, sedimentary, and metamorphic rocks are formed.

Pupils are expected to meet the objectives through reading the text, doing the activities, and using whatever supplementary materials are available. This is done one section or lesson at a time.

Each section or lesson is likely to have three parts:

1. Introduction. (You prepare pupils to do activities and read.)

2. Developing the idea. (Children do activities and read.)

3. Summarizing and extending the learning. (You help pupils generalize and apply what they have studied.)

The teaching suggestions for lessons, and many additional aids, are found in a teacher's edition of the pupil's textbook. Here's a list of what it's likely to have:

■ Science content background material

■ Lesson objectives

■ Lesson generalizations

■ Materials needed for activities

■ Lesson procedures

■ Evaluation questions and tests

■ Ways to help pupils with special needs

■ Ways to integrate other subjects

■ Model bulletin board

■ Model learning center

■ Enrichment activities

■ Home activities

■ Activity worksheets

The last three items may also appear as ditto masters or in separate pupil workbooks.

Despite this abundance, there are several ways in which a textbook unit can be enhanced. Your district may have a curriculum guide for the purpose, but if it does not, you can do the job yourself. Let's look first at how a curriculum guide can help you get the most from a text unit.

SCHOOL DISTRICT CURRICULUM GUIDES

Years ago, curriculum guides of large school districts were likely to contain comprehensive resource units organized around common science topics. They required enormous effort to assemble and seldom met expectations. As text programs gradually improved, fewer and fewer districts made the effort.

Modern guides typically have two uses: they state the district's policies for science, and they supplement the adopted science program by showing how local resources fit into lessons.

Local Policies

We live in a time of accountability. Seldom now in well-managed districts can a teacher select science topics or units simply from preference or interest. For the most part, this is a good thing. Can you imagine the state of mathematics or reading education if everyone operated solely from personal choice?

Many state departments of education have curriculum standards and guidelines that local districts use in adopting a science program. There may also be state or district achievement tests whose objectives are aligned with the guidelines. District leaders naturally want to see a match between what is taught and what is measured on tests. To help ensure this, the local curriculum guide may point out what text chapters to stress, the best sequence to use, and recommend time periods for different chapters.

The guide is also likely to give district policy on safety, such as what animals are acceptable for classrooms, and field trip requirements. Further statements may cover how to group pupils, order materials, correlate subjects, and other practical matters.

Local Resources

Most school districts accumulate sizable collections of audiovisual materials, trade (library) books, teacher reference books, models, microcomputer software, and the like. Many nearby community resources may beckon for firsthand learning experiences: wildlife sanctuary, water filtration plant, aerospace center, zoo, museum, and so on. There may also be a list of community volunteers who are willing to share their expertise with pupils. How can these resources be best used? This is always a question when a new science program is adopted.

The usual job today of a science curriculum guide committee is to supplement text units: It plugs local resources into appropriate places and suggests further activities when those in the text seem sparse. Notice how this is done on a page from a typical guide (Figure 7-1).

Reading from left to right, let's look at the first lesson: "Living Things Need Energy." It can be found on pupil text pages 48–49. The district's objective is for pupils to be able to compare the roles of producers and consumers. A related activity,

"Plants that animals eat," Copy Master page 26, is a reproducible page from a booklet in the text program, and is designed to promote critical thinking. The last column contains the title of a district film whose length is five minutes.

Note in the resource column symbols "PW" and "SEE." These are for *Project Wild,* an environmental studies activity book widely available in the district; and *Science in Elementary Education,* which is this book. Further resources used by the committee in other units included another activity book and materials from a popular math/science project.

Also not shown on the guide page are resources found in each school's instructional materials center. Trade books that can be used with the unit, for example, can be selected by pupils themselves from the center's collection. In other districts, a collection of trade books on a unit topic may be boxed at a central materials center and delivered to a school when needed.

Not all curriculum guides look alike. And a textbook unit might be more than a single chapter. For example, it can be several chapters united by a topical title:

Unit: Earth and Its Neighbor

    Chapter 1: Earth in Space

    Chapter 2: The Moon

    Chapter 3: Rocketing to the Moon

Still, the basic organization as presented shows how many text authors and curriculum guide committees do their work.

As you might expect, the quality of curriculum guide resource help varies from superior to awful. It's clear that an excellent resource supplement takes care of many instructional problems. But what do you do when the guide at hand is little more than a declaration of good intentions, or when there are no resources stated at all? One answer is, do what a guide committee does, only on a smaller scale.

SCIENCE CURRICULUM EXTENSIONS PACKET

Chapter 3: Food Chains and Food Webs   Grade 4

Lesson	Text Page #	Objective	Related activity	Resource	AV/Media Support	Length
1. Living Things Need Energy	48–49	Compare roles of producers and consumers.	Plants that animals eat	Copy Master p. 26	What do they eat?	5
2. Animals and Their Food	50–53	Classify animals according to what they eat.	Classification of animals	Copy Master p. 28	Animals and their foods, Rev. ed.	10
			Finding out	p. 53	Battle of the bugs, 2nd ed.	11
			Deadly Links	PW, pp. 197–200	Plankton: Pastures of the ocean	10
3. Food Chains	54–57	Show how members of a food chain affect each other.	How do food chain members affect each other?	p. 57	World of plant and animal communities	14
			What is a food chain?	SEE, p. 420	Pond-life food web	12
			Foods from plants	Copy Master p. 29		
4. Food Webs	58–61	Understand the relationship between food chains and food webs.	What did your lunch cost wildlife?	PW, pp. 215–216		
			Oh Deer!	PW, pp. 131–134		

FIGURE 7-1
Page from a curriculum guide.

HOW TO SUPPLEMENT TEXTBOOK UNITS

To supplement a textbook unit, consider these suggestions:

1. Thoroughly read the unit, as shown in the child's text and teacher's edition, to grasp what it is about. (Ordinarily, the teacher's edition includes the pupil material.)

2. Look for places where you can use local resources—field trips, audiovisual materials, kits, trade books, speakers, computer software, and so on. (Have on hand the district's instructional resources catalog to consult.)

3. Look for opportunities to integrate reading, math, language, and other subjects into lessons. (These are often mentioned in the teacher's edition, but you will need to address your group's specific needs.)

4. Look for chances to open-end some concrete activities now present, or add a few. (Have on hand this book or others in the bibliography to consult.)

5. Estimate the total time needed to teach the unit, then fit the text's lessons into the block of available time. (We will detail block planning later in this chapter.)

6. Order district instructional materials for times needed and gather other materials for activities. (Your pupils can help gather everyday things.)

When teaching a text unit for the first time, be sensitive to what you can handle. Just try a few of the enrichment ideas in the teacher's edition and those stated above in items two through four. Follow the suggested lesson procedures as found except for the few places where you have amended the lessons.

As you gain experience and confidence, adopt more of the foregoing suggestions and extra helps in the teacher edition. Continue to add more of your own ideas and local resources. The improved results that come from supplementing the text should please both you and your pupils.

Many teachers are satisfied with teaching from a supplemented text. They often cite convenience and time saved as reasons. Since elementary teachers plan and teach about eight additional school subjects besides science, this is understandable.

Other teachers, though, feel restricted by the book format, even an improved one. Without the publisher's full array of multimedia resources to draw from, they see mostly closed-ended activities that illustrate ideas in the book rather than broad chances for real inquiry. They see relatively short, tightly controlled lessons when they want pupils to ask more questions and pursue strong interests over longer periods of time. These teachers are aware of some ways to augment the book unit, but for them these measures don't go far enough. They want the book to be one tool among several, rather than the main event. What they *really* want is a practical way to design their own multimedia unit, and a format that allows them to work flexibly with their pupils.

Making a unit from scratch is generally impractical for teachers because it demands much time, effort, and expertise. But there is rarely a need for it. You can usually assemble what you want in several hours if you start with a well-organized base. The teacher's edition of almost any modern textbook series can give such a base.

HOW TO MAKE YOUR OWN TEXTBOOK-BASED UNITS

Three main things you need to know to make a textbook-based unit are:

■ How to determine which *generalizations* to use.

■ How to gather more *activities*, if needed, to teach each generalization.

■ How to introduce, or *bridge* into, each generalization's sequence of activities.

Determining Generalizations

The chapters or units of most textbooks are organized around from about 3 to 10 large generalizations. (These may be called "concepts.") Rarely are there fewer or more than this, and the average seems to be about five. The teacher's editions of most books contain outlines with the large generalizations clearly labeled. When this is the case all that is needed next, if the scope seems satisfactory, is to look up a few more activities. In other series, generalizations are sometimes too detailed and should be combined to make a broader statement. For example, take these generalizations:

The faster something vibrates, the higher a sound it makes.

Smaller things vibrate faster than larger things.

The tighter something is, the faster it vibrates.

You could combine them to read:

Speed of vibrations affects pitch; smaller, tighter objects sound higher because they vibrate faster.

These statements are mainly for your guidance as you put together the unit, so their exact form does not matter if they make sense to you and reflect the material.

Make a tentative list of such generalizations. Then go through the text chapter to see if they reflect the main parts of the chapter. Big topical headings and the number of pages devoted to each are the main indicators. Change the generalizations as needed to match what you find, if you want to stick closely to the textbook's contents. Your task is to wind up with the fewest big ideas possible without combining unrelated ideas. Don't worry about losing track of details. Those will come out in the activities.

It is easy to think from looking at these suggestions that you need a long time to decide on the large ideas. This is unlikely. Pick out a chapter in a child's text and carefully read it along with the accompanying section in the teacher's guide. After doing so, with average ability in outlining, you can probably pin down the main generalizations in 10 to 20 minutes on your first try.

Whether you use one or several text chapters as a base for a unit or as the entire program, *it is important to think through their basic organization.* When making a unit, you need to know the generalizations to compile extra activities, but the importance of analysis goes beyond this. It boosts your confidence by providing a sense of direction. It leads to the feeling that, if needed, you can make a few changes and add some children's ideas. It helps you to decide what is important and what is not. In contrast, when merely following the book, you go wherever it goes.

Getting Activities

One advantage in using the book as a base is the assurance that at least some activities are "automatically" available and tied to each generalization. The pupil text contains reading matter, pictures to examine, and other things to do. It is your job, then, to expand its present inventory of activities and take advantage of local resources. The more numerous the activities, the easier it is to select exactly what is most fitting at the time of planning specific lessons.

The teacher's edition should have additional activities. Some programs include the teacher's edition in an expanded teacher's resource package, held together by a three-ring binder. It may include blackline masters and further activities. These sources may give you most of what you need. By arranging their offerings in lessons of your own design, they may better suit your purposes.

Many school districts also provide books and catalogs that contain collections of activities. The following resource books contain hundreds of experiments, demonstrations, and other things to do:

Gega, Peter C. *Concepts and Experiences in Elementary School Science.* 2d ed. New York: Macmillan, 1994.

Lowery, Lawrence F. *The Everyday Science Sourcebook: Ideas for Teaching in the Elementary and Middle School,* Palo Alto, CA: Dale Seymour, 1985.

Strongin, Herb. *Science on a Shoestring.* Reading, MA: Addison-Wesley, 1991.

Further references can be found in the bibliography.

Having a sourcebook that contains many activities can enable you to find what you want without wasting time, if the generalizations selected are broad, basic ones. Especially watch for open-ended activities, since these experiences are most likely to accommodate pupils' individual differences.

How many open-ended investigations should you plan for? That depends a lot on the kinds of pupils you have. Gifted and talented children are able to do, and require, much more open-ended work than other children. At the other extreme, the educable mentally handicapped profit most from direct teaching and narrowly defined activities. A worthy goal is to reserve about 40 to 50 percent of unit time for hands-on science experiences, both closed- and open-ended.

Besides a good activity sourcebook, consult your school's audiovisual catalog and other resource catalogs, if any. Note under each generalization what experiences will help you to teach it. Also, record possible study trips.

Perhaps other local facilities can be used, such as the school building and grounds, and local resource persons. It may be worthwhile to check a free-materials catalog for other possibilities.

Children's trade books may be available on the subject at the school library, district library, or local public library. Beyond the primary grades, encyclopedias are worthwhile for additional information. Further, children can check newspapers and magazines for stories and pictures. Extra reading matter can do much to extend children's learning. It takes care of a practical matter, as well. Because fast readers can devour the regular assignment in the class science text within minutes, they need supplementary reading to be challenged.

Take care not to rush into reading activities. Most of the time reserve these for the end of study of each generalization. Our ability to understand words relates directly to our experiences. Let reading activities reinforce and extend these experiences.

There are many chances in a unit to integrate other subjects besides reading into lessons. Now is a good time to consider them. What do the children need more practice with? Oral language? Applied math? Writing? Other skills? What other activities might children do for enrichment? Paint a large mural on butcher paper? Perform a dramatic play? Sing or make up songs or verses about an interesting animal? If you know your pupils well, chances for subject enrichment and practice of basic skills can easily come to mind. However, don't forget to keep the focus on *science*.

After you have grouped some good learning activities under each generalization, arrange them in some logical teaching order. The sequence of content in the class textbook can provide the overall direction here. Remember to cluster concrete activities ahead of reading and other second-hand activities when possible.

Does noting activities seem lengthy and time consuming? It does not have to be. Most of your references will be within easy reach on your desk throughout the unit, so write down only as much as you need to plan with. Then, consult your references for details as required.

Determining Bridges (Introductions)

Now that you have located some activities for each generalization, you will need some way to introduce each of these main parts of the unit to pupils and move smoothly into each accompanying set of activities. Some teachers call this phase "bridging" because it takes the children from where they are to the beginnings of where they need to go.

A useful introduction, or bridge, relates to pupils' experiences and present understandings. It stimulates them to use their present schemata as you interact with them. Pupil responses and questions give you some insight into what they already know about the generalization or topic to be studied, including their misconceptions. The last part of the bridge also leads into the first activity in each sequence.

You may want to introduce the children to the entire unit at one time by asking questions based on all the generalizations. However, many teachers believe it is easier and more meaningful to the children to introduce only one section at a time. Of course, a brief statement about the overall unit topic should be made in any case.

Ideas for bridging into each set of activities usually can be found in the textbook or its teacher's edition. Most modern programs reflect the constructivist view of learning, as described by Piaget and later researchers (Chapter 2). They are likely to begin a unit or lesson with an opportunity for the teacher to find out what children already know and relate this to what they will learn. In most texts, a stated purpose or questions open a topical section. In some textbooks, a section may begin with an activity.

Bridges do not have to be elaborate. Often, they are easiest to do and most effective if you begin with concrete materials or familiar objects. Following are three examples.

In a primary-level unit on magnets the beginning generalization is "Magnets attract objects made of iron and steel." The teacher has gathered some magnets; others have been brought in by children. The teacher points to a pile of miscellaneous objects and the magnets and says to the class:

What are some things people can do with magnets? (A brief discussion follows.) *See what you can find out with these magnets and things. Let's work for a while. Then, be ready to tell what you found. Also, you may have questions about magnets to ask then.*

In a middle-level unit on "The Earth's Changing Surface," the beginning generalization is "Weathering and erosion constantly wear down the earth's surface." The teacher mentions to the class that the soil and broken rock they see on the earth's surface extend downward only a short distance. Below is solid rock. The teacher then asks:

What are some ways rock may get broken up and moved around on the surface?

In an upper-level unit on "Light Energy," the beginning generalization is "When light strikes a mirror at a slant, it is reflected at the same slant in the opposite direction." Each pair of children has a small mirror. Most of the mirrors have been brought from home. The teacher writes on the chalkboard:

Can you spy on your partner with a mirror without him or her being able to see you looking? (A brief discussion follows.) *To try this, tape your mirror flat against the wall. Stand in whatever places you like. Be ready to discuss what you found out.*

In each of these three examples, the children discuss what they know already or have found out in the beginning activity. When misconceptions surface, the teachers note them because they might interfere with concepts taken up in the lessons ahead. Some children have questions. Several questions will be answered in other activities of the first generalization. Some questions can be covered in other generalizations of the unit. A few questions will need individual attention. All these questions are noted by the teachers for follow up.

For additional examples of bridges, see the investigations in Appendix A of this book. Notice how each bridge ends with an "Exploratory Problem," which leads into the first activity of the investigation.

A Sample Unit

For a sample unit developed in this way, see Figure 7-2 (pages 171–5). Notice that it is written on cards. This is a convenient way to keep track of your generalizations, activities, and bridges. Suggestions for using the format follow.

Write one broad generalization at the top of each five- by eight-inch card. *This is for your reference only,* not for teaching to the children. Sections of the book may be headed by problems, topics, or themes. If one seems useful, you might prefer to first write this heading, then the generalization. Next, write your sequentially arranged activities under each generalization, leaving a space for the bridge. Then write the bridge. Be sure to relate the last part of the bridge to the first activity, so you can move smoothly into it.

The use of cards has advantages. They can be shuffled in any desired sequence. It is easy to add and take away generalizations and activities. Special sections can be fitted in: bulletin board ideas, news clippings, notes, or whatever else is desired to make the unit complete and easier to teach.

Also, notice in Figure 7-2 marginal notes for science processes written next to some

EARTH'S CHANGING SURFACE

This is a fourth-grade unit on the forces that tear down and build up the earth's surface. Children also learn how rocks are formed and several ways soil is conserved.

Fifteen periods of about 50 minutes each are planned for the unit. (See block plan on back of this card.)

(Front of card)

	April 6–10	April 13–17	April 20–24
M	Generalization I, activity 1 (Ask class for materials, act. 2.)	Gen. II, act. 1	III, act. 3 (Ask for rocks and jars Gen. IV., act. 2, 4.)
T	I, act. 2 (See custodian for mat., I, act. 3.)	II, act. 2	III, act. 6, assess. (Ask for rocks and jars, IV act. 2, 4.)
W	I, act. 3 (Ask class for materials act. 6.)	II, act. 3 or 5	Gen. IV, act. 1, 2
Th	I, act. 4 or 5 (Ask class for mat. 6.)	II, act. 4, assess.	IV, act. 2, 3
F	I, act. 5 or 6, assess. (Ask for mat. Gen. II, act. 1, and milk cartons cafeteria.)	Gen. III, act. 1, 2 (Ask volunteers project act. 3 to bring mat.)	IV, act. 4, 5 assess. (Follow up on crystal growth next week.)

Order library books. Also AV materials by March 6 for I (4), II (3), III (1, 2). Phone II (5), III (4).

(Back of card)

FIGURE 7-2

When developing your own textbook-based unit, it's convenient to keep track of everything on five- by eight-inch cards.

Gen. I. Weathering and erosion constantly wear down the earth's surface. (Class text pages 61–68.)

Bridge
How far down do you think the soil goes? What is beneath the soil? What are some ways rock may get broken up? How might broken up rocks and soil be removed? What does weathering mean? erosion?

Activities

(obs.)	1. Define weathering and erosion. Tour school grounds for examples. (Open-ended.)
(exp.)	2. Plants break rocks experiment, text p. 63. (Open-ended.)
(infer.)	3. Dirt mountain erosion demonstration, Schmidt p. 56.
	4. Films: Face of Earth (15 min.), Work of Rivers (10 min.).
	5. Read text pp. 61–68 and library books. SUMMARIZE weathering and erosion forces.
(classif.)	6. Kids find and sort picture examples of forces that bring change. Display. (Open-ended.)
	7. Haiku poetry on forces that change the earth's surface.

(Front of card)

Materials
2. Plaster of paris; bean seeds; paper cups.
3. Shovel; hose. (See custodian.)
4. MP204; MP206 (AV center).
6. *Nat'l Geographic, Arizona Highways* back issues; scissors; construction paper; paste.

Assessment
How many examples of weathering and erosion on the school grounds can you find? Find some examples we did not observe on our first tour. Make a record.

Also use end-of-section questions, p. 68.

(Back of card)

FIGURE 7-2
continued

Gen. II. Topsoil is composed of mineral, vegetable, and animal matter; topsoil is conserved in several ways. (Pages 69–77.)

Bridge
What are some reasons farmers might be interested in erosion? How might they guard against soil erosion? What makes up soil? Let's see for ourselves.

Activities
(classif.) **1.** Small group analysis of soil samples. Sort objects found. (Open-ended.)
(exp.) **2.** Plant seeds in poor and good soil samples, text p. 72. (Open-ended.)
3. Introduce six study prints on soil erosion. See "Conserving Our Soil" videotape.
4. Read text, pages 69–77, and library books. SUMMARIZE ways to conserve soil.
5. Possible visit agent, Soil Conservation Service. (Practice interview and listening skills.)

(Front of card)

Materials
1. Magnifiers; old spoons; sack of good topsoil; newspapers; clean pint milk cartons.
2. Bean seeds; sack each of good and bad soil; milk cartons.
3. SP (set of 6) 117; Vid. 440.1 (AV center).
5. Bill Johnson, Soil Cons. Service, 283-6600.

Assessment
What are some ways you might prevent erosion on our school grounds? Think about the examples you found before. Discuss these ways with two partners. Then give a report.

We don't live on farms. What difference would it make to us if most farm soil erodes?

Also use end-of-section questions, p. 77.

(Back of card)

FIGURE 7-2
continued

Gen. III. Lava flows and crustal movements continually build up the earth's surface. (Pages 77–84.)

Bridge

Does anyone know what a volcano is? What do you think makes a volcano happen? What is an earthquake? Has anyone been where there was an earthquake? Let's find out some surprising ways the earth's surface changes.

Activities

1. Film: Earthquakes and volcanoes (30 min.).
2. Film: Trembling Earth (25 min.).

(meas.)
3. Make clay models of volcanoes, p. 79. Also "seismograph," special project Hone, p. 28. (Art and construction.)
4. Guest speaker with northern California earthquake slides. (Or locate earthquake pictures.)
5. Use maps to locate active volcanoes.
6. Read text, pages 77–84, and library books. SUMMARIZE how mountains are formed.

(Front of card)

Materials

1. MP 254 (AV center).
2. MP 261 (AV center).
3. Two colors of clay; newspapers; rulers; scissors. (Seismograph volunteers, check Hone book for materials.)
4. Orville McCreedy, 286–6147. (Or, past *Nat'l Geographics,* 1989 issues.)

Assessment

Children will construct cutaway models of volcanoes and, using the models, be able to explain how volcanoes may happen.

Also use end-of-section questions, p. 84.

(Back of card)

FIGURE 7-2
continued

Gen. IV. Three kinds of rocks are formed as the earth's surface wears down and builds up.

Bridge
Thank you for bringing so many different rocks. What makes them look different? Which of these might have come from volcanoes? How else might some have been made? Before we find out, let's see how many different properties of these rocks you can observe.

Activities
(commun.)   **1.** Partners do rock description game. (20 questions—lang. develop.)
(exper.)   **2.** Crystal growing activity, p. 91. (Open-ended.)
             3. Read text, pages 85–93, and library books.
(classif.)   **4.** Sort rocks as to basic type, p. 90. (Open-ended.)
             5. SUMMARIZE gen. IV and whole unit.

(Front of card)

Materials
2. Baby food jars; string; paper clips; sugar; hot plate; teakettle; newspaper.
4. Children's rock samples—stress variety; heavy paper sacks; several hammers.

Assessment
Children will be able to control the size of "rock" crystals by varying the cooling rates of hot sugar solutions.

Children will be able to identify some properties of rocks and explain how these are clues to the rocks' formation.

Also use unit test questions, p. 93.

(Back of card)

FIGURE 7-2
continued

activities. These can remind you of what to stress in such activities. Several "open-ended" notes serve the same function. Open-ended activities are often the easiest and best way to meet pupils' individual differences in unit teaching.

Finally, note that there is a specific assessment section for each of the four main parts of this unit. For generalizations I and II, assessments are stated as questions. For III and IV, they are stated as pupil behaviors to observe. Which method do you prefer? Some teachers use both. (Details about objectives and assessment appear shortly in this chapter.)

A fine unit does not spring full blown from its first organization. The more you teach it, the more you will want to modify it. Activities may be strengthened, the teaching order changed, scope increased, and so on. With experience, you can often detect from inspection alone where your first organization will falter with your class. In the meantime, you learn largely from teaching it and noting what happens.

The Planning/Teaching Order

When you *teach* a textbook-based unit as described here, you *reverse* the order in which it was planned. Look at it this way—

In *planning* the unit, you determine:

G eneralizations, then

A ctivities for each generalization, then a

B ridge for each generalization's set of activities.

But in *teaching* the unit, you begin with a:

B ridge, which leads into the first of several

A ctivities, which lead into an understanding of each

G eneralization in your unit.

In other words, this is a GAB–BAG approach to planning and teaching a text-based unit. It turns what may be expository and deductive

textbook lessons into inductive lessons that can be front-loaded with concrete activities before reading and other vicarious learning take place. You don't have to be a science prodigy to teach this way. Nearly everything in the unit comes from others. The specific organization, though, is uniquely yours.

Some Further Considerations in Making Textbook-Based Units

Activity Availability. A Slavic proverb says, "To eat bread, there first must be bread in the basket." The main reason to make a text-based unit is to free yourself from text-bound teaching. But to do so requires first that some appropriate activities are available.

If you want numerous *concrete* activities, there will be few for young children in such topics as heredity, atoms, the earth's interior, space travel, cell structure of living things, animal migration, and so on. An easy way to know the topics for which much *is* available is to check the contents of a recent resource activities book, such as those listed on page 168. These are likely to be useful guides. Be wary of topics that do not appear in such books.

If you want supporting materials such as AV aids, models, and so on, check early on to see what the district or school instructional resource center offers. When the center offers little or nothing and few concrete activities are available, trying to make a textbook-based unit is apt to be frustrating and unproductive.

Which Format Works Best? An easy way for an argument to start between two science educators is for one to claim a better way of laying out a textbook-based unit. You, too, may want to rearrange or add elements in the format I have presented. My basic format, and three workable variations for you to consider, are listed in Table 7-1. Of the three variations, many of my students like the last one (far right) most. But before you make changes, please read the rest of this chapter for additional perspective.

TABLE 7-1
Four ways to lay out a textbook-based unit.

generalization	objective(s)	generalization(s)	topic or problem
bridge	bridge	objective(s)	objective(s)
activities	activities	assessment	introduction
materials	materials	introduction	activities
assessment (based on "constant" objectives)	assessment	activities	materials
		materials	assessment

LESSONS AND BLOCK PLANS

How is a lesson organized? How do you distribute the lessons of a whole science unit among the daily or other periods available for instruction? We will consider both matters in this section and begin with the parts of a lesson. Let's consult again the completely planned unit (Figure 7-2) on pages 171–175 of this book. It is a realistic model designed to contain both good and improvable features—the kind often developed by a student teacher or beginning teacher.

Notice that this unit is organized around four generalizations. For our purposes, think of each generalization and its activities as a separate subunit, or *one complete lesson*. Therefore, four lessons make up this unit. Although it is customary to think of a "lesson" as a daily planned period, you will find it easier to teach and plan with broader learning segments in mind.

One complete lesson has three phrases:

1. *Introducing* phase: Meaning and purpose for study are established.
2. *Finding out* phase: Children engage in purposeful activities and gradually develop knowledge of concepts and generalizations.
3. *Summary/applying* phase: They summarize, apply, and assess what they have learned.

Seldom in true *unit* teaching will you go through all three phases of the lesson cycle in one daily time period. Developing purpose within a meaningful context may take only a few minutes, but it can take considerably longer. The finding out phase may take several hours. The summary/applying segment may vary from a half hour to an hour or more. Following is your possible role in each of the three phases.

Introducing

When you begin a lesson, you start out with a certain amount of goodwill from the children. Whether it grows or vanishes depends on the interest and meaning worked into the lesson.

An introduction that gets pupils to think about their experiences, or that provides an experience, builds interest and usually reveals what they already know—including misconceptions. It may also provoke some pupil questions that can be added to those you raise in the introduction. Many teachers write these questions on a chart, so they can be addressed during the lesson or rest of the unit. To answer questions may require some planning: how to find out, materials needed, and so on. Much of this can be done before the finding out segment begins.

A key to success in this phase is to connect with children's prior knowledge. To do this, apply the concept or generalization to be learned in a problem that makes sense to them. "How can a small child lift a large adult on a seesaw?" is a challenge they are likely to eagerly try to explain, show on the chalkboard, and demonstrate on the playground. Learning that "The force of a lever can be increased by moving the fulcrum closer to the load" will come in the next phase, after further challenges and activities with levers that look nothing like a seesaw.

You might begin this phase in any of several ways. Interesting challenges can come from applying a concept to everyday events, exploring science materials, from a news event, a short story, a demonstration that works or doesn't work ("How can you get the siphon to work?"), a discrepant event ("What makes the ice cubes sink in one glass of clear liquid and float in the other one?") and so on. What you want is something meaningful to think about that relates to the organizing concepts or generalization.

The beginning part of the lesson, then, is where you pose an understandable problem, listen to learn what pupils already know, probably raise further questions from them, and help pupils plan to find out in an overall sense. When you make a text-based unit, *the introducing phase of a lesson and bridging are the same.*

Finding Out

The next part of the lesson is where children pursue their purposes and challenges you raise for activities you've selected. They do experiments, investigate, see demonstrations, explore sequences and frames of a videodisc, view a videotape or filmstrip, read trade books and the class text, and perform other activities. Notice that I've placed the hands-on activities before the more passive ones. First-hand experiences usually provide the background and vocabulary for better understanding vicarious instructional materials that may follow—videotapes, filmstrips, and books, for example—that explain and reinforce the ideas being studied.

Some science programs make a clear distinction between first- and second-hand activities. They divide the finding-out part of the lesson cycle into two phases: a discovery phase, for first-hand activities only; and a concept development or elaboration phase, for working with instructional materials such as books or videotapes that more fully explain the ideas that pupils began to form during their first-hand investigations. This results in a four-part lesson cycle: introducing, discovering, elaborating, and summary/applying.

Summary/Applying

The last part of the lesson is when, through discussion and other means, you help children build a clearer and more general understanding of the concepts and generalization they are constructing. You want them now to see the forest, after they have lingered long among the trees. This is the time to apply and extend what they have learned and, in the process, assess how well they grasp the big ideas.

You might have pupils read or review the pertinent textbook section just before this phase, so information is fresh in mind. Questions not already answered are addressed now. Children may also give reports and show models or drawings to explain the big ideas. You might ask pupils to define in their own words a concept studied. (What does *erosion* mean to you?) Or have them complete a concept map (see page 186) that shows how concepts they have studied are related. This is the time to bring up new examples of applications, and encourage pupils to find more. These actions can be even more productive if done in cooperative groups, because then pupils will continually interact with others to share and sharpen ideas. You might also give a test in which children need to apply their knowledge. (You'll see more detailed ways to assess learning later.)

All of the preceding actions allow you to assess what children have learned, including misconceptions. At the same time, they induce children to build new knowledge and refine what they have already constructed. This is consistent with the constructivist approach to learning.

How to Make a Block Plan

Before we consider the details of how much time to allow for teaching different parts of a unit, reread the sample unit (Figure 7-2) to get a sense of the following features. First, notice that the topic is a broad one. This is typical of a text-based unit. If you go for more depth by adding activities to those of the text's, something has to give. You have only so much time to teach science. It may be best to downplay or even drop one or two generalizations rather than to skim over the entire unit.

How do you decide which generalizations to cut down or drop? Look for those that offer the least chance for children to have concrete experiences. In our unit example, the third generalization on mountain building offers the fewest concrete possibilities for nine-year-olds. But *volcanoes* and *earthquakes* are part of the mountain-building process! Their spectacular qualities make them highly interesting. Also, your pupils may be living in an area that has occasional earthquakes. In cases like this, you need to use judgment. Probably it would be better to downplay this generalization than to eliminate it. Do you agree?

Please turn now to the block plan for this unit on page 171. It was made by a student teacher. She has selected most of the activities in the unit to teach to a particular class within a given time frame. Given another class or time limit, she might choose to teach fewer or more activities, which would cause her to change the present block plan. Overall, she has done a good job of allocating activities and planning ahead. Notice how she allows lead time to ask children for some common materials.

Can you see any places where you would have planned differently? Probably she will need more time for the summary/applying phase in several lessons, so a few more activities will need to be omitted. If she heeds the children's interests, she may also need more time for the rock-collection activities (1, 4) in generalization IV.

When you have a block plan like this, based on generalizations and organized as suggested, you will probably find that you can soon teach well *without making formal plans for each scheduled science period.* So a block plan can save you much time.

Here are some things to consider when you work on block plans. It is better to reserve large blocks of time for daily study than to schedule science for 20 minutes or so a day, 2 or 3 days a week. A few experienced teachers seem to do much even within short sessions. However, it usually takes too much time to set up and distribute materials in a hands-on program for short periods to work well. Forty minutes is a more practical time period at the primary level, with up to an hour for older pupils.

A daily contact with ideas and activities of the unit gives continuity and reinforcement to learning. It also heightens the child's continuing sense of participation and interest. Notice that the *total* time allotted to science during the year, say 60 hours, need not be greater with large blocks of time for units. While science may not be taught during part of the school year as a result, it still uses the available time more efficiently.

There is an exception to these suggestions about time. When the class grows plants or otherwise waits for slow changes to take place, an every-other-day schedule may be more workable, for example. In most cases, it will be best to let the condition of the objects influence when lessons are taught. Even careful advance planning seldom guarantees that living things will act in predictable ways.

The planning shown in the block-plan example does not mean rigid restrictions have been placed on the time, activities, or sequence involved. Flexibility is really a requirement, rather than an option. If the videotape you requested does not arrive on time or the sun fails to shine for the solar heat experiment, something else needs to be ready. And although a certain amount of time is set aside, it may need to be expanded or cut down, depending on what happens in the classroom. So the block plan you start with may look quite different by the time the unit is completed. How things go from day to day will probably cause you to continually modify the plan.

Should everyone put into block plans what appears in this one? Planning is a highly individual matter. Thirty experienced teachers in one college summer session course were asked to make a block plan for a science unit. Wide differences appeared in the notes they felt were necessary for their own guidance. All but one teacher strongly endorsed the making of a block plan. But few agreed as to exactly what it should contain.

HOW WELL CAN YOU CONSTRUCT SCIENCE UNITS?

Making and teaching a unit is a surer way to become competent than merely reading about it. If you do go ahead, some guidelines can help you judge your unit. Following are some questions you can ask yourself to evaluate your work. They reflect most of the important points so far in this chapter and preceding ones. Look over the list carefully. You may want to omit some questions, add a few of your own, and arrange some order of priority among them. Concentrate at first on what you think is most important. In revisions and in later units, work on other points. It takes a lot of practice to do *everything* well.

1. Is the unit based on a small number of basic generalizations (or problems or topics or themes)?

2. Do the lesson bridges relate to pupils' experiences, provide feedback about their present knowledge, and move smoothly into the first activity of each sequence?

3. Are some open-ended activities included?

4. Can a variety of science processes be used in the activities?

5. Are the activities appropriate for the pupils' abilities?

6. Do reading and other second-hand activities, when used, usually follow concrete activities?

7. Are useful activities from other subject areas integrated into learning sequences?

8. Do pupils *apply* their knowledge in assessments or simply recall it?

9. Does the block plan allot enough time for children to learn what is proposed?

10. Does the block plan anticipate needed materials far enough in advance?

OBJECTIVES AND THE ASSESSMENT OF SCIENCE LEARNING

When you design and teach units and lessons, it is important to keep objectives in mind. In most units, you will want children to achieve both knowledge and process objectives and gain positive attitudes. Usually, the science curriculum guide or textbook manual contains statements of possible objectives. From these sources, you can select those that seem to suit your pupils. Sometimes, though, the stated objectives are not much help. They may be vague or stated in such detail that you lose your overall sense of direction.

This brings up a related issue: Should you rely heavily on detailed statements of objectives written by others? Although these may be helpful, you are likelier to get better results if your mind is organized than if the organization is only on paper.

Knowledge

One good way to ease the load of coping with many objectives is to reduce their number. You can cut down knowledge objectives by working toward concepts and generalizations rather than isolated facts. Some teachers recognize this, but then wrongly conclude that they can bypass the facts and directly teach these abstractions. This is unfortunate because what children know about concepts and generalizations depends much on what they construct from the concrete facts they study.

Take, for example, the primary-level generalization "Magnets attract things made of iron or steel." Children begin their study with concrete materials that bring out a fairly large number of facts. The children learn that a magnet attracts nails and metal coat hangers and that these are made of iron. They find that scissors and some pins are attracted and that these are made of steel. They test other metal and nonmetal objects and discover that these are not attracted.

As pupils learn these facts, vocabulary is introduced by the teacher as needed to label emerging concepts. Words such as *steel, iron,* and *rubber* are used by children as they mentally combine objects made of similar materials. Gradually, they also combine these concepts, and so a hazy approximation of the generalization develops in their minds.

But don't expect children to neatly state the generalization. This may not reveal their true understanding. Stating generalizations properly often requires formal operational thinking. Instead, ask children to demonstrate their knowledge by *applying* it in observable ways. This means they should do more

than simply recall some facts. A higher level of understanding is revealed if they can use their knowledge of a generalization to *explain, predict,* or *control* objects and events, preferably those that are new to them. You may recall that this is also how scientists use these abstractions, but of course at more complex levels.

To "explain" is to tell how objects may have interacted to cause or prevent change. Children also explain when they give and justify new examples of a concept.

To "predict" means to forecast, using present information, a future observation of an object or event.

To "control" means to show how an object or event can be changed, or how a change can be slowed, speeded up, or prevented.

In a scientific view, to explain, predict, or control objects and events is *the* performance objective of all knowledge objectives. Consider it a "constant" objective, since it does not change, while individual generalizations do. If you keep this in mind, it becomes easier both to state and keep track of objectives. Notice next how this works.

Suppose your school requires statements of observable performance objectives in lesson plans, or you wish to state them. Here is how you might do so with the magnet example used previously:

Pupils will

■ Explain why some objects are not attracted.

■ Predict some objects that will and will not be attracted.

■ Show how to prevent a magnet from picking up an attractable object.

Suppose a middle-grade unit generalization is "Weathering and erosion constantly wear down the earth's surface." Your stated objectives might be as follows:

Pupils will

■ Explain why some rocks weather more than others.

■ Predict places where gullies may form.

■ Draw a sketch that shows two ways to slow erosion on a bare hillside.

Suppose in an upper-grade unit on the human body a generalization is "Automatic reflex actions (blinking, reaction to sudden pain, etc.) have survival value." Your stated objectives might be as follows:
Pupils will

■ Explain why automatic blinking has greater survival value than conscious blinking.

■ Predict two situations that will trigger an automatic reflex.

■ Make a sketch that shows how an injury might prevent a reflex action.

Notice that in the preceding sample objectives, no mention was made of how well a child should do or under what conditions evaluation should take place. Because of the many differences in pupils, we must rely on our judgment in these matters. This is true whether we are concerned with knowledge or process objectives.

For more samples of knowledge-type performance objectives for assessment, see the investigations in Appendix A of this book. The generalizations for these investigations include objectives typically patterned after the explain-predict-control model.

Science Processes

You can also reduce to manageable size the number of process objectives you work with. Remember, there are only about seven broad processes in most programs: classifying, observing, measuring, inferring and predicting, communicating, and experimenting (COMIC–E). These, too, are "constant" objectives in that we want children to constantly apply them in activities and so become ever more competent in their use. Each of these broad categories of processes can help you to recall a cluster of related subprocesses, if these have been learned reasonably well. To do this, you will want to refer to the list of processes on page 90 from time to time. The investigations in Part II of this book can also furnish many chances to practice the teaching of these processes. Notice that in both places they are stated as observable pupil actions. You can easily convert these statements into performance objectives for your own units, if needed.

Process objectives are assessed by providing a situation that requires the child to use the process. Most teachers appraise these objectives by observing children in action during the regular activity time. But don't expect dramatic changes in a pupil's general ability to apply a broad process from one lesson to the next. This kind of growth requires long periods of time and practice in a variety of subject-matter contexts.

Whenever you plan a science activity, try to think of the broad thinking process involved. Then, decide which specific subprocesses, such as those on page 90, can be used in the activity. As you work with children, ask questions from time to time that generate these actions in the children. (For in-context examples, see the marginal notes in the investigations of Appendix A. Also check the accompanying samples of objectives.)

Scientific Attitudes

Recall from Chapter 4, page 97, that scientific attitudes of children are often shown by their behaviors in four broad categories: curiosity, inventiveness, critical thinking, and persistence. The sample behaviors listed under these categories are the kinds of actions you look for when you appraise growth in attitudes. As with process, good times to do so are during hands-on activities and discussions. Additional opportunities will be described in more detail shortly. Remember, though, that broad attitudes cannot be developed quickly. They are a long-range byproduct of the quality of learning activities and general atmosphere of your classroom.

Putting Assessment Into Perspective

"I can show you how to assess pupil achievement in many valid and reliable ways, but I can't tell you what grades to give." An outstanding test specialist began his college class on assessment techniques with those words a long time ago. As a fledgling student of education in that class, I didn't understand at first what he meant. After all, wasn't the *purpose* of assessment to give (teacher) and get (student) grades?

Some test experts see a difference between *assessment* and *evaluation,* even though the two terms now generally mean the same thing. To them, assessment is finding out *what* pupils have achieved. Evaluation is placing a *value* or "grade" on what is achieved.

There are only two basic ways to grade. We can compare a child's achievement to that of others in a defined population and place a value on it. ("Jim got more right than two-thirds of the class on this test—that ought to be an A. But this class didn't do as well as last year's—I'd better make it a high B.") Or we can define and pose some objectives for pupils and place a value on how many objectives were achieved. ("Ann met 7 out of 10 objectives—that deserves an A. But maybe only 9 or more should count as an A. Should I get an opinion from another third-grade teacher?")

The point is that placing a value on achievement (A, B, C or Superior, Good, Fair, etc.) is arbitrary. It depends on who makes the rules and how consistently they are followed. We typically are required to do some type of grading, of course, but this is best done within school district guidelines. Decisions on pupil promotion, retention, remedial instruction, and the like are strongly linked to grades. The lack of a common policy among and within schools in a district only invites trouble. Does teacher consistency in grading mean that grades awarded will be perceived by everyone as "fair"? It definitely helps; but fairness, to borrow from a favorite cliché, is in the eye of the beholder.

This chapter reflects the view that the primary purpose of assessment is to improve pupil achievement. By finding out what and how well students achieve, we can improve our teaching.

Is assessment something you do *to* children or *with* them? Each emphasis reflects a different outlook. Have you ever been asked to do something important without knowing exactly how your performance was going to be appraised? Do you like the feeling? When we work out standards or expectations *with* pupils, they usually achieve more and see the assessment process in a different light. It puts their intelligence to work, so they can better guide their own learning within the limits of their maturity and experience. If you want to maximize your teaching effectiveness, make clear to children what makes up success in *everything* they do in your science program. You'll need then to assess together a broad array of their work, not simply tests.

Even the noblest of intentions must heed the limits of time. In a previous section, you saw some ways to zero in on objectives that are most likely to yield a rich payoff. Using time productively requires making many further judgments. It will help now to see when chances for assessment generally arise.

We have three main opportunities to appraise pupils' abilities: before, during, and after teaching the activities in each lesson. The introduction or bridge of a lesson is a good place to assess pupils' present knowledge, including misconceptions. This is called *diagnostic* assessment. It can be done in a written pretest, but usually the questions you put to the children serve better, because you can follow up what they say.

Appraising pupils' work behaviors during activities is *formative* assessment. This is an apt word, since what we observe helps to shape or form our immediate, responsive teaching behaviors. This quick feedback to pupils, in turn, helps them to form improved learning behaviors.

Finally, when we assess pupil achievement after activities, we practice *summative* assessment. To do so, we can ask questions when we summarize and review previous activities. We can also appraise children's projects or other completed work, and use tests. Let's now examine in more detail ways to assess science achievement.

WAYS TO ASSESS PUPIL ACHIEVEMENT

Publisher's science programs have traditionally been weak on assessment. They are now far better. While some testing of facts and simple understandings is still found, newer programs are likely to offer many chances to appraise broad concepts and science processes, and supply more worthwhile material than you probably will have time to use. So rather than having to *create* assessment tools, you'll typically need to judge which is best to apply.

Teacher guides or packets may provide materials and guidelines for all of these assessment possibilities and more:

- Teacher observation
- Written tests
- Performance tests
- Journal writing/Activity logs
- Concept maps
- Projects
- Portfolios

See now some things that are good to know within each of these chances for appraisal.

Teacher Observation

The job of teaching is inexact at best. We might view it as a series of consecutively developed hypotheses. That is, each thing we do or say is a kind of hypothesis that we are uncertain will be "accepted" (learned) by the children. If much teaching takes place before feedback shows that learning has occurred, we may make many unwarranted assumptions.

We can observe, and often help pupils stay on track, in whole-class settings, but the most productive times are likely to be in individual and small-group situations. There are many chances for informal teacher–child contacts during the finding out or activity times in lessons. Notice what your pupils say and do when they interact with you, a partner, or other members of a small group. What you observe gives you data for fast self-correction or for assisting individual pupils, if needed.

The quickest way to find out if pupils grasp concepts and processes is to ask questions and listen carefully to responses. By fashioning further questions to follow up responses, you can detect misconceptions and may be able to quickly address them. You can also discover much more about what students are learning.

Time will prevent you from getting around to each pupil in every science period, but there is rarely a need for that. If you have organized your class into cooperative learning or other groups, it's usually enough to check what each is doing and to question individual pupils as warranted. When possible, distribute your questions evenly among individuals and groups over each week or so. This will give you a reasonably complete picture of how all your pupils are doing. To make this a habit, try using a chart on which you place a check after working with someone or a group. Don't be surprised if you overlook many children at first. It often takes a systematic effort to properly sample everyone's learnings.

Written Tests

You'll find a variety of tests in the teacher guides and assessment guides of science programs. Written tests are typically found at ends of lessons or chapters and units. They are designed to assess pupil understanding of science words, concepts, and generalizations; the ability to apply them; and ability to do some critical thinking. Besides objective items, such as multiple-choice questions, most programs now include open-ended or essay questions for pupils at grade three and above.

Paper-and-pencil tests can be another useful tool in assessing learning, but should not be used as the only or main means of appraisal. A big drawback of tests is that the results come too late to affect the way the unit or lessons are taught. The immediate, corrective feedback necessary for effective teaching is absent if we rely on tests alone. Since only limited time is available, it's not always possible to go back and effectively take care of incompletely understood or misconceived material.

Another drawback of written tests is that it's hard to test science processes in that format. The processes are used most often in a context where children manipulate science materials. In other words, they perform some observable actions that demonstrate their ability to apply one or more processes, usually with their knowledge of a concept. Process is better appraised in a *performance test*.

Performance Tests

For a quick reminder of a wide range of operations pupils may demonstrate in performance tests, look at the summary of science processes on pages 90–91. Assessing these operations requires pupils to be placed in contexts that allow them to gather and process data.

In its purest form, a performance test has the child demonstrate operations with concrete materials. For instance, the test may ask a child to *measure* several, irregularly-shaped rocks to find the one with the greatest volume. Besides the rocks, materials might include a wide-mouth, clear plastic cup, spoon, marking pen, and container of water. To demonstrate this process, the child might partly fill the cup and mark the water level with the pen. Next, she might slowly submerge and remove each rock with the spoon, taking care each time to mark the water level and not spill water. If the process is performed properly, the child identifies the rock with the highest water level as having the most volume and the test item is scored correct.

Another performance test might ask a pupil to *infer* the identity of three unknown leaves by consulting a chart with descriptions of leaves. A variation might ask the pupil to *classify* a half-dozen leaves, by putting them into two or more groups and stating the observable property or properties she used to do so. If the groupings are consistent with the stated properties, the answer is scored correct.

Working with concrete materials is not always necessary. Pupils may classify pictures of leaves or animals, for instance. Or a chart may be supplied that shows data from an investigation, and the child asked to interpret the data and draw a conclusion.

When children are capable writers, some performance tests may be completed entirely with words. For *experimenting*, this problem might appear:

> Suppose you want to find out whether bean plants will grow faster with Fertilizer A than with Fertilizer B. How could you set up an experiment to find out?

Or, the problem could address a specific part of the experiment:

> What variables do you need to control?

In some tests with similar problems, the child needs only to select the best answer from several options supplied in a problem—a form of multiple-choice item, though longer than most.

Performance tests with concrete objects obviously take the most time to set up, but those you are likely to see require only a few and easily found materials. And multimedia programs may offer assessment kits that include everything needed. Directions are clear and scoring uncomplicated.

Even so, some teachers with active, hands-on science programs bypass performance tests. They believe that they get all the assessment data they need by observing children at work and interacting with them during regular activity times and follow-up discussions. This may be possible with a wide array of process-rich activities and systematic observing. But mandated performance tests are becoming more prevalent at school district, state, and national levels. Avoiding them entirely in the regular science program may cause pupils to do less well on such tests.

Activity Logs and Science Journals

You saw earlier (pages 80–81) that recording data from an activity in a notebook or log is usually necessary when observations occur over time. Doing so makes it likelier that pupils will keep track of changes, observe more carefully, and think about what they are doing. Teachers may also ask children to respond in writing to questions in activities, for similar reasons. Notice how often questions appear in the investigations and activities of Appendix A in this book. This practice is typical of elementary school science. Pupils can appraise their recordings by comparing them with those of other group members. When data conflict, it's only natural for them to pursue reasons.

Today the concept of *writing to learn* is applied in all subjects. It holds much value for science. Many teachers have their pupils keep a science journal, which also may serve for recording data. A journal offers opportunities to improve science learning and practice important writing skills at the same time. Writing requires thinking, which changes with different purposes.

Descriptive writing can be used, among other possibilities, to identify things: "Can you describe an animal (plant, habitat, etc.) so well, without naming it, that your partner can tell what it is?" Or, "Make a chart that shows the properties of these rocks. Can your partner match the rocks to your descriptions?" Assessing these writings is straightforward. If there is a problem, both partners can work to figure out why.

Defining concepts in writing, before and after instruction, enables children to assess for themselves what they have gained from their studies. The questions, "What is soil? What is it made of?" may yield quite different results before and after lessons.

Creative writing also can and should be linked to concepts being studied. If your pupils are writing a story about an imaginary visit to an outer planet, you might ask them to correctly use recently learned words, such as orbit, acceleration, and zero gravity. Cooperative learning groups can judge whether concepts are used correctly and consult with you as needed.

You can also ask pupils at different levels to write summaries of what they have learned in a lesson, give an opinion and defend it, write a persuasive letter, compose interview questions, and do much other writing. Each form can be assessed for clarity, logic, and completeness.

It is important to have your pupils assess their own writing as much as possible, through clear directions and standards. You'll probably want to *sample* their work from time to time, but don't end up *doing* their work.

Concept Maps

One message from researchers in human learning is especially clear: Organization and meaning go together. The better we are able to relate new information to what we already know, the easier it is to remember and use it. Science programs now commonly employ several different graphic organizers to help children construct meaningful relationships among the facts and concepts they learn. The *concept map* is probably the most used organizer. It's also an excellent means to assess conceptual knowledge.

Figure 7-3 shows a simple concept map that pupils might complete after some in-

FIGURE 7-3

A concept map.

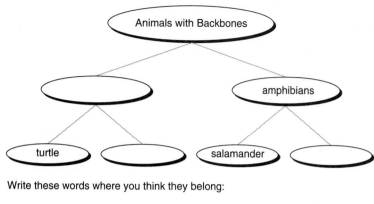

Write these words where you think they belong:

frog   reptiles   lizard

struction on body structures and functions of amphibians and reptiles. Notice that, under "amphibians," pupils need only to supply another example: "frog." On the left, both the larger concept of "reptile" and then "lizard" are needed. Other ways to assess understanding would be to omit all the words now in the map, or have children make their own map.

Pupils often make different concept maps after receiving the same instruction. This happens even when they understand all the concepts in the way you intend. They may simply view relationships among the concepts differently. So it's important for them to regularly compare their maps with partners and interact with you to more fully assess what they have learned.

Projects

It's a good idea to view science projects as normal and regular extensions of concepts and generalizations studied by the whole class. This offers many chances for pupils to take on projects, and they are more likely to do their own work. It also makes assessment simpler, less formal, and more frequent than when projects are reserved for science fairs.

A good project usually requires self-assessment from start to finish. If guidelines are simple, and your comments regarding

success are consistent, pupils will develop judgment in assessing their efforts during projects and when reporting them. Let's look again at the simplified project form introduced in Chapter 6, with its first three steps now stated in the present tense, to see how it may further this goal. Questions in parentheses after each step are assessment criteria for you to consider, and for teaching to children when appropriate.

What do I want to find out? (Is the problem clear? Is there enough time to find out? Is it too easy or hard?)

What materials do I need? (What substitute materials can be used, if necessary?)

What do I do? (What exact steps are needed? What's the best order?)

What did I find out? (Does this answer the problem? Is this jumping to a conclusion?)

When you appraise project reports, either written or oral, consider keeping in mind the process acronym, COMIC–E. It can help you to determine if and how children use the processes.

Projects also give many chances for pupils to display the scientific attitudes of *critical thinking* (Are the parts of the report logical? consistent?), *persistence* (Is there evidence that the child overcame difficulties?), *inventiveness* (Was the child resourceful in substituting materials, or otherwise imaginative?), and *curiosity* (Does the child ask further questions, and want to find out more from books, people, or another project?). When you notice behaviors like these and give positive comments, you reinforce them.

As mentioned before, children do better at oral than written reports. But not all oral reports are artfully constructed models of clarity. If I were asked to say only one thing about oral reports it would be this: Encourage children to give them in their own words, with only occasional glances at notes, if possible. It's your best assurance that they understand, and others will comprehend, what they are saying.

Student Portfolios

Would you like to cultivate more self-assessment abilities in pupils? motivate increased effort in learning? show parents tangible and understandable evidence of what their children are learning? If so, consider a *portfolio* for each child. This is a sampling of work over time, collected and stored in a folder. It gives observable evidence of knowledge, processes, and attitudes gained by the child over one or more science units. The work record may appear in any or all of these forms:

- Tests—end of lesson, unit, performance
- Activity log pages
- Project reports
- Book reports
- List of books read, with annotations
- Concept maps, other graphic organizers
- Charts
- Graphs
- Science journal pages
- Creative stories
- Science words learned
- Artwork

These materials may be stored in a standard expandable folder, or a larger folder cut from poster board. Should you have a separate science portfolio? Or is it better to reserve a section for science in a more comprehensive portfolio? Primary-level teachers lean more toward the comprehensive type. Unless some material is sent home periodically or discarded, either type gets overstuffed and hard to store or manage.

Both the child and you should select items for the portfolio. Everything should be dated, so common items in a category can be paired or otherwise put in order by time, and progress observed. Guide children to look for improvements in their work, and to discuss examples they have selected with their groups. Encourage them to pair an original effort with an improved version whenever possible. This can make them more conscious of their progress and help develop pride in work done well. It can also provide incentive for producing more work of good quality.

To help children set goals for themselves, periodically have them review and think carefully about their work samples. This might be done monthly or at the end of a unit. Some teachers ask their pupils to write thoughtful responses to these two questions:

What do I feel good about?

What do I want to improve?

Responses to the second question can make it easy to set goals with children. At the next periodic review, they can examine their portfolios for evidence that the goals were met.

SUMMARY

Teaching that gets good results requires organization. How we organize depends on whether we work with an activity-centered program, a multimedia program, a curriculum guide, or science textbooks.

Activity-centered programs feature hands-on science and use methods compatible with those described in this and other recent books on elementary science education. Typically produced after years of development and try-outs, they offer many rich opportunities for children to learn science through first-hand experiences.

Multimedia programs offer a wide array of materials and methods. They may be organized around a core of books or a set of videodiscs. A complete program offers a wealth of possibilities for first-hand and vicarious learning, but some schools may adopt only part of a program, usually a series of textbooks or the equivalent.

School district curriculum guides are likely to have two uses. They contain local policies for science teaching, and they supplement adopted textbooks with locally available resources.

Modern textbook series offer excellent teaching aids in the teacher editions that accompany pupil books. Still, almost any text can be usefully supplemented by integrating local resources and some open-ended activities.

Some teachers want a more inductive and flexible approach to science than is possible with a textbook format. This can be done, while keeping the benefits of structure and well-written subject matter, by making a textbook-based unit. Its quality, though, is strongly linked to the availability of local teaching resources. The acronym GAB–BAG is an easy way to remember how to make and teach a textbook-based unit.

Lessons ordinarily have an introductory, finding out, and summary/applying phase. In unit teaching, only rarely are all three phases of a lesson cycle completed within a daily science period of 30 to 60 minutes. A block plan is an efficient way to organize what, within a unit, will be taught to a particular class in a given time period. It may change as time and classes vary.

Effective teaching is more likely when we have objectives in mind rather than if they are only on paper. Essentially, we want children to be able to *apply* knowledge and science processes, within a context of appropriate attitudes. The explain–predict–control model for knowledge and the COMIC–E acronym for processes are simply devices to help you keep these "constant" objectives in mind. Assessment of objectives occurs mainly at three times: before activities (diagnostic assessment), during them (formative assessment), and after activities (summative assessment).

This chapter reflects the view that the primary purpose of assessment is to improve pupil achievement. By finding out what and how well students achieve, we can improve our teaching. Pupil achievement can be appraised in many ways, including teacher observation, written and performance tests, journal and activity log writings, concept maps, projects, and portfolios.

SUGGESTED READINGS

Barnes, Lehman W. and Marianne B. Barnes. "Assessment, Practically Speaking." *Science and Children* 28(6):14–15 (March 1991). (An introduction to performance testing.)

Elliott, David, and Kathleen Carter. "School Science and the Pursuit of Knowledge—Deadends and All." *Science and Children* 24(8):9–12 (May 1987). (Points out some of the inadequacies of straight textbook teaching. Shows how to enrich lessons.)

Hein, George (Ed). *The Assessment of Hands-On Elementary Science Programs.* Washington, DC: National Science Teachers Association, 1990. (New assessment approaches for grades K–8 that focus on thinking processes.)

James, Robert K., and Shirley M. Hord. "Implementing Elementary Science Programs." *School Science and Mathematics* 88(4):315–34 (April 1988). (Detailed analysis of what it takes to ensure the fullest and best use of a quality science program.)

Linn, Marcia C. "Free Choice Experiences: How Do They Help Students Learn?" *Science Educa-*

tion 64(2):237–48 (April 1980). (Direct teaching of how to experiment was more effective than when students freely chose activities for the same purpose. But a combination of direct teaching first with free-choice activities afterward was best. Implications here for combining structured unit teaching with follow-up learning center and project activities.)

Mechling, Kenneth R., and Donna F. Oliver. *Science Teaches Basic Skills,* Handbook 1, Principals' Project. Washington, D.C.: National Science Teachers Association, 1983. (Shows many ways to incorporate the 3 Rs and other subjects into science units and lessons.)

Sample Investigations and Activities

□ ACTIVITY: How Are the Colors Made in Comic Strips?

NEEDED

colored comic strips from different newspapers   strong hand lens

TRY THIS

1. Study different comic strip pictures with a hand lens.

2. Notice how many colors are made from only a few colors.

3. Notice that some dots may be printed side by side. Or, one colored dot may be printed partly over another.

4. Observe how different shades are made by changing the distance between dots.
    a. What side-by-side colored dots do you see? What colors do they make?
    b. What overprinted colors do you see? What colors do they make?
    c. In what ways are cartoon colors from different newspapers alike? Different?

(*Teaching Comment:* An opaque projector is ideal for analyzing colored comics. Projecting the picture greatly magnifies it and makes the color printing techniques easier to notice.)

■ INVESTIGATION: The Makeup of Colored Liquids

You know that a colored liquid can be made by mixing two or more colors. Most inks and dyes are made in that way. Some of the colors mixed to make another color are surprising.

EXPLORATORY PROBLEM

How can you find out the colors that make up a colored dye or ink?

NEEDED

food coloring (red, blue, green, yellow)   scissors
four toothpicks   baby food jar, half full of water
waxed paper   white paper towel

TRY THIS

1. Cut some strips from a white paper towel. Make them about 10 by 2 centimeters (4 by $\frac{3}{4}$ inches).

2. Put one drop of red food coloring and one of blue on waxed paper. Mix them.

3. Touch the toothpick to the coloring. Make a sizable dot on the middle of one strip.

4. Hold the strip in a small jar that is about half full of water. The colored dot should be just above the water level (Figure A-1).

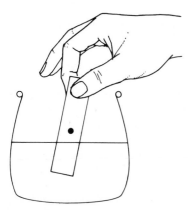

FIGURE A-1

5. What happens to the coloring as water is soaked up past the colored dot? (This may take a minute or longer.) How many colors appear as the colored dot spreads out?

DISCOVERY PROBLEMS

observing   **A.** What colors are in other food coloring samples? How are different brands of the same colors alike or different?

inferring   **B.** Try a game with a partner. Mix drops from several food colors, then test them on strips. Keep a record. Remove the tested strips from the jar and let them dry. Can your partner tell which food colors were mixed for each strip? Switch places with your partner. Can you tell what mixed colors were used for your partner's strips?

observing   **C.** What colors make up some inks? Also, do different brands of the same colored ink contain the same colors? Get some washable colored inks and test them.

observing   **D.** What colors are in some colored fruits and vegetables? Try beets, red cabbage, blueberries, and other examples. Crush a bit of the food in water. Let the colored liquid stand overnight before testing. How are the colors of some foods alike? Different?

TEACHING COMMENT

PREPARATION AND BACKGROUND

The basic process of this investigation is called paper chromatography. The separate pigments that make up the color of a dye are adsorbed at slightly different rates by the paper. This has the effect of spreading out the pigments, which makes them visible. Only washable (nonpermanent) dyes will work.

Blank newspaper strips cut from page edges are sometimes satisfactory for the process. But thick, porous white paper towels are likely to work better.

GENERALIZATION

The colors that make up a dye may be discovered through paper chromatography. Most dyes contain several blended colors.

SAMPLE PERFORMANCE OBJECTIVES

Process: Given the materials, the child can demonstrate how to use paper chromatography to analyze the colored pigments in a dye.
Knowledge: The child can predict the colors blended in several common dyes.

□ ACTIVITY: What Happens When Your Eyes Tire from Seeing One Color?

NEEDED

construction paper—blue, yellow, red	scissors
white paper	watch with second hand
pencil	

TRY THIS

1. Pencil an *x* in the center of the white paper.
2. Cut out one small (5-centimeter, or 2-inch) square each of blue, yellow, and red paper.
3. Put the blue square on the *x*. Look at it steadily for 30 seconds.
4. Remove the square and look at the *x*.
   a. What color appears at the *x*?
5. Rest your eyes for a minute or so. Then, try the yellow and red squares in the same way.
   b. What color appears after the yellow square? red square?

■ INVESTIGATION: A String Telephone

Have you ever used a "string telephone"? It's a handy way to talk to someone far across a large room without shouting.

EXPLORATORY PROBLEM

How can you make a string telephone?

NEEDED

two sturdy paper cups

strong string, about 8 meters (26 feet) long

nail

two paper clips

partner

TRY THIS

1. Punch a hole into the bottom center of each cup using a nail.

2. Put a string end into each hole.

3. Tie each string end to a paper clip. This will keep the string from slipping out of each hole.

4. Stretch the string tightly between you and your partner.

5. Speak into one cup while your partner listens with the other cup (Figure A-2).

FIGURE A-2

DISCOVERY PROBLEMS

observing **A.** Can you hear better through the string telephone than through the air? Whisper softly through the phone. Do it a little louder until your partner hears you. Then whisper to him or her at the same loudness without the telephone.

experimenting **B.** How can you stop a sound from reaching you on the string telephone?

experimenting **C.** Suppose two other children have a string telephone. How can you make a party line?

experimenting **D.** What can you do to make your phone work better? Try containers of different sizes and materials. Try different kinds of string and waxing the string with candle wax.

TEACHING COMMENT

PREPARATION AND BACKGROUND

Holding the string or letting it sag will dampen or stop sounds. So will touching the vibrating cup bottom. For a party line, cross and loop around once the lines of two sets of phones.

Cylindrical cereal boxes (for example, Quaker Oats) and salt boxes work well for string telephones. Metal can bottoms are too thick and rigid to vibrate well. Hard string or waxed string is superior to softly woven string.

Some children might believe the string telephone works like a real one. In the regular phone, sound vibrations are changed into electrical vibrations, or tiny spurts of electricity. These vibrations zip through the wire at almost the speed of light to the receiving phone. This phone changes the electrical spurts back into sound vibrations. Help children to realize that in the string telephone, only sound vibrations are transmitted.

GENERALIZATION

Sound vibrations can travel through string and other solid materials.

SAMPLE PERFORMANCE OBJECTIVES

Process: The child can discover through experimenting at least one way to improve the performance of a string telephone.
Knowledge: The child can explain how sound travels from one string telephone to another.

FOR YOUNGER CHILDREN

Younger pupils can construct and explore how to operate a string telephone. But they are less likely than older pupils to find ways to improve the telephone's performance.

■ INVESTIGATION: A Bottle Xylophone

Do you know what a xylophone looks like? This instrument has a row of different-sized blocks of wood. The player makes sounds by striking the blocks with two special sticks. You can easily make an instrument that works like a xylophone. But instead of wood, you can use bottles of water.

EXPLORATORY PROBLEM

How can you make a bottle xylophone?

NEEDED

eight matched soda bottles   pencil and paper
water

TRY THIS

1. Put different levels of water in each bottle.

2. Line the bottles in a row (Figure A-3), in any order.

3. Tap each of the bottles lightly with a pencil. Notice how high or low each sound is. This is called *pitch*.

FIGURE A-3

DISCOVERY PROBLEMS

observing   **A.** How much water is there in the bottle of highest pitch? lowest pitch?

classifying   **B.** Can you put the bottles in order from lowest to highest pitch?

experimenting   **C.** What must you do with the bottles to make an eight-note scale?

observing   **D.** Can you play a simple song? Put paper slips in front of the bottles. Number them from 1 to 8, for an 8-note scale. Notice the numbers of the notes you play.

communicating   **E.** Can you write a song so someone else can play it correctly? Write on paper the numbers of the notes to be played. Use your own made-up song or a known song. Observe how well the song is played.

hypothesizing   **F.** How can you improve the way you wrote your song?

predicting   **G.** Suppose you blew over each bottle top. Now the air inside would vibrate rather than the water. How do you think that would affect each pitch? Try it and see.

TEACHING COMMENT

PREPARATION AND BACKGROUND

Bottles made of plain glass make clearer, purer sounds than those made of rippled glass. If you or a child can play the piano, children may enjoy playing this eight-note xylophone either as an accompanying or leading instrument. Children may also enjoy singing with the instrument.

GENERALIZATION

An instrument's pitch depends on how much mass vibrates. As mass increases, pitch lowers. With less mass, the pitch gets higher.

SAMPLE PERFORMANCE OBJECTIVES

Knowledge: The child can predict which of two unevenly filled bottles will sound lower when struck.
Process: The child can correctly order an eight-note scale with proportionately filled bottles of water.

FOR YOUNGER CHILDREN

Try the basic activity, plus A and B.

■ INVESTIGATION: How to Make a Bulb Light

Have you ever used a flashlight? The electricity to light the bulb comes from one or more batteries. You don't need a flashlight to make the bulb light. You can do it with a single wire and a battery.

EXPLORATORY PROBLEM

How can you light a flashlight bulb with a wire and a battery?

NEEDED

D-size battery   2 wires, 15 centimeters (6 inches) long
two flashlight bulbs   paper and pencil

TRY THIS

1. Remove the insulation from both ends of the wire.
2. Put the bulb bottom on the raised button end of the battery. (See Figure A-4.)

FIGURE A-4

3. Touch one wire end to the metal side of the bulb.
4. Touch the other wire end to the battery bottom.

DISCOVERY PROBLEMS

experimenting **A.** How many other ways can you light the bulb? Keep a record of what you do. Make drawings.

predicting **B.** Study each of the drawings in Figure A-5. Which ways will light the bulb? Which will not? Record what you think. Then find out.

FIGURE A-5

experimenting **C.** How many ways can you light a bulb with two wires? (Use one battery.) Record what you do.

experimenting **D.** How many ways can you light two bulbs with two wires? (Use one battery.) Record what you do.

TEACHING COMMENT

Use number 22 or 24 bell wire, available at most hardware or electrical supply stores. Be sure that the plastic covering is stripped well back from both ends of the wire to ensure good contact. The D-size flashlight cell is most often used, but other sizes also work well.

Probably most children will need a partner when working with two bulbs or wires. It is hard for one pair of hands to connect everything.

Caution: Advise pupils to quickly notice, and discontinue trying a connection, if the wire they use to connect the bulb and battery begins to get warm. This happens when the bulb (resistor) is bypassed and the wire ends touch only the battery terminals—a type of short circuit. A short quickly wears down a battery and, if continued for some time, may make the wire uncomfortably hot.

GENERALIZATION

Electricity flows when there is a complete circuit; there are several ways to light a bulb.

SAMPLE PERFORMANCE OBJECTIVES

Process: The child can connect a battery and bulb with wire in several different ways to light the bulb.
Knowledge: The child can describe the bulb and battery parts that must be connected for a bulb to light.

FOR YOUNGER CHILDREN

Many younger pupils can do the exploratory activity and, in a limited way, Discovery Problems A and B. However, they may have some trouble in manipulating the materials.

□ ACTIVITY: How Can You Make an Electric "Nerve Tester" Game?

NEEDED

60 centimeters (2 feet) of bare copper bell wire	clay
number 22 or 24 insulated wire	flashlight bulb
sticky tape	bulb holder
heavy cardboard	scissors

TRY THIS

1. Put two lumps of clay on some cardboard as shown in Figure A-6.
2. Bend the heavy bare copper wire as shown. Stick each end into a clay lump.
3. Cut three pieces of the lighter insulated wire as shown. Bare the ends.
4. Attach the three wires to the bulb holder and battery. Attach the free end of the battery wire to the end of the heavy wire. Twist it around and push the twisted wires slightly into the clay.
5. Bend the free end of the light bulb wire around a pencil to make a slightly open loop. Touch the loop end to the heavy wire. See if the light goes on.
6. To play the game, carefully place the open loop over the heavy wire so the wire is inside the loop. Move the loop from one end to the other and back without

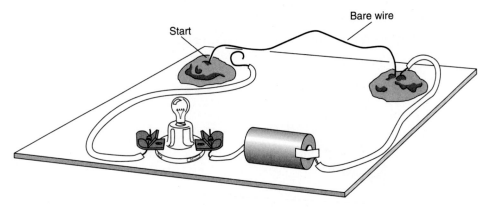

Start

Bare wire

FIGURE A-6

touching the heavy wire. If it touches, the light will go on. The person who lights the bulb least often wins.

a. Who has the steadiest nerves in the class?

b. How does practice help?

c. Is your left hand shakier than your right hand?

d. Are people shakier before or after lunch? What other things might affect how shaky people are?

e. How can you explain this circuit to someone?

(*Teaching Comment:* Any single-strand, somewhat stiff wire will serve for the heavier wire. Even a piece cut from a wire coat hanger will work if the paint is sanded off. To make the bulb light more brightly when the wire is touched, use two batteries in series.)

■ INVESTIGATION: Wheel-Belt Systems

Have you ever noticed how bicycle gears turn? The two gears are connected by a chain. When you push one gear around, the other moves, also.

A gear is just a wheel with teeth. There are many ways to connect wheels. Often, they are connected with belts. Several connected wheels are called a *wheel-belt system.* You can make your own wheel-belt system with spools and rubber bands.

EXPLORATORY PROBLEM

How can you make a wheel-belt system?

NEEDED

four empty sewing spools
crayon
four rubber bands

four finishing nails
board (about the size of this page)
hammer

TRY THIS

1. Pound four nails into the board as shown in Figure A-7.

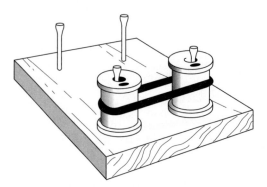

FIGURE A-7

2. Make one crayon dot on the rim of each spool.

3. Put a spool on each of two nails.

4. Place a rubber band around the two spools.

5. Turn one spool. Watch the other spool turn also.

DISCOVERY PROBLEMS

predicting **A.** How will the spools turn when connected in different ways? Notice the drawings in Figure A-8. Each set of spools starts with the left spool. An arrow shows how each is turning. Another spool in the set has a question mark. It is next to a dot on the spool rim. See how the spools are connected.

Will the dot on the rim turn left or right? Make a record of what you think. Then, use your wheel-belt board to find out.

predicting **B.** Notice the Figure A-9 drawings. How should the spools be connected to turn in these ways? How many different connections can you think of? Make drawings of what you think. (Do not cross any rubber bands more than once.) Then, use your wheel-belt board to find out.

experimenting **C.** What wheel-belt systems can you invent? Make up and trade some problems with friends. Fix your board so you can use more spools.

TEACHING COMMENT

PREPARATION AND BACKGROUND

Part of an end piece from a discarded vegetable crate is ideal for the wheel-belt system base. Be sure that only finishing nails are pounded into the wood. These nails have small heads, allowing the spools to slip easily over them.

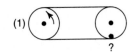

(1)

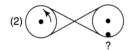

(2)

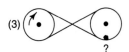

(3)

(4)

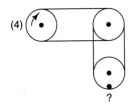

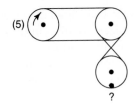

(5)

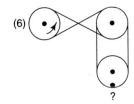

(6)

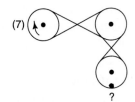

(7)

(8)

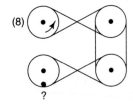

FIGURE A-8

(1)

(2)

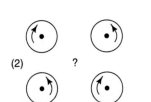

(3)

(4)

FIGURE A-9

Note that this investigation deals only with the direction the spools turn. By using different-sized spools, children also can study how size governs the speed of turning. Because much slipping will happen with the rubber bands, the size–speed relationship cannot be determined accurately. Children can get the idea better by inverting a bicycle and studying the relative turnings of the large gear and the small gear.

GENERALIZATION

A wheel-belt system can be used to change the direction of a force.

SAMPLE PERFORMANCE OBJECTIVES

Process: When shown a two-, three-, or four-wheel-and-belt system, the child can predict the direction each wheel will turn.
Knowledge: The child can point out some everyday examples of wheel-belt systems or their equivalents.

FOR YOUNGER CHILDREN

Many primary pupils work well with wheel-belt systems. But use fewer spools than with older children.

■ INVESTIGATION: Pendulums

Have you ever seen an old-fashioned grandfather clock? One kind has a long weighted rod underneath that swings back and forth. The swinging part is called a *pendulum*. You can keep time with your own pendulum made with a string.

EXPLORATORY PROBLEM

How can you make a string pendulum?

NEEDED

thin string, about 1 meter (or yard) long
meter stick or yardstick
pencil
three heavy washers

paper clip
clock or watch with second hand
sticky tape
graph paper

TRY THIS

1. Tape a pencil to a table edge so it sticks out.

2. Bend a paper clip into a hook shape. Tie one string end to the hook.

3. Loop the free end of the string once around the pencil. Tape the string end to the table top.

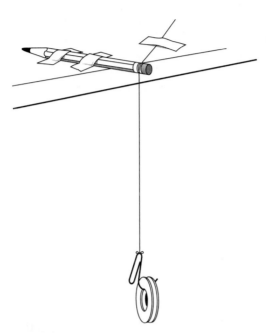

FIGURE A-10

4. Put two washers on the hook (Figure A-10).
5. Move the washers to one side and then let go. Each time the washers swing back to that side, count one swing. Be sure the string does not rub against the table edge.

DISCOVERY PROBLEMS

measuring **A.** How many swings does the pendulum make in one minute? Have someone help by observing the second hand on a clock. Then you can count the swings.

hypothesizing **B.** Do wide swings take more time than narrow swings? Suppose you let go of your pendulum far to one side. What difference might that make in the number of swings it takes in one minute?

hypothesizing **C.** Does the amount of weight used change the swing time? What might happen if you use a one-washer weight? a three-washer weight?

hypothesizing **D.** Does the length of string used make a difference in swing time? (Measure length from the pencil to the end of the washers.) What might happen if you use a short string? longer string?

experimenting **E.** How can you get your pendulum to swing 60 times in 1 minute?

inferring **F.** Suppose you had a grandfather clock that was running slow. What could you do to its pendulum to correct it? What if it was running fast?

communicating **G.** How well can you predict with your pendulum? Make a graph such as the one shown in Figure A-11.

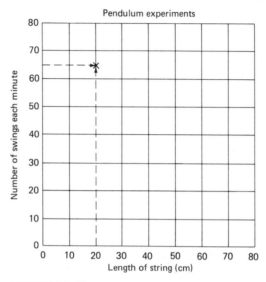

FIGURE A-11

Try several string lengths for your pendulum. Count the swings for each length. Let's say you find that a 20-centimeter string swings 65 times in 1 minute. Make a mark on your graph where lines running from these two numbers meet. (See the graph.) Make marks for three or four other string lengths and their swings. Then draw a straight line between the marks.

predicting Suppose you know the length of a pendulum, but you have not yet tried it. How can you use your graph to predict its number of swings?

predicting Suppose you know the number of swings of a pendulum, but you have not yet measured its length. How can you use your graph to predict the pendulum's length?

experimenting How can you make your predictions better and better?

TEACHING COMMENT

PREPARATION AND BACKGROUND

The timing of events is possible with a pendulum because its to-and-fro motion recurs with near-perfect regularity. Through manipulating variables, children can discover that the *length* of the weighted string affects the swing rate, or period, of a pendulum.

Be sure your pupils realize that one complete swing consists of the swing out *and* return movement.

Should washers be unavailable, substitute other small, uniform weights. You can hang a small paper cup from the hook and put marbles, dominoes, or checkers, and the like inside. Some pupils may need help constructing the graph. However, they should be able to follow through on the predicting part after becoming familiar with its construction. The way to more accurate predictions with graphs is to increase the valid data one works with.

GENERALIZATION

A pendulum is any object that swings regularly back and forth; its length affects its swing rate.

SAMPLE PERFORMANCE OBJECTIVES

Process: The child can accurately predict the swing rate of a pendulum for one minute by using graph data.
Knowledge: The child can state how to increase and decrease the swing rate of a pendulum.

FOR YOUNGER CHILDREN

An easy way for younger pupils to see the effect of manipulating a variable is to set up two identical pendulums to start. When both are set to swinging, they should perform in the same way. Thereafter, change only one variable at a time with one pendulum—weight or width of swing or length—so its performance may be contrasted with the unchanged pendulum. This strategy can keep the investigation concrete and understandable from the beginning through Problem D or E.

■ INVESTIGATION: The Growth of Seeds

Where do green plants come from? Have you planted seeds? What did you do?

EXPLORATORY PROBLEM

How can you plant seeds so they may grow?

NEEDED

soil	bean seeds soaked overnight in water
water	paper towel
pencil	topless milk carton or paper cup
pie pan	

TRY THIS

1. Poke holes into the carton bottom with a pencil or nail.

2. Put the carton on a pie pan.

3. Fill the carton almost full with soil.

4. Water the soil slowly until water leaks into the pie pan.

5. Poke a hole in the soil. Make it about as deep as the seed you plant is long (Figure A-12).

FIGURE A-12

6. Put the seed into the hole. Cover it with wet soil. Tap the soil down *lightly*.

7. Water the soil when it feels dry to your touch, but not more than once a day.

8. Measure your growing plant three times a week. Put a strip of paper alongside. Tear off some to match the plant's height. Date the strips and paste them on a large sheet of paper. What can you tell from this plant record?

DISCOVERY PROBLEMS

experimenting **A.** Try some experiments with more materials. In what kind of soil will a seed grow best? Try sand, sawdust, or soil from different places. Or, mix your own soil from some of these.

experimenting **B.** Will a seed live and grow if you water it with salt water? How much salt can you use?
What else might you use to "water" a growing seed?

experimenting **C.** Will a broken or damaged seed grow?
Will a seed that was frozen or boiled grow?
Will a seed grow if the seed cover is taken off?

experimenting **D.** Does the position of a seed make a difference? For example, what will happen if you plant a seed upside down?

experimenting **E.** What other experiments with seeds might you try?

TEACHING COMMENT

PREPARATION AND BACKGROUND

A seed that is soaked before it is planted will sprout faster than one planted dry. But don't leave a seed in water more than overnight. It may die from insufficient air.

GENERALIZATION

Some plants grow from seeds; proper conditions are needed for seeds to sprout and grow.

SAMPLE PERFORMANCE OBJECTIVES

Process: The child sets up an experiment to test a condition that may affect seed growth.
Knowledge: The child describes how seeds may be properly grown into plants.

FOR YOUNGER CHILDREN

Most intuitive thinkers can do the foregoing activities. However, they will be unable to control variables unless guided. Be sure that these children learn right away how to properly plant and care for a growing seed. Then they will see an experiment with another seed as a variation to be compared with their "good" one. This approach makes sense to them. It also ensures that most children will feel successful and encouraged rather than frustrated and disappointed.

☐ ACTIVITY: In What Places Are Seeds in the Soil?

NEEDED

shoe boxes   outdoor places
clear kitchen wrap   small shovel
plastic bags

TRY THIS

1. Line some shoe boxes with plastic bags.
2. Half-fill each shoe box with bare soil from a different place. Record where each place is on the box. Try garden soil, soil where weeds grow, and other bare soils.
3. Water the soil so it is damp. Cover each box with clear kitchen wrap.
4. Leave each in a warm, well-lighted place for several weeks or more.
   a. In which box do you expect seeds to grow?
   b. In which box, if any, did seeds grow?
   c. Will wild plants grow in the exact places from which you took soil? Observe these places from time to time.

■ INVESTIGATION: The Properties of Leaves

Have you ever collected different kinds of leaves? There are more than 300,000 different kinds! How can you tell one leaf from another? What do you look for?

EXPLORATORY PROBLEM

How can you describe the properties of leaves?

NEEDED

six or more different leaves   partner
pencil and paper

TRY THIS

1. *Size:* How large is the leaf? Compare their sizes with things everyone knows.
2. *Shape:* What is the shape of the leaf? Some are oval; some are almost round. Others are shaped like a heart, star, or other figure.
3. *Color:* What is the color of the leaf? Most fresh leaves are green, but some are darker or lighter than others. Some leaves have other colors.
4. *Veins:* These are the small tubes that carry liquid throughout the leaf. How do the veins look? In some leaves, they are side by side. In others, the veins look like many Vs in a row with a main center vein. Some leaves have several long veins with Vs. In a few leaves, veins cannot be seen.
5. *Edges:* What do the leaf edges look like? Some are smooth. Some edges are wavy. Other leaf edges look like saw teeth (Figure A-13).

FIGURE A-13

6. *Feel:* How does the leaf feel to you? Is it rough? smooth? waxy? hairy? slippery? sticky?

7. *Smell:* What does the leaf smell like? Some leaves may not have a noticeable smell.

DISCOVERY PROBLEMS

classifying

inferring

A. Play a game with a partner. Sort your leaves into two groups according to one property (shape, veins, and so forth). Let your partner study your groups. Can he or she tell which property you used to sort your leaves? Try other properties. Take turns with your partner in this sorting game.

communicating

B. Play the "I'm-Thinking-of-a-Leaf" game with a partner. Place four or more leaves in a row. Think of just one leaf and its properties.

inferring

Can your partner find out what leaf you have in mind? He must ask you only questions that can be answered by yes or no. Example:
"Does the leaf have veins?" (Yes.)
"Does the leaf have smooth edges?" (No.)
When your partner finds out the right leaf, switch places. How many questions must you ask to discover the leaf your partner is thinking of? The person who needs to ask fewer questions wins.

communicating

C. How well can you describe your leaves? Can you make a chart that someone else can use to identify them?

Make a chart of all the properties you observe about your leaves. Call your leaves A, B, C, and so on. Try to remember which is which.

Leaf	Shape	Veins	Edges	Size	Feel
A	Like a star	Like Vs	Sawtooth	Medium	Smooth
B					
C					
D					

inferring

Give your completed chart and your leaves to your partner. They should be out of order, so your partner must study your chart to tell which leaf is A, B, and so on.

communicating

Which chart descriptions were helpful? Which confused your partner? How could these be made clearer?

TEACHING COMMENT

PREPARATION AND BACKGROUND

Important: To further the processes of careful observing and communicating, use only leaves that are roughly similar in this investigation. You want different kinds of leaves, but if each is grossly and obviously different from others this will defeat the purpose of the investigation.

It is best to do this investigation with fresh, unblemished leaves. Weed leaves will do. Leaves may be kept fresh for several days by placing them in plastic bags.

GENERALIZATION

Leaves vary in size, shape, color, texture, vein pattern, and other properties; no two leaves are identical.

SAMPLE PERFORMANCE OBJECTIVES

Process: The child can communicate leaf descriptions that enable other persons to identify the leaves.
Knowledge: The child can state at least five of the general properties that can be used to describe leaves.

FOR YOUNGER CHILDREN

Most primary-level children should be able to do Discovery Problem A, and some should be able to do B.

■ INVESTIGATION: Mealworms and What They Do

Have you ever seen a mealworm? You can buy them at a pet store to feed to lizards and fish. It's fun to observe mealworms and what they do.

EXPLORATORY PROBLEM

How can you find out about mealworms and what they do?

NEEDED

mealworms	spoon
three rulers	small card
shoe box lid	small jar of bran
magnifier	cotton swab
rough paper towel	ice cube
straw	black sheet of paper

TRY THIS

1. Put a mealworm in an upturned shoe box lid (Figure A-14).

2. Use a spoon and card to move it to where you want.

3. Use a hand magnifier to see it more clearly.

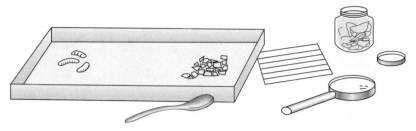

FIGURE A-14

DISCOVERY PROBLEMS

observing   **A.** What do you notice about the mealworm? How many legs does it have? How many feelers on its head? What is on its tail end? How many body segments, or parts, does it have?

inferring   **B.** Put it on a rough paper towel, then on a smooth surface. On which does it seem to travel easier?

observing   **C.** Put a few more mealworms in the shoe box lid. Observe how they look and act. In what ways can you tell different mealworms apart?

experimenting   **D.** In what ways can you get a mealworm to back up? Which way is best?

observing   **E.** Suppose you place them on a slant. Will they go up or down? Does the amount of slant make a difference?

measuring   **F.** How far can a mealworm go in half a minute?

observing   **G.** Which food do they seem to like best? Try cornflakes, flour, bread, crackers, and other foods.

hypothesizing   **H.** Suppose you put two mealworms into a narrow straw, one at each end. What do you think will happen when they meet?

experimenting   **I.** Do mealworms like moisture? How could a cotton swab be used to find out? How else might you find out?

experimenting   **J.** Will a mealworm move to or away from a cold place? How could an ice cube be used to find out?

experimenting   **K.** Will a mealworm move to a dark or light place? How can black paper be used to find out?

predicting   **L.** Which way will a mealworm go each time (Figure A-15)?

experimenting   **M.** How can you get a mealworm to go in a straight line for at least 10 centimeters (4 inches)? No fair touching it!

hypothesizing   **N.** What are some more questions about mealworms you would like to investigate?

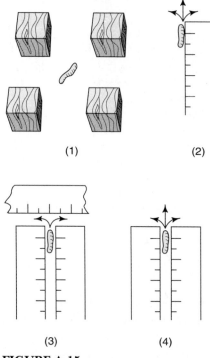

(1)   (2)

(3)   (4)

FIGURE A-15

TEACHING COMMENT

PREPARATION AND BACKGROUND

Mealworms are the larval stage of the grain beetle, an insect often found in rotting grain or flour supplies. They may be bought cheaply at pet stores and are fed to a variety of small animals, including some fishes.

Mealworms can be kept in a closed glass jar containing bran or other cereal flakes. Punch small holes in the jar lid for air. A potato or apple slice can be added to provide extra moisture. When the old bran looks powdery, dump out everything, then wash and dry the jar. Put back into the jar fresh bran and the live, healthy-looking mealworms. In this way, you should be able to maintain a mealworm culture for many months.

It is possible to observe the entire life cycle—egg, larva, pupa, and adult beetle—of this interesting creature in six to nine months. The children will notice quickly how a mealworm sheds its skin as it grows larger. Only the egg stage is hard to observe, because the eggs are tiny. This animal is harmless to handle at all stages.

Children usually try a variety of interesting methods to influence a mealworm's behavior. To make it back up, they may try touching it, blowing light puffs of air through a straw, making a tapping sound, or using a flashlight, heated nail, or cotton swab soaked in vinegar, ammonia, or water. To test for moisture preference, they may stick one moist and one dry cotton swab into a container of bran and mealworms. Whatever methods they use, try to get them to treat these animals humanely. While gentle touching is all right, direct contact with heat or chemicals may be harmful to mealworms.

GENERALIZATION

Some behaviors of an animal are inborn, and some are influenced by its environment.

SAMPLE PERFORMANCE OBJECTIVES

Process: The child can test the preferences of mealworms as to temperature, light, food, and moisture.

Knowledge: The child can state the apparent preferences of mealworms as to temperature, light, food, and moisture.

FOR YOUNGER CHILDREN

Younger pupils should be able to do most of the activities in the investigation, although with less precision than older children.

□ ACTIVITY: How Useful Are Your Thumbs?

NEEDED

paper clip   pencil and paper
tape

TRY THIS

1. Make a list of some things you can do now with one or two hands.
   a. Which do you think you cannot do without thumbs? Which might you do less well? Which might you do as well?
2. You might record what you think on a chart. You can make a check mark first for what you think, and then an *X* for what you find out.

Can Do with Thumbs	Without Thumbs: Can't Do	Do Less Well	Do as Well
Pick up paper clip	✔	X	
Tie shoelace			
Write my name			
Shake hands			
Button a shirt			
Etc.			

   ✔: I think.   X: I found out.

3. Ask someone to tape your thumbs to your hands.
4. Try doing the things on the list without using your thumbs.
   b. What surprises, if any, did you find? How do your thumbs help you?

■ INVESTIGATION: How Practice Improves Learning

Suppose you learn to do something one way, and then someone says you must learn to do it in another way. Why might this be hard to do? How might learning to draw or write backward be a problem? How might practice help?

EXPLORATORY PROBLEM

How can you learn to do mirror drawing or writing?

NEEDED

small mirror	paper
clay	pencil
book	ruler
watch or clock with second hand	graph paper

TRY THIS

1. Draw a triangle on paper, no larger than the one in Figure A-16.

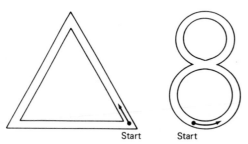

Start   Start

FIGURE A-16

2. Arrange the paper, a mirror, and a book as in Figure A-17. Use two pieces of clay to hold up the mirror.

FIGURE A-17

3. Sit so you must look into the mirror to see the triangle.

4. Place your pencil point on the triangle corner at "start."

5. Observe a watch and notice the time.

6. Draw a line inside and around the whole triangle. Look at the mirror to see what you are doing. Keep the line between the triangle's inside and outside borders. If you go beyond the borders, stop drawing. Start again from the place where you left the border.

7. When you complete the drawing, check the time again. Record in seconds how long it took for this first trial.

DISCOVERY PROBLEMS

measuring **A.** How will practice affect the time needed to draw around the triangle? How much faster will your second trial be? third trial? fourth trial? Make a record like this of what you find out:

Number of Trials	Time to Finish (Seconds)
1	160
2	140
3	100
4	70

communicating **B.** Make a graph of your findings. Notice how to do this on the graph in Figure A-18. Suppose it took 160 seconds to finish the first trial.

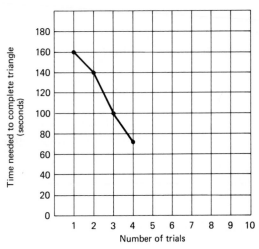

FIGURE A-18

Put your finger on 1 at the bottom. Follow the line up to and opposite 160. A dot is placed where the two lines cross. Check to see how the other figures are recorded. See how a line has been drawn from one dot to the next. This line is called a *curve*. The graph tells about learning, so the line may be called a *learning curve*.

predicting **C.** Study your own learning curve. How fast do you think you can draw the triangle after six trials? seven trials? eight trials? nine trials? ten trials? Record your findings on your graph and complete your learning curve.

inferring **D.** How does your learning curve compare to those of others? Do some people learn mirror drawing faster than others? If so, how can you describe them?

predicting **E.** Try a mirror drawing of another figure, such as a large 8 (Figure A-16). What shape will your learning curve be for this figure? Will people who learned fast before learn fast again?

hypothesizing **F.** What other problems about learning mirror drawing can you investigate?

TEACHING COMMENT

PREPARATION AND BACKGROUND

You may have to help some pupils with the line graphs if they lack experience. Also, expect some pupils to have trouble deciding how many seconds it takes to draw completely around each figure.

GENERALIZATION

An earlier learning may interfere with a later learning. Proper practice can improve one's performance.

SAMPLE PERFORMANCE OBJECTIVES

Process: The child can record data accurately on a graph.
Knowledge: The child can predict when an earlier learning is likely to interfere with later learning.

FOR YOUNGER CHILDREN

This investigation is too abstract for young children in its full form. But if the exploratory problem is presented as a hand–eye coordination activity, young pupils will enjoy it.

☐ ACTIVITY: Which Foods Have Starch?

NEEDED

iodine
medicine dropper
tiny pieces of foods, such as white
   bread, rice, macaroni, cheese, potato,
   cereals, etc.

piece of white chalk
cornstarch
teaspoon
waxed paper

TRY THIS

1. Place a bit of cornstarch on waxed paper. Crush a small piece of white chalk next to it with a spoon.

2. Put one drop of iodine on each. Notice how the cornstarch turns purple-black. The chalk should look red-brown. When a food turns purple-black, it has starch.

3. Test your food samples with the iodine. Crush each sample first with the spoon. Wash it off each time.

   a. Which samples seem to have starch? Which do not?

4. Try the starch test on part of an unripe banana. Then test part of a very ripe banana. Taste a little of each.

   b. What difference do you notice? When does a banana seem to have more starch? When does it seem to have more sugar?

■ INVESTIGATION: How Water Sinks into Different Soils

Some of the rain that falls on soil runs off it into streams. Some rain also soaks into the ground. This water can help crops grow. If water sinks deep below the surface, it may be pumped to the surface for many uses. How fast water soaks into soil depends on several conditions. You can find out some for yourself.

EXPLORATORY PROBLEM

What can you do to test how fast water sinks into soils?

NEEDED

two matched cans, one with both ends
  removed
different outdoor places with soil

watch with second hand
water

TRY THIS

1. One can should be open at both ends. Scratch a mark sideways on the can's side 2.5 centimeters (1 inch) from one end.

2. Go to a place with soil outdoors. Use your foot to press the can into the soil up to the mark.

3. Have the second can filled with water. Pour the water into the first can without spilling any (Figure A-19). With a watch, check how long it takes for all the water to sink in.

DISCOVERY PROBLEMS

measuring **A.** How much time is needed for the water to sink into the soil?

measuring **B.** Compare the sink times of different soils. How will soil with grass compare to the same kind of soil without grass?

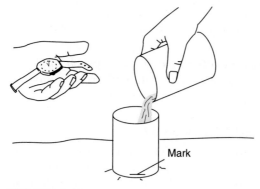

Mark

FIGURE A-19

measuring   **C.** How will sandy soil compare with sticky soil?

measuring   **D.** How will hard-packed soil compare with loose soil?

measuring   **E.** How will soil that is usually in the sun compare with soil that is usually in the shade?

measuring   **F.** How will soil on a hill compare with soil that is on a flat surface?

inferring   **G.** What are some things about soil that seem to make water sink in quickly? slowly?

TEACHING COMMENT

PREPARATION AND BACKGROUND

A steel can is likely to hold up better than an aluminum can for this activity. Some hard soils may require an adult's weight to push the can down to the mark.

GENERALIZATION

Permeable soils tend to be loosely packed and composed of coarse mineral particles with little or no humus.

SAMPLE PERFORMANCE OBJECTIVES

Process: The child can measure and compare the permeability of several different kinds of soils.
Knowledge: The child can explain the conditions that are likely to be found in highly permeable soils.

FOR OLDER CHILDREN

To make this investigation into an experiment for older students, start with Discovery Problem G. Then, after discussing hypotheses, ask, "How can we find out?"

☐ ACTIVITY: What Happens to Water Pressure with Depth?

NEEDED

tall, empty milk carton   nail (or sharp pencil)
sink   water

TRY THIS

1. Punch a nail hole in the carton's side, halfway up, from the inside out.

2. Punch another hole above it and a third hole below it, from inside out.

3. Cover all three holes tightly with three fingers. Fill the carton with water. Keep it in the sink.
   a. If you take away your fingers, what do you think will happen?

4. Remove your fingers quickly from the three holes.
   b. What happened? In what part of the carton was the water pressure the greatest?

   (*Teaching Comment:* Sometimes the torn edges of the holes will impede the flow of water. Punching the holes from the inside out makes this less likely.)

☐ ACTIVITY: How High Can Water Flow Compared to Where It Comes From?

NEEDED

rubber tube, 1 meter (or 1 yard) long   container of water
funnel that fits the tube   sink

TRY THIS

1. Stick the funnel end tightly into a tube end. Do this activity in a sink.

2. Hold up the funnel. Have someone pour water into it.

3. When water comes out of the tube, pinch it off.

4. Have someone fill the funnel with water. Keep the tube end pinched off.
   a. How high will you be able to hold the tube end and still have water come out? Higher than the funnel? as high? lower?

5. Let go of the tube end. Try holding it at different heights.
   b. What did you find?

☐ ACTIVITY: How Can You Show That Air Takes Up Space?

NEEDED

large, deep glass bowl   water
two small glasses   paper towels

TRY THIS

1. Fill the bowl three-fourths full with water.

2. Hold a glass with the open end down. Push it straight down into the water.

3. Put a second glass in the water sideways, so it fills with water.

4. Now tip the first glass. Try to "pour" the air up from the first glass into the second glass (Figure A-20).

FIGURE A-20

    a. What happens to the water in the higher glass?
    b. What happens in the lower glass?
    c. How can you get the air back into the first glass?
    d. Suppose you put a crushed paper towel in the bottom of a glass. How could you put the open glass underwater without getting the towel wet?

(*Teaching Comment:* If no air bubbles are lost in the process, the air may be transferred from one glass to the next indefinitely. Because air is lighter than water, the air-filled glass will always need to be below the water-filled glass during the transfer.)

☐ ACTIVITY: How Can You Tell If Air in a Balloon Weighs Anything?

NEEDED

two matched balloons	scissors
meter stick or	sticky tape
yardstick	string

TRY THIS

1. Hang a meter stick evenly from a doorway or other place. Use a string and tape.

2. Attach a string loosely to each of the two deflated balloons.

3. Tape each string to an *end* of the stick. Be sure the stick is level after the balloons are hung. If not, place a partly open paper clip on the stick where needed to balance it (Figure A-21).

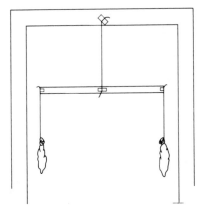

FIGURE A-21

  a. What will happen if you blow up one balloon and rehang it?
  b. In what ways can you make the stick level again? The strings must stay at the ends of the stick.

  (*Teaching Comment:* Be sure the balloon strings are always affixed to the stick *ends* to help assure balance. In b, the deflated balloon can be blown up like the inflated one. Or, the inflated balloon may be slowly deflated by puncturing it at the neck with a pin.)

▪ INVESTIGATION: Evaporation

Many persons hang wet clothes on a clothesline. After a while, the clothes are dry. What do you think happens to the water? When water disappears into the air, we say it *evaporated.* You can find out more about evaporation by drying wet paper towels.

EXPLORATORY PROBLEM

How can you get a paper towel to dry? How long will it take?

NEEDED

plastic bowl of water   piece of cardboard
paper towels   two aluminum pie plates

TRY THIS

1. Put a paper towel underwater to soak it.

2. Bunch the wet towel in your fist. Squeeze out all the water you can.

3. Open the towel and lay it on a pie plate (Figure A-22).

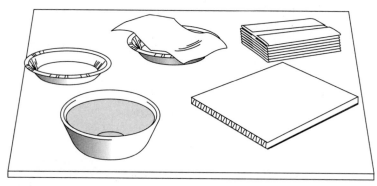

FIGURE A-22

4. Leave the plate on your desk. Check the time.

5. Every so often feel the towel to see if it is dry. Check the time again when it is all dry.

DISCOVERY PROBLEMS

predicting **A.** Suppose you put one wet towel where it is shady and cool, and another where it is sunny and warmer. Which wet towel do you think will dry first?

communicating **B.** What can you do to show that a dried-out towel is completely "dry"? How many others agree with you?

predicting **C.** Suppose to make it windy, you fan one wet towel with cardboard. You do not fan a second wet towel. Which towel do you think will dry first?

predicting **D.** Suppose you spread out one wet towel and leave another bunched like a ball. Which towel do you think will dry first?

predicting **E.** Suppose you leave one wet towel on top of a plate. You leave a second wet towel under another plate. Which towel do you think will dry first?

experimenting **F.** Play a game with a friend. Who can dry a wet paper towel faster? How can you make the game fair?

experimenting **G.** What is the longest you can keep a wet paper towel from drying?

TEACHING COMMENT

PREPARATION AND BACKGROUND

The foregoing sequence gives several chances for children to manipulate conditions that affect the evaporation rate of water. The last two activities encourage them to manipulate these conditions creatively. Discovery Problem C calls for fanning one wet towel with cardboard to simulate a windy condition. Clipping the towel to the pie plate with several paper clips will keep it from blowing off the plate.

GENERALIZATION

Wind, heat, and an uncovered and spread-out condition all help to make a wet paper towel dry faster.

SAMPLE PERFORMANCE OBJECTIVES

Process: The child can vary and control at least one condition to increase the drying rate of a wet paper towel.
Knowledge: The child can state at least one condition that will change the drying rate of a wet paper towel.

FOR OLDER CHILDREN

Invite older children to do the activities with more precision. For example, they might attempt to predict the drying times in each of the activities.

Have them calculate the drying *rate* of a wet towel or sponge by using a beam balance. Let them suspend a wet towel from one end of the beam, and clay or another object on the other end to achieve a balance. Then, as the towel dries and lightens, the beam will begin to tilt up. Pupils can add water to the towel with an eyedropper, one drop at a time, to keep the beam level.

Ask questions such as, How many drops evaporate in one minute? Does spreading out the drops you add make a difference in the evaporation rate? Will half of a wet towel have half the evaporation rate of a whole towel? and so on. If you do not have a beam balance, just suspend a meter stick or dowel from a string. Your pupils will be delighted at the dramatic effect of the evaporation rate. It takes only a few minutes, under usual conditions, for it to be noticeable.

☐ ACTIVITY: How Can You Measure Changes in Air Pressure?

NEEDED

glass jar	balloon
rubber band	scissors
straw	file card
glue	

TRY THIS

1. Make a *barometer.* Cut out a large part of a balloon. Stretch it tightly over the jar opening. Use a rubber band to hold it fast.

2. Pinch one straw end flat. Cut a point with scissors at this end.

3. Glue the straw's other end to the center of the stretched balloon.

4. Fasten a file card to a wall. Place the barometer by it. Have the straw pointer centered on the card and almost touching.

5. Make a mark on the card where the straw points each day for a week (Figure A-23).

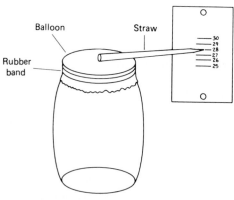

Balloon   Straw

Rubber
band

30
29
28
27
26
25

FIGURE A-23

a. On what day was the air pressure the highest? lowest?
b. When, if at all, was there no change in air pressure?

(*Teaching Comment:* Increased air pressure pushes down harder on the balloon diaphragm. This makes the straw pointer go up. Decreased air pressure causes the higher pressure inside the jar to push up on the diaphragm, so the pointer goes down. The movement can be increased a bit by gluing a piece of matchstick under the straw at the jar rim. You might challenge pupils to calibrate their barometers. They can note the daily barometric pressure in the newspaper or phone the weather bureau. After a week or so of recording the official pressure next to their own recordings, they may be able to predict roughly the official pressure from their own barometers. Place this kind of barometer where it will have the least change of temperature. Otherwise, the air in the jar may expand and contract so much that the effects of changing air pressure will be obscured.)

□ ACTIVITY: What Does the Moon Look Like from Day to Day?

NEEDED

day or night moon   paper and pencil

TRY THIS

1. Draw neat circles in a row on paper. To do so, trace around a coin or other round object.

2. Look at the moon each day for several weeks. Draw inside a circle what you see each time and date each circle.

3. When you cannot see the moon, leave a circle blank, but date it, also.

4. After several weeks, look carefully at your drawings.
   a. What pattern of shapes do you see?
   b. How can your pattern help you to draw the right shapes in the dated, blank circles?

Professional Bibliography

GENERAL SOURCES OF ACTIVITIES

Bybee, Rodger, Rita Peterson, Jane Bowyer, and David Butts. *Activities for Teaching About Science and Society.* Columbus, Ohio: Merrill, 1984. (Activities that relate to social needs and problems.)

DeVito, Alfred, and Gerald H. Krockover. *Creative Sciencing: Ideas and Activities for Teachers and Children.* Glenview, IL: Scott Foresman (Goodyear), 1991. (About 160 activities designed to stimulate creativity.)

Freidl, Alfred E. *Teaching Science to Children, An Integrated Approach.* New York: Random House, 1986. (A large array of hands-on activities for children, including many discrepant events.)

Gega, Peter C. *Concepts and Experiences in Elementary School Science.* 2nd ed. New York: Macmillan, 1994. (Many open-ended investigations and activities keyed to basic concepts.)

Lowery, Lawrence F. and Carol Verbeeck. *Explorations* (3 volumes: *Earth Science, Physical Science, Life Science*). Carthage, IL: Fearon, 1987. (48 process-oriented activities for grades 1–3.)

Strongin, Herb. *Science on a Shoestring.* Reading, MA: Addison-Wesley, 1991. (Easy-to-do investi-gations with readily-found, inexpensive materials.)

Van Cleave, Janice P. *Science for Every Kid* (5 volumes: *Biology, Chemistry, Earth, Astronomy, Physics*). New York: Wiley, 1989–1991. (Each volume has 101 activities for grade three and beyond, many of which are suitable for science fair projects.)

PERIODICALS (Teachers)

Discover, Time, Inc., 3435 Wilshire Blvd., Los Angeles, CA 90010. (Monthly. Interesting, up-to-date information about developments in science.)

Journal of Research in Science Teaching, John Wiley and Sons, Inc., 605 Third Ave., New York, NY 10158. (Quarterly. Scholarly articles on research and practice.)

Natural History, American Museum of Natural History, Central Park West at 79th St., New York, NY 10024. (Monthly, 10 issues a year. Interesting articles on a variety of natural subjects, including ecology.)

School Science and Mathematics, School Science and Mathematics Association, P.O. Box 1614, Indiana University of Pennsylvania, Indiana, PA 15701. (Monthly, nine issues a year. Includes articles on methods and research.)

Science, American Association for the Advancement of Science, 1515 Massachusetts Ave., N.W., Washington, DC 20005. (Monthly, except bimonthly Jan./Feb. and July/Aug. Accurate, up-to-date nontechnical information about developments in science.)

Science Activities, Science Activities Publishing Company, Skokie, IL 60076. (Ten issues a year. Useful activities for teachers of the upper grades and beyond.)

Science and Children, National Science Teachers Association, 1742 Connecticut Ave., N.W., Washington, DC 20009. (Monthly, eight issues a year. Articles of interest and practical value to elementary school teachers.)

Science Education, John Wiley and Sons, Inc., 605 Third Ave., New York, NY 10158. (Quarterly. Reports of research and essays on the teaching of elementary and secondary school science.)

Science News, Science Service, 1719 N Street, N.W., Washington DC (Weekly. Brief, easy-to-read reports on current findings of scientific research.)

PERIODICALS (Children)

Digit, P.O. Box 29996, San Francisco, CA 94129. (Six issues a year. Computer games, ideas, challenges. Upper elementary.)

Enter, One Disk Drive, P.O. Box 2686, Boulder, CO 80322. (Ten issues a year. Computer games, ideas, challenges from the producers of the Children's Television Workshop. Upper elementary.)

National Geographic World, National Geographic Society, Department 00481, 17th and M Streets N.W., Washington, DC 20036. (Monthly. Articles on environmental features of interest to children.)

Odyssey, AstroMedia Corp., 625 E. St. Paul Ave., P.O. Box 92788, Milwaukee, WI 53202. (Bimonthly. Full-color astronomy and space magazine for children 7 to 13.)

Ranger Rick's Nature Magazine, National Wildlife Federation, 1412 Sixteenth St., N.W., Washington, DC 20036. (Monthly, for children of elementary school age. Interesting stories and pictures on natural subjects, including ecology. *Your Big Backyard,* also 10 issues, is for preschool and primary-level children.)

Scienceland, 501 Fifth Ave., Suite 2102, New York, NY 10017. (Monthly, eight softcover booklets issued a year. Well-received magazine for children, preschool to third grade.)

Science Weekly, P.O. Box 70154, Washington, DC 20088. (Twenty issues a year. Current science developments for children in grades one through six.)

3-2-1 Contact, Children's Television Workshop, P.O. Box 2933, Boulder, CO 80322. (Ten issues a year. Experiments, puzzles, projects, and articles for children 8 to 14.)

PROFESSIONAL TEXTS

Abruscato, Joseph. *Teaching Children Science.* Englewood Cliffs, N.J.: Allyn & Bacon, 1992. (Methods, activities, and content for elementary school science.)

Blough, Glenn O., and Julius Schwartz. *Elementary School Science and How to Teach It.* New York: Holt, Rinehart and Winston, 1990. (Methods and comprehensive coverage of subject matter content.)

Cain, Sandra E., and Jack M. Evans. *Sciencing: An Involvement Approach to Elementary Science Methods.* Columbus, Ohio: Merrill/Macmillan, 1990. (A methods text organized into six broad units to develop teaching competencies.)

Carin, Arthur A. *Teaching Science Through Discovery.* 7th ed. Columbus, Ohio: Merrill/Macmillan, 1993. (Methods and activities, with emphasis on discovery teaching.)

Esler, William K., and Mary K. Esler. *Teaching Elementary Science.* Belmont, Calif.: Wadsworth, 1989. (Methods and subject matter. Exemplifies and applies three kinds of lessons.)

Gabel, Dorothy. *Introductory Science Skills.* Prospect Heights, Ill.: Waveland Press, 1984. (A laboratory approach to learning science and mathematics skills, and basic chemistry.)

Good, Ronald G. *How Children Learn Science.* New York: Macmillan, 1977. (Research on children's mental development and recommendations for teaching science.)

Harlan, Jean. *Science Experiences for the Early Childhood Years.* Columbus, Ohio: Merrill/Macmillan, 1992. (Everyday science activities for younger children.)

Henson, Kenneth T., and Delmar Janke. *Elementary Science Methods.* New York: McGraw-Hill, 1984. (Methods and activities for elementary schoolchildren.)

Jacobson, Willard J., and Abby Barry Bergman. *Science for Children.* Englewood Cliffs, N.J.: Prentice-Hall, 1987. (Methods and content of elementary-school science.)

Peterson, Rita, Jane Bowyer, David Butts, and Rodger Bybee. *Science and Society: A Source Book for Elementary and Junior High School Teachers.* Columbus, Ohio: Merrill, 1984. (Content and comprehensive methods. Emphasizes science's impact on society.)

Renner, John W. and Edmund A. Marek. *The Learning Cycle and Elementary School Science Teaching.* Portsmouth, N.H.: Heinemann, 1988. (Emphasizes methods that match children's cognitive processes for successful science teaching.)

Victor, Edward. *Science for the Elementary School.* 7th ed. New York: Macmillan, 1993. (Methods, content, and activities. Features an extensive scope of subject matter in outline form.)

Wassermann, Selma, and J. W. George Ivany. *Teaching Elementary Science.* New York: Harper & Row, 1988. (Stresses informal, inquiry-type science experiences for children.)

Wolfinger, Donna M. *Teaching Science in the Elementary School.* Boston: Little, Brown, 1984. (Extensive treatment of the basic, causal, and experimental processes of science. Integrates much research on science teaching.)

Zeitler, William R., and James P. Barufaldi. *Elementary School Science,* New York: Longman, 1988. (Modern methods for teaching science. Contains a variety of illustrative lessons.)

Some Major Project-Developed Programs

ACTIVITIES FOR INTEGRATING MATHEMATICS AND SCIENCE PROJECT (AIMS) Grades K–8

This program, developed at Fresno (California) Pacific College, was originally funded by the National Science Foundation to train a group of teachers in the rationale and methods for integrating science and mathematics in Grades 5–8. The classroom testing of written materials produced such positive results, a full-fledged writing project was launched to develop 15 teaching booklets. Materials are now available for K–8.

The rationale for AIMS includes these points: (1) Math and science are integrated outside the classroom and so should also be integrated inside it; (2) as in the real world, a whole series of math skills and science processes should be interwoven in a single activity to create a continuum of experience; (3) the materials should present questions that relate to the student's world and arouse their curiosity; (4) the materials should change students from observers to participants in the learning process; (5) the investigations should be enjoyable because learning is more effective when the process is enjoyed.

For more information, write to AIMS Education Foundation, P.O. Box 8120, Fresno, CA 93747.

EDUCATION DEVELOPMENT CENTER INSIGHTS   Grades K–6

The Education Development Center is in Newton, MA. The program contains 17 activity-based modules that can be used separately within another science curriculum, or as a full curriculum within the life, earth, and physical science areas. Each module is organized around four phases of instruction: Getting Started, Exploring and Discovering, Organizing and Processing for Meaning, and Applying and Extending Ideas. Six major science themes are incorporated into the program: systems, change, structure and function, diversity, cause and effect, and energy. Content and process skills are balanced across the curriculum. Material from other school subjects is integrated into many activities to give an overall understanding of how they normally relate.

The activities, often open-ended, focus on experiences that draw on the urban environment. Playground apparatus, toys, and the pupils themselves may serve as resources for learning science concepts. Instructional materials are designed for both the inexperienced teacher and the veteran who seeks innovative strategies to develop critical and creative thinking in pupils.

An advisory group of teachers from seven major urban areas continually gave feedback to program developers about the quality of learning and assessment activities.

The commercial distributor is Science Kit, Elementary Science Division, 777 East Park Drive, Tonawanda, NY 14150.

ELEMENTARY SCIENCE STUDY (ESS)   Grades K–6

ESS was begun in the 1960s as a curriculum improvement project of the Education Development Center, a nonprofit organization devoted to generating new ideas for education.

The program consists of 56 units of instruction that cover a wide range of science subjects. Each unit has a teacher's manual, and most units have an accompanying kit of materials. No fixed master plan exists for scope and sequence. The developers felt that each school district was best qualified to assemble its own curriculum from the units to meet local conditions.

ESS is intentionally child centered. Activities are designed to reflect the wonder, curiosity, and natural play of childhood. While the teacher guide for each unit suggests an overall structure, the pupils help determine in which directions the activities go and how much time is spent on each

activity. So most classroom procedures are exploratory and open-ended. ESS believes that learning happens best when children are free to use their own styles without overstructuring and premature closing from adults.

Materials are available from Delta Education, Inc., P.O. Box 915, Hudson, NH 03051.

FULL OPTION SCIENCE SYSTEM (FOSS) Grades K–6

This program is designed to serve both regular and most special education pupils in a wide cross-section of schools. Developed at the Lawrence Hall of Science, Berkeley, California, the program features several modules at each grade level that include science lesson plans in the earth, life, and physical sciences, and extension activities in language, computer, and mathematics applications.

The laboratory equipment includes several package options, from complete kits to individual items. Materials assembly directions show how teacher and pupils can gather and construct equipment for many activities. A correlation table tells how to integrate activities with other programs and state department of education guidelines for science.

Much care is taken to have a suitable match between activities and pupils' ability to think at different ages. Further work has been done to make the program easy to instruct and manage. Provisions for preparation time, ease of giving out and retrieving materials, cleanup, storage, and resupply have continually guided program developers.

The commercial distributor of FOSS is the Encyclopedia Britannica Educational Corporation, 310 South Michigan Avenue, Chicago, IL 60604.

NATIONAL GEOGRAPHIC KIDS NETWORK
Grades 4–6

The National Geographic Kids Network is a program that has children gather data on real science problems and then use a computer network to share their data with a scientist and children in other locations. The developer is the Technical Education Resource Center (TERC), in partnership with the National Geographic Society, which publishes and distributes the program.

Each of the instructional units is six weeks long and focuses on a central science problem. Children learn to ask questions and gather data in scientifically acceptable ways. The data are transmitted to an interested scientist who analyzes the data, answers children's questions, and then sends back an overview of all the collected information from cooperating schools.

Curriculum materials include children's handbooks that have background information on the topic of study, teacher guides, and computer software. The software is made up of a word-processing program, data charts, and a computer map of North America, all of which are used to ready and transmit data.

For details, write National Geographic Society Educational Services, 17th & M Streets, Washington DC 20036.

NUFFIELD SCIENCE 5–13
Grades K–8

Science 5–13 is a series of reference and resource publications for the teacher that suggests an open-ended, child-centered approach to elementary science. ("5–13" signifies the age span of the children served.) This program was begun as a curriculum project at the Nuffield Education Foundation of Great Britain.

The basic set of teaching units is composed of 20 volumes. Some unit titles are: "Working with Wood"; "Science, Models, and Toys"; "Structure and Forces"; "Children and Plastics"; "Trees"; and "Ourselves." An additional set of six titles in environmental education complements the basic program.

A major contribution of Science 5–13 is how it takes children's beginning experiences with everyday things and freely extends them in many directions. All the while, children's intellectual development is carefully considered.

In the United States, the distributor is Macdonald-Raintree, Inc., 205 W. Highland Ave., Milwaukee, WI 53203.

OUTDOOR BIOLOGY INSTRUCTIONAL STRATEGIES (OBIS)
Ages 10–15

Developed at the Lawrence Hall of Science, University of California (Berkeley), OBIS is designed for use with community youth organizations and schools that want to offer outdoor laboratory experiences. Four activity packets offer a broad selection of interesting, firsthand activities for studying ecological relationships in different environments: desert, seashore, forest, pond and stream, city lots, and local parts.

Each activity card consists of background information for the leader, description of materials needed, what advance preparation may be required, a lesson plan, and several follow-up suggestions. Each activity can be used alone or as part of a developmental sequence.

The commercial distributor is: Delta Education, Box 915, Hudson, NH 03051

SCIENCE FOR LIFE AND LIVING   Grades K–6

The full name for this curriculum is "Science for Living: Integrating Science, Technology, and Health." The developer is the BSCS Group, a nonprofit foundation for science education.

After readiness activities at the kindergarten level, these concepts and skills form the main curriculum structure: order and organization (Grade 1); change and measurement (Grade 2); patterns and prediction (Grade 3); systems and analysis (Grade 4); energy and investigation (Grade 5); and balance and decisions (Grade 6). Children build their own understanding of an integrated world of science, technology, and health as they work through activities that bring out the concepts and skills.

Each complete lesson contains five consecutive phases: (1) An *engagement* activity begins the lesson. Children connect what they know to the present material and reveal their prior knowledge, including misconceptions. (2) *Exploration* follows, in which pupils explore the materials or environment and form a common base of experience. (3) Next, an *explanation* phase gives pupils a chance to describe what they are learning, and the teacher is given an opportunity to state the intended learning. (4) *Elaboration* then provides activities that extend understandings and give further chances to practice skills. (5) The last phase, *evaluation*, allows pupils and teacher to assess what has been learned.

Published materials are available from the Kendall/Hunt Publishing Company, 2460 Kerper Blvd., Dubuque, IA 52001.

SCIENCE AND TECHNOLOGY FOR CHILDREN (STC) Grades 1–6

The developer of this curriculum project is the National Science Resources Center, established in 1985 by the National Academy of Sciences and the Smithsonian Institution to improve the teaching of science and mathematics in the nation's schools. The project's mission is to significantly increase the number of schools that offer hands-on science programs to children, and to interest more females and minority members in science.

Teaching units include such titles as *Weather and Me* (Grade 1), *The Life Cycle of Butterflies* (2), *Plant Growth and Development* (3), *Electric Circuits* (4), *Microworlds* (5), and *Magnets and Motors* (6). They are designed to focus on easy-to-use materials and integrate science with other areas of the curriculum. Each unit includes a teacher's guide; pupil activity booklet; a description of needed materials; and annotated lists of recommended trade books, computer software, and audiovisual materials.

The developers sought to make the management of materials and activities as practical as possible. In the field testing of units, evaluation procedures monitored how well the units worked under a wide variety of classroom conditions.

For details, contact the National Science Resources Center, Arts and Industries Building, Room 1201, Smithsonian Institution, Washington, DC 20560.

SCIENCE—A PROCESS APPROACH (SAPA) Grades K–6

SAPA has a unique structure. It uses process skills rather than subject-matter content as the base for its scope and sequence. Subject matter is used mainly as an aid to developing the skills, although much content is presented.

Eight "basic" processes are taught in grades K–3: observing, using space/time relationships, using numbers, measuring, classifying, communicating, predicting, and inferring. In grades 4–6, five "integrated" processes are taught that build on and extend the basic processes: formulating hypotheses, controlling variables, interpreting data, defining operationally, and experimenting. The method used to organize the development of the skills was to identify the process behaviors of scientists, and then to logically break down the behaviors into sequences through which they could be learned by children.

SAPA II, a more recent version of this program, has a more flexible structure than the first edition. Alternate procedures have been provided to allow the teacher more leeway in meeting pupils' individual differences and organizing teaching.

The commercial supplier is Delta Education, Inc., P.O. Box 915, Hudson, NH 03051.

SCIENCE CURRICULUM IMPROVEMENT STUDY (SCIS)   Grades K–6

SCIS is organized on a base of powerful and modern science concepts. Each of 12 instructional units features a central concept, with supporting subconcepts and process skills integrated into the activities.

Lessons have three parts: exploration, invention, and discovery. In the exploratory part, children are given objects to observe or manipulate. At times these observations are guided by the teacher; otherwise, the children observe and manipulate the objects as they wish.

Explorations allow firsthand contact with the material under study and provide a basis for children to use language. At the same time, the need arises for an explanation to make sense out of what has been observed.

This is taken up in the second part of the lesson sequence. After discussion, the teacher gives a definition and a word for the new concept.

This "invention" of a concept sets up the third part of the lesson. Now, the children are given a variety of further experiences within which they discover many applications of the concept. These extend and reinforce their knowledge and skills.

An updated version of this program, *SCIS3*, is available from Delta Education, Inc., P.O. Box 915, Hudson, NH 03051.

UNIFIED SCIENCES AND MATHEMATICS FOR ELEMENTARY SCHOOLS (USMES)   Grades K–8

The USMES project was funded by the National Science Foundation to develop and try out interdisciplinary units of instruction involving science, mathematics, social sciences, and language arts. The units are centered on long-range investigations of real and practical problems geared to the local environment. Twenty-six in all, the units may be used by local school planners to design different curricula to meet their needs but yet commonly reflect a problem-solving approach.

Several kinds of materials are provided for planners and teachers: an introductory guide to USMES, a teacher resource book for each major problem, background papers, a design lab manual (that tells how to set up and make needed apparatus), and a curriculum correlation guide.

More information may be gotten from ERIC, Ohio State University, 1200 Chambers Road, Columbus, Ohio 43212.

Commercial Suppliers of Science Materials and Equipment

(*Note:* The following classifications of suppliers may not be entirely accurate because suppliers often change offerings with business conditions. A current catalog should reveal the full scope of materials for sale in each case. Use school stationery when requesting free elementary-level catalogs. An annual, comprehensive listing of suppliers accompanies each January issue of *Science and Children*.)

General Supplies—Physical and Life Science

Carolina Biological Supply Company
2700 York Road
Burlington, NC 27215

Delta Education, Inc.
P.O. Box 915
Hudson, NH 03051

Edmund Scientific Company
101 E. Gloucester Pike
Barrington, NJ 08007

Frey Scientific Company
905 Hickory Lane
Mansfield, Ohio 44905

Learning Things, Inc.
68A Broadway
Arlington, MA 02174

Life Science Supplies

Carolina Biological Supply Company
2700 York Road
Burlington, NC 27215

Connecticut Valley Biological Supply
    Company
Valley Road
Southampton, MA 01073

Ward's Natural Science Establishment
5100 West Henrietta Road
P.O. Box 92912
Rochester, NY 14692

Balances

Ohaus Scale Corporation
29 Hanover Road
Florham Park, NJ 07932

Microscopes

American Optical Corporation
Eggert and Sugar Roads
Buffalo, NY 14215

Bausch & Lomb, Inc.
1400 North Goodman Street
Rochester, NY 14602

Swift Instruments, Inc.
P.O. Box 95016
San Jose, CA 95016

Microprojectors

Ken-A-Vision Manufacturing Company
5615 Raytown Road
Raytown, MO 64133

Aquaria, Terraria, Cages

Carolina Biological Supply Company
2700 York Road
Burlington, NC 27215

Jewel Aquarium Company
5005 West Armitage Avenue
Chicago, IL 60639

Science Kit, Inc.
777 E. Park Drive
Tonawanda, NY 14150

Kits and Models

Delta Education, Inc.
P.O. Box 915
Hudson, NH 03051

Denoyer-Geppert Company
5235 N. Ravenswood Avenue
Chicago, IL 60640

NASCO Company
901 Janesville Avenue
Fort Atkinson, WI 53538

Science Kit, Inc.
777 E. Park Drive
Tonawanda, NY 14150

Summary of Children's Thinking in Three Piagetian Stages*

*Based on a format suggested by Robert Mele.

Thought Process	Intuitive Thought[*]	Concrete Operational	Formal Operational
Cause and Effect	Logic often contradictory, unpredictable. Events may occur by magic or for human convenience.	Contradictions avoided. Physical objects are linked to show cause and effect. Commonsense explanations may be wrong but logical.	Can separate logic from content. Systematic control of variables possible, plus hypothetical "thought experiments," to test ideas.
Relative Thinking	Egocentric perceptions and language. Little grasp of how variables interrelate. Physical properties viewed in absolute, not relative, ways.	Perceptions of position and objects more objective. Aware of others' views. Some understanding of interrelated variables, when connected to concrete objects and pictures.	Understand relative position and motion. Can define and explain abstract concepts with other concepts or analogies. May temporarily show some egocentricity in propositions.
Classifying and Ordering	Sort one property at a time. Little or no class inclusion. Trial-and-error ordering in early part of stage.	Understand class inclusion principle. More consistent seriation with diverse objects. Can follow successive steps—less discrete thinking.	Can recombine groups into fewer, more abstract categories. Can form hierarchical systems.
Conservative Thinking	Mostly do not conserve. Perceptions dominate thinking. Center attention on one variable and do not compensate. Little or no reverse thinking.	Can reverse thinking, consider several variables and compensate. Conserve most of the Piagetian test concepts.	Conserve all of the Piagetian test concepts, with displaced and solid volume usually last.

[*]Intuitive thought is the last period of the preoperational stage.

Index